To Emilie
from Mom and Dad
for your 21ST
birthday .

Japan Diaries

A Travel Memoir

Geraldine Sherman

McArthur & Company
Toronto

Canadian Cataloguing in Publication Data

Sherman, Geraldine
    Japan diaries

ISBN 1-55278-090-2

1. Japan – Description and travel. 2. Sherman, Geraldine – Journeys – Japan. 3. Fulford, Robert, 1932-   -Journeys – Japan. 4. Sherman, Geraldine – Diaries. I. Title.

DS812.S53 1999   915.204'49   C99-931744-X

Typesetting and Design by Mad Dog Design Connection Inc.
Cover Design by Linda Pellowe / Mad Dog Design
Printed in Canada by Transcontinental Printing

McArthur & Company
322 King Street West, Suite 402
Toronto, ON M5V 1J2

10 9 8 7 6 5 4 3 2 1

For my partner in all things, Robert Fulford

"Japan offers as much novelty
perhaps as an excursion to
another planet."

— Isabella Bird
*Unbeaten Tracks in Japan: An Account
of Travel on Horseback in the Interior* (1885)

INTRODUCTION

I can't remember the first time I allowed myself to dream of going to Japan. I do have an early memory from 1955, when I was fourteen. In high-school art class in Chatham, Ontario, we were asked to draw a face. What came to mind was not my face or the face of anyone I'd ever seen, but the face of a Japanese woman. Her hair was in an elaborate bun adorned with lacquer combs, her neck framed by a loose kimono. She was peeking out from behind a fan that I'd painted red and gold.

I knew no one who was Japanese. Among my friends, I was considered slightly foreign — an awkward, overweight kid, one of fifty Jews adrift in a sea of 23,000 Gentiles. But to me, the Japanese were the quintessential "other." Their ancient and complex civilization appeared to have evolved a distinct way of being human. It seemed admirable to me. My youthful judgment no doubt was influenced by Japan's refined aesthetics — manicured gardens, embroidered silk, and delicate manners. Apart from that, I longed to be somewhere else, as far from Chatham as possible.

In Montreal, studying sociology and anthropology at McGill, I was intrigued by the Japanese ability to absorb wave after wave of incoming culture — borrowing, adapting, and reinventing to create a unique society. From China and Korea they acquired a written script, a legal code, Buddhism, and art forms later described as "typically Japanese." Following the arrival of the first Europeans in 1543, Christianity and Western science and technology threatened to bring irreversible change. After less than sixty years of contact, Japanese authorities recognized the threat and banished most outsiders (*gaijin*).

For the next 250 years, the shoguns ruling Japan preserved their country's splendid isolation. That ended forever in 1853 when Commodore Matthew Perry of the US navy piloted his gunboats into Edo Bay. The Americans ushered in the industrial revolution and the speediest social transformation in history.

All of this was background to the controversial classic *The Chrysanthemum and the Sword: Patterns of Japanese Culture* by Ruth Benedict. In 1944, the US government commissioned Dr. Benedict, a cultural anthropologist, to study the Japanese so that Americans could better understand their puzzling, little-known enemy. She defined the differences between the West and Japan in terms of guilt and shame. She argued that we in the West are guided by strong personal standards and that when these are violated by "sinful" behaviour, we feel guilt. In the East, however, the principal concern is maintaining appearances and earning the good opinion of others. If one errs, the culturally appropriate feeling is shame. Individual feelings come after duty to one's family and society.

Although at the time she wrote the book Dr. Benedict had not set foot in Japan — she based her work on interviews with Japanese-Americans — its effect was profound in the United States and to elsewhere. When it was translated into Japanese in 1949, it became a bestseller. *The Chrysanthemum and the Sword* appealed to me, and others of my generation, because it questioned blind allegiance to individualism on the one hand and submission to external authority on the other.

At the McGill Film Society, I fell under the spell of Akira Kurosawa's movies, especially *Rashomon*, a magical blend of feudal Japanese life and modern Western relativism. The screenplay, adapted from stories by Ryunosuke Akutagawa, explores the elusive nature of reality and morals. Four characters give different accounts of the same events — robbery, rape, murder, and abandonment. Kurosawa blended Japanese craft and history with Western literature and cinema, adding Shakespeare and Dostoyevsky, Eisenstein, and Ford to his own national pantheon. In *Seven Samurai* he transformed six-shooters into swords and sheriffs into samurai, as seven ragged warriors come to the aid of beleaguered villagers and, in the process, save their own humanity.

At the end of the 1960s, when I was a young radio producer getting to know the man I would marry, we worked together on a documentary about suicide. We both agreed that besides being inevitable, death, with luck and determination, could — in fact, *should* — be controlled. If people in the West were taking charge of their lives, why did they seem content to abandon control of their deaths? The program made the case for dying as a part of life: bring it back into the home, reinstate some of its natural progression, and perhaps adorn it with wit and style comparable to other human milestones. In Japan, both ancient and modern, there seemed a greater awareness of the fleeting nature of life, epitomized by the fragile beauty of cherry blossoms, and of its corollary, death. Suicide offered an honourable escape from a hopeless situation and could be enacted without shame for the deceased or their survivors. I found this admirable, as did my husband-to-be, Robert Fulford.

In 1969, I planned to make my first trip to Japan for a series of radio documentaries before the Osaka World Fair, but had to cancel due to illness. Twelve years later I returned to the subject as producer of a five-part CBC *Ideas* series: *Canada and Japan: Images and Realities*, written and presented by Ken Richard and Ted Goossen, two Toronto professors who are experts on Japan. They understood my passion for a country I'd never seen and encouraged me to go.

The Asia Pacific Foundation was offering grants to journalists to explore an Asian country of their choice. Bob and I applied — he in the print category and I for electronic media. We rehearsed our answers for an inevitable question: "If one of you got the fellowship, would the other go along?" (In other words, two for the price of one.) "Well," eyes lowered, "that's hard to say..." was our reply, designed to leave the strong impression that the answer really was, no. Happily, we were both winners – a return economy ticket and ten thousand dollars for each of us, more than enough for six weeks, even in Japan. When we applied, Bob didn't know that by the time we boarded the plane he would have ended a nineteen-year period as editor of *Saturday Night*. And I didn't know that soon after our return I would leave the CBC after twenty-two years to become a freelance writer. In many ways the 1987 trip was the beginning of a new chapter in our life together.

Ten years later, the Japan Foundation made it possible for us to return to Tokyo for two months. We were doubly lucky.

I do not speak or read Japanese, which is both a hindrance and a blessing. I have learned to use my eyes in ways I might not have done otherwise. I was able to see beauty in neon signs and ignore their shrill messages. I could people-watch with impunity, taking advantage of my outsider status to break free of social conventions. And, unlike younger tourists or language teachers, I had money to do what I wanted.

This book grew from my belief that the unexamined journey is not worth taking. I kept a daily journal on both trips. Taken together, these two Japan diaries reveal some of the changes the Japanese have experienced in recent times and some of the hurdles they have yet to overcome on their way from isolated island nation to respected world power. The diaries reveal changes in my life as well.

There are those who argue that Japan is like an onion — peel away the layers and there's nothing left. This may be true, but it hardly matters. To anyone who loves to contemplate Japan, there's so much to enjoy along the way, so many subtle questions raised, so many answers possible. Could there be a more absorbing activity than watching Japan reveal itself? Not for me. I remain enchanted. I doubt that will ever change.

Part 1

SATURDAY, SEPTEMBER 12, 1987

As we pulled out of the driveway this morning, they were on the front steps — my mother, Helen, and our two daughters, Rachel, fifteen, and Sarah, thirteen. They know that this is really my trip: Bob is coming along as a willing but somewhat sceptical companion. He's curious about Japan but fearful, I think, of the crowds so often featured in television coverage, hordes of commuters being shoehorned into subway cars.

At the airport in Toronto, a young mother and her newborn son stood near us in line. I asked her where they were going and she said, "Hong Kong. To visit his mother — I mean his grandmother. And grandfather." Obviously, a new mother. According to a friend on the Immigration Appeal Board, it's quite common for a Hong Kong family to send a pregnant woman to Canada. She remains, on an extended visit, until she gives birth. They expect that this Canadian child can then sponsor his family when the colony reverts to China in 1997. Whether or not this scheme will work, I admire its boldness and the young woman's bravery.

Perhaps because my grandparents were immigrants from Eastern Europe, the changing mix of people is one of the great attractions Canada holds for me. Japan, on the other hand, appears to welcome visitors and foreign ideas, but not immigrants. I'm curious to experience life in a monoculture, even though I don't think I approve.

The plane landed in Vancouver. We'd decided to splurge — a stopover to break up the trip, and an upgrade to business class for the long flight across the Pacific. I can't believe this is happening to me.

We're in the Empress Lounge in the Vancouver airport. Our plane is an hour late. No matter: I have rediscovered the joys of the self-service bar and an endless supply of Bloody Marys. We'd just settled in when "Mr. Sherman?" rang out over the public address system. My heart stopped. What could it be? The announcement repeated, almost correctly this time: "*Mrs.* Sherman?" We made our way to the desk. "We'd like to upgrade you to first class, if that's all right?" Indeed. Row 11 traded for row 2. Who could object? Then the woman looked at Bob, rather spiffy, I thought, in his blue blazer and striped shirt. "Oh," she remarked, "you don't have a tie!" This was not news to us. It *was* news that first class required ties. Rock stars, for God's sake, travel first class. (Of course, they do pay for their tickets.) "I was just going to buy him a tie at Duty Free," I lied. Had I kept my promise, Bob would have been the only Caucasian in first class, other than the steward, wearing a tie.

Two hours later we were nestled into two of the twelve first-class seats. They were huge, and covered in the sort of lambskin recommended for the infirm. The service was unrelenting; the movie screen crystal clear. The first course in the endless ritual called dinner was smoked salmon garnished with caviar, chopped egg whites, sour cream, and chives, and the ubiquitous capers. (I washed it all down with straight vodka lest we have to make an emergency landing in Vladivostok.) Bob asked if I knew where capers come from. I answered, with great authority, "They grow." (Actually, I have never seen a caper bush, but I knew that Bob would be even more ignorant on this subject than I.)

The next course was Consommé de Queue de Boeuf au Porto — the key word being "queue" — which, with my Grade 12 French, I recognized meant "tail." Before we left Toronto, we had been given an entire book on combating jet lag. I was now engaged in breaking every written rule, but was perfectly prepared to spend two days in bed as punishment. The entrée was a great slab of Chateaubriand Béarnaise. I managed to eat my way through seven courses, coffee, and liqueur. I was deliriously happy, thankful that I was not Henry Kissinger or the Pope — not expected to perform when I deplane.

I was the only woman in first class. I wonder how often I will be "the only woman" during this trip? I don't expect to meet many independent women — artists, diplomats, politicians. Certainly very few my age, forty-six. From all I've read, marriage is still the prime goal of young Japanese women. When my former CBC Radio boss, Margaret Lyons, returned from attending a broadcasting conference in Japan, she reported that she'd felt slighted at every turn because she was a Japanese-Canadian who couldn't speak Japanese — but more important, because she was a woman.

In the Empress Lounge we'd spoken briefly with two thirty-five-ish men who had perfected Canadian bureaucratese. They work for the Federation of Municipal Governments, with headquarters in Ottawa, and were on their way to China for three weeks, via Japan. After the Upgrade Incident, several Bloody Marys, two coffees, and a package of Oreos to steady my nerves, I was able to give them my full attention. They were keen on a program called "Aid and Trade," and the twinning of cities, something I never understood, even as a former town planner. They were so well groomed and nattily dressed, I naturally assumed they were gay. (But then I think *everyone* is gay.)

I'm curious to see the celebrated tolerance of the Japanese to a wide range of sexual practices. Homosexuality and cross-dressing receive less disapproval than in other countries, at least according to Ian Buruma, author of *The Japanese Mirror*. He wrote about sexual patterns of all sorts, including the obsession Japanese men have with breasts, particularly their mother's breasts — the source of unconditional approval. (I wonder if women have similar needs, and if they do, how they satisfy them.)

I skimmed through a Japanese comic, or *manga*, on the plane. I couldn't read the text but the drawings said it all — the blonde heroine with her enormous breast thrust into the mouth of a Japanese man carrying a sword. He could have been carrying a briefcase.

While breasts are apparently a suitable object for erotic fantasies, pubic hair is not. Recent censorship battles converged on this single anatomical feature. In 1985, the French lent the Japanese a series of nude Man Ray photographs from the 1930s. In this celebrated but not unusual case, customs officials seized the pictures, saying that they "failed to comply with local standards." They insisted on blacking out the tangly bits; the French resisted and prevailed. The Americans have not had similar success. Magazines such as *Playboy* are occasionally detained while the abhorrent hairs are painstakingly scratched out by teams of incorruptibles. Pubic hair in films is also scratched out, frame by frame, or blurred with drops of glycerine. These erasures result in risible physical oddities for Japanese audiences, and provide one more anomaly to baffle *gaijin*, as foreigners are commonly called.

Before leaving for Japan, we talked about the surprising inconsistencies in Japanese life when Peter Day, a friend and colleague, brought John Randle to our house. He's the co-author with a Japanese woman, Mariko Watanabe, of *Coping with Japan*, a skill, he confessed with typical British self-deprecation, he never quite mastered. I've brought the book along. It's full of sensible advice, including how to order in a restaurant when there's no English menu: go with the waiter to the window where plastic replicas are displayed and point. The book explains that this custom began in the nineteenth century "to help the Japanese identify new foods from the West."

In today's *New York Times*, an op-ed piece acknowledged that Japanese post-war economic goals have been met, even exceeded: "But what kind of nation does this make Japan, and what kind of culture is Japanese culture?" These are certainly the questions that interest me, but this writer already had his answers, and they were laced with vitriol.

Only a few hours into the flight and one of the Japanese passengers was asleep, the first in our cabin to conk out. I walked to the back of the plane, down rows of sleeping Japanese. The women had their own slippers, sweet little things with gold thread or golf tassels, all about size 4.

I remembered my standard line when friends asked if I was excited in the months leading up to this trip: "No," I answered. "I haven't let myself get excited yet. I won't until I'm buckled in." But on the plane, I was excited. Truly excited. I did wish, though, that it was 1868 and I was the first Western woman to arrive in Japan in hundreds of years.

Isabella Bird, the redoubtable global traveller, visited Japan in 1878, only ten years after it opened to the West. In her book, *Unbeaten Tracks in Japan*, she complains that cities such as Yokohama and Tokyo have "undergone marked changes in a few years," and she longs to "get into the real Japan!" Everyone, it seems, complains about arriving too late in Japan.

MONDAY, SEPTEMBER 14

I must stop saying, "I can't believe it!" At the airport we did exactly as the guidebook and our friends instructed, and it worked perfectly. We rode the bus to the Tokyo City Air Terminal. There we loaded our stuff into a taxi, mindful not to open or close the passenger doors because this is the driver's job. He controls the doors from his seat and only pops out to help with the luggage. This is all part of the service, and we were not to tip. Ever.

The taxi came equipped with cotton seat covers in the front and a lace version in the back, both dazzling white. Ken Richard, our friend and a University of Toronto professor of East Asian studies, had made reservations for us at Seifuso, a Japanese inn, or ryokan, in the heart of Tokyo. He'd given us one of their cards with a small map on the back and told us to place it in the white-gloved hands of our driver. We did. After about forty-five seconds of serious examination, he bounded out of the cab and left us, with the meter running, for what seemed like five minutes. When he returned, he made it clear that he had telephoned to find out how best to get us to our destination. And no wonder. In the last block he was forced to back into a tiny laneway in almost total darkness.

We had arrived at a most remarkable place: part East, part West, everything sort of jumbled as you come in — shoes at the door, slippers waiting a few steps up, and in the air, a unique cooking smell. (Oil and soy sauce, with a hint of the sea?) We took off our shoes and changed into the largest plastic slippers available.

The inn is family run — the mother, son, and daughter who greeted us at the door were friendly and curious, surprised to see that we had business cards printed in English on one side and Japanese on the other. A houseboy took our bags, and we followed him down a stone path set in sand. We had to leave our first pair of slippers in the hall outside our room and transfer to inside-the-room slippers. (I later discovered yet another change of slippers for toilet purposes.)

Inside the large room stood a low table holding a tea set (a Thermos of hot water, tea bags, and two cups), a television on its own table, and cushions. Not a single chest of drawers or chair with legs. There were a few hangers on a hook on the wall, right next to a calligraphy scroll. One wall turned out to be a large closet with sliding doors in which bedding was stored. The futon quilts are taken out at night and laid on the floor, which is entirely covered with thick, springy rice-straw mats (tatami) edged in cloth, each one about six feet long and three feet across. This is how we'll sleep for most of our time in Japan.

There's also a small hallway with a sink and off the hall, two enclosed rooms — one with a Western-style toilet, the other with a deep Japanese-style bath. The ceilings are low and threaten to smack Bob (who's almost six feet tall) in the head each time he moves. The lighting is subdued, verging on dismal. Our bags seem to eat up the entire space, which is not tiny by Japanese standards — about fourteen tatami mats, which is how rooms are measured. No question: this is exactly where I want to be.

Gave up unpacking and went down to the restaurant at the front of the inn — *chirashi-sushi* (raw fish on cold rice) for me, tempura for Bob. Managed to spill an entire bowl of miso soup over my jean skirt. Exhaustion was clearly setting in. Inched back to the room, where our bedding had been laid out, and crawled in. Local time, 9:30 p.m. Outside our window there's a garden. Lying on the futon, I see branches of a gnarled old tree. I'm living inside a haiku.

TUESDAY, SEPTEMBER 15

Today was Keiro no Hi, "Respect for the Aged Day," a national holiday to honour Old People. Despite the venerable name, this is not an ancient holiday but one instituted after the Second World War. The reasons for such a holiday? One can only imagine. Perhaps traditional filial devotion died with the Second World War. Perhaps, as with busy people everywhere, family responsibilities are hard to fulfil and need formalizing. Some practical person said, "The Japanese can use any holiday they can get!"

We started the day with a short stroll around the streets near our ryokan, a mix of houses, shops, and offices. Soon we stumbled on a neighbourhood gathering of children, their parents, and grandparents in front of a portable shrine called a *mikoshi*. Every neighbourhood, even the most densely urban, maintains a shrine to its local tutelary deity, or *kami*. Once a year, the *kami* is said to enter the *mikoshi* and is carried through the streets, blessing the residents. Today was our *kami*'s turn.

The young men were binding a wagon together with heavy twine, tightening each corner by twisting a mallet until there was no more slack. They passed the mallet back and forth as the children banged a huge drum mounted on the wagon. Old people, in casual traditional dress, sat in the shade of a nearby tent, drinking tea. Although the men chosen to carry the *mikoshi* are often reputed to be scantily dressed and overly sloshed, we saw none of this in *our* neighbourhood. Mind you, we didn't stay long.

Respect for the Aged Day could not have come at a better time: it meant that official business could be postponed. The Foreign Press Club and the Japan Tourist Office were closed, but the department stores in Ginza were not. We tackled the immense but well-organized subway system at our leisure and without panic. As we confronted our first automated ticket machine, two young men, one British, the other American, asked if they could help. They did, a bit, but mostly they helped build our confidence. "It's really remarkable that you're out on the subway on your first day." The American added: "I knew a couple of Manhattanites who landed at Narita airport, went to the nearest hotel, and just stayed there for two weeks!" Here less than twenty-four hours and we're laughing at other tourists.

We visited two major department stores — Takashimaya and Mitsukoshi, the birthplace of the Mitsui conglomerate. The founder, Takatoshi Mitsui, after travelling abroad, revolutionized the selling of silk for kimonos: he charged a fixed price, cash up front. (Before, customers ran up a tab that was collected twice a year and included arbitrary carrying costs.) In 1868, Mitsui was ready: he diversified, establishing Japan's first department store, the first to sell imported goods, and the first to hire saleswomen. To survive, Mitsui had transformed old ways into new, and others followed. Invention, Japanese style.

Both Takashimaya and Mitsukoshi contain multitudes. The top floor of each store, the eighth, was devoted to bonsai trees, carp tanks, a kids' play area, and a performance space for concerts. In one store, a group called Five Cool Guys was scheduled to appear. Judging by their posters, they might have chosen a more appropriate name — four guys were dressed in powder blue suits, their leader in red, all with matching bow ties and greased-back hair. Their tape, playing in the background, was no more attractive than the singers themselves. Most of the audience paid little

attention and looked as if they simply wanted a place to rest in outdoor shade.

The first floor sold French, Italian, and American designer items at dreadfully inflated prices. The children's clothes were exquisite, and the food halls in the two basement levels were worthy rivals of Harrods of London. Much of the food I couldn't identify specifically, but there was lots of seaweed and other marine life in wooden barrels at one end, delicate pastries and chocolates in dreamy little boxes at the other. It was lunchtime, and we desperately needed a place to sit down.

On a side street we found a restaurant with plastic models of familiar dishes in the window and followed the recommended method. "Window?" we asked. The waiter knew the drill and with good humour followed us outside where we pointed to two appetizing bowls of noodle soup, reminders of *Tampopo*, the movie directed last year by Juzo Itami. So glad we saw it. To me, it illustrates the Japanese obsession with craftsmanship, even though in style it's an homage to the American Western: a truck-driving stranger in a black Stetson enters the roadside restaurant of a struggling widow and helps her discover the secrets of the perfect noodle soup. Bob suggested it reflects the realities of post-war Japan, when people were hungry well into the 1950s. Perhaps both readings are correct. The soup was delicious.

Earlier in the day, we'd heard from David Bond, a former student of Ken Richard, now a trade commissioner with Ontario House, our provincial representative in Japan. He and his wife, Jill, invited us to their apartment for dinner. After we met him at Exit 3 of the Ginza subway station, we walked together through dark streets, in an area of deserted office blocks, until we stopped near the American embassy. (Like American embassies everywhere, it's a heavily fortified bunker.)

Inside the Bonds' modern apartment, surrounded by their oversized furniture, I felt I'd never left Toronto. After grace — Jill's the daughter of a clergyman — we tucked in to roast beef and potatoes, and to learning more about our hosts. They'd first come to Japan as newlyweds — he in business, she to teach — intending to tour Asia. But they'd been so fascinated by Japan they stayed for a year and a half, learned a bit of the language, and returned to Toronto for more study. After a brief stint as a civil servant at Queen's Park, David was appointed to this new job and arrived in April; Jill joined him six weeks ago.

She teaches English at a women's university that sounds like a high-class secretarial school. "All the students are pretty rich," Jill explained. "They didn't get into a good university, so they'll go there for four years. Then, if they're lucky, they'll go abroad for a while — but not for *too* long." Staying away *too* long apparently spoils your attitude and makes you an undesirable wife. The idea is to return quickly and marry well. "By the third year, a lot of them get really depressed and lack motivation." She doesn't think that they would do much better if they went to a real university.

She told us that this was the time of year when those who will graduate in the spring look for jobs. "They spend a lot of time and money on the right clothes. And I go over what they should say." Then she told us an incredible story. "One of my girls came back last week and told me that she thought her interview was going well until she was asked her blood type. I said, 'Blood type?' 'Oh yes,' she said. 'I'm A-positive and he said they already had too many A-positives. They were looking for an O.'"

Jill and David explained that the Japanese believe blood type indicates character, in much the same way some people think there are "typical Libras," or "confused Geminis." It all began in 1931 when a Japanese psychologist, Takeji Furukawa, published his research in the *Journal of Applied Psychology*, linking personality with blood type. This notion captured the imaginations of other medical types — now called blood-group biopsychologists — in other parts of the world. Since the 1970s, the Japanese have soaked up hundreds of pop-psychology books that "prove" blood type affects everything a person does. In Japan, people also pay attention to your Chinese birth year: hypothetically, people born in the year of the Horse might not be compatible with people born in the year of the Rat.

We made plans to meet again on Sunday and go to a flea market on the grounds of a shrine. David's passion is swords; he's one of only two Westerners ever invited to join an exclusive Japanese society of sword collectors. They're both fascinated with the Meiji-era general, Maresuke Nogi and his wife, Shizuko, who, upon hearing of the death of their emperor in 1912, committed what appeared to be *junshi* — suicide in which the vassal follows his lord into death. Nogi died by *seppuku*, slitting his abdomen, then falling on his sword, while his wife stabbed herself several times above the heart — surely an agonizing death.

David explained that Nogi was a strong believer in Bushido, the code of the samurai, which demanded willpower, courage, and absolute loyalty to one's feudal lord. While Nogi's death was widely celebrated in myth and song, he had, in fact, committed an illegal act: Bushido had been outlawed in the middle of the seventeenth century when the Tokugawa shoguns turned the lords' domains into prefectures and their samurai into bureaucrats serving the central authority.

Only in 1934, with the publication of Nogi's suicide note, were the complex motivations for this deadly act revealed: they pointed to a blend of professional regret ("Since I lost the regimental colours in the battle of 1877, I have searched in vain for an opportunity to die"), and personal melancholy ("I've become old and weak"). His death was stripped of noble implications and downgraded to *jisatsu*, simple suicide. Nevertheless, the general's home has been preserved and once a year is open to the public. This year Jill and David were there.

WEDNESDAY, SEPTEMBER 16

An exhausting day of peaks and troughs. We were scheduled to go to the Canadian embassy at 10 a.m. Before we left, I called Ted Goossen, a friend doing research in Japan, and arranged for him to meet us at our place at about five to go out for dinner. For breakfast, Bob foraged around the neighbourhood, as is becoming his pattern, and returned with sticky buns for ¥250 each (about $2.50) from a nearby kiosk and McDonald's pale coffee. They're the only places open early.

The temperature was cooling down, and rain threatened. I took great pleasure plotting our route to the embassy, smug in the belief that I could do better than follow the advice given last night by the Bonds. (Arrived only slightly late.) The embassy is a story in itself: located on a piece of prime commercial land on Aoyama-dori, opposite Akasaka Palace, home to many members of the present royal family, it was built in 1933, under the supervision of, and with a sizeable contribution from, our first ambassador, Herbert Marler. (One hesitates to guess its worth, which must be something like half of Manhattan.)

In stark contrast to the American embassy, tightly wrapped in a mesh fence, ours is guarded by a small sentry box, standing empty this morning.

The all-white chancellery, home of our current ambassador, Barry Steers, stands in splendour in a park-like setting; the working offices next door are another matter entirely — cramped, a shamble of boxes and crates lining the walls, and above them dull prints, crooked and dusty. On a round Formica table in the middle of the office, a pile of booklets rested at a frightening tilt. Never mind. The information inside was out-of-date. Our guide, a man newly transferred, he told us, "from politics to culture," looked harried and embarrassed. He seemed at a loss to explain not only what *we* were doing there but what *he* was doing.

"We have this slide show we're supposed to show you. Sorry about that. Everyone has to see it. I'll be with you in a minute." Out he went and returned some minutes later. "Sorry, but we have to go to this rather large boardroom. It's the only one we have, so we have to use it for everything." (His string of apologies made me feel close to Canada, where regret is a national preoccupation.)

As a journalist, I found the show excruciating: tons of text over a single, unidentified slide of boats in a harbour, for instance, followed by a dozen more slides that might have been interesting if someone had told us what we were looking at. The script, written by two staff members, was replete with sentences such as: "Although the Japanese gross national product at seven trillion yen is the highest among the twelve top economic nations, her defence spending, governed by the 1947 treaty with the victorious Americans, remained at 1 percent until 1984, when it slipped upward to 2.4 percent, making Japan, in real dollars, the world's third-largest investor in arms in the world, a fact which makes some of those who remember the Pacific War, and those newly developing nations in the Pacific, uneasy." Yes, that was one sentence.

Before the show started, I asked, with the requisite number of Canadian *mea culpas*, if there was even a slight chance, if it wasn't too much trouble, could I, could *we*, please, have a cup — *two* cups actually — of coffee? "Yes, of course," our host replied, "but I hope you won't mind the service — cardboard and Styrofoam, that sort of thing."

When the show ended, we were joined by a Japanese woman who really did know something about Japanese culture — a subject entirely missing from the audiovisual presentation we'd been subjected to. She said she could arrange tickets for us to theatre, traditional and contemporary, and dance. She offered to check with the Tokyo International Film Festival about our accreditation and their program.

They're showing five Canadian films this year, including *I've Heard the Mermaids Singing*, *Un zoo la nuit* — an entry in the very Japanese blood-and-guts category, Special Effects — and *Housekeeping*, directed by Bill Forsyth, a Scot, based on a novel by Marilynne Robinson, an American, shot in British Columbia. The embassy staff was a bit surprised when we told them about the national confusion in *Housekeeping*. They were planning a gala in honour of the director for September 29, or thereabouts.

Finally we were introduced to the minister in charge of culture, a Dickensian sort of character, all muddle and bluster. The competent Japanese woman left, no doubt to rescue one of her less competent bosses. "Terribly sorry," Mr. Minister began, "we were to go to lunch, just the four of us, but it seems that the ambassador is sick and he was supposed to do this do, the head table sort of thing, at this meeting of the Canadian Chamber of Commerce in Japan. Now, you can say no, and I'll just tell them I'm busy. But if you'd care to come, we'd be delighted to have you."

"That would be fine," chimed in the trooper I married. I piped up, "But don't you need a tie?" thinking, hoping, that tielessness would work in our favour this time. However, our intrepid minister pulled a slightly soiled red one from his closet and off we went to the Tokyo Hilton. Outside the hotel, a small group of teenagers and photographers had gathered to catch a glimpse of Michael Jackson and his travelling zoo. Zoo, as in animals. As in monkeys.

The after-lunch speaker was to be a member of the Diet, from the Nakasone faction in the Liberal Democratic Party. We were told he was a brilliant and outspoken man, a graduate of George Washington University in the United States, as well as "the best" Japanese schools, which I guess meant Tokyo University. Since Prime Minister Yasuhiro Nakasone cannot run again, there's a leadership race in the ruling LDP. His topic — "Who will succeed Nakasone?" — seemed to excite the interest of Canadian business and government types.

As we sat at our tables in the cavernous gold ballroom, the theme song for *Masterpiece Theatre* played over and over. I asked the bureaucrat next to me if he knew the reason for the choice.

"No," he replied. "But when you rent the hall, you always need two mikes — one for the head table, one for the lectern, so it always comes with taped music." This didn't exactly answer my question, but I appreciated the sample of arcane information that fills a diplomat's pouch.

Lunch was vintage Western hotel with everything from damp salad to pulverized meat, sugary ice cream, coffee, and plenty of booze. The speaker came to our table, was introduced to Bob, and they exchanged business cards. The fellow was listed as chancellor of Temple University, Japan. He wore a powder blue suit and was accompanied by a pretty, elegantly dressed woman I assumed was his wife although she might have been an assistant, or something between the two. He did not introduce her, and paid no attention to her throughout the event. She sat at the back of the room and spoke French to one of the Chamber members. As the politician rose to speak, she moved to the front and began to take photographs of him. When the sound of the snores nearly overpowered his delivery, she moved further forward and set her camera on the lectern, which I took to be a signal that he should speed up. (We were told later that sleeping at public events is not considered impolite in Japan.)

The speech was expected to last ten minutes. No speaker ever sticks to ten minutes, certainly not a politician, but nothing could have prepared me for the forty-five minutes that lay ahead. He began by holding up a revised copy of a book he'd written with an American, *The Internationalization of Japan*, I believe it was called. Then he confessed he'd been visiting his constituents the night before and since it took longer to get from there to Tokyo than from Vancouver to Tokyo, he was hoping we would understand if his delivery showed signs of his fatigue. He was, he said, one of the few English-speaking members of the Diet — a scary thought, since his version of the language required the full participation of the listener.

Those who stayed awake heard that Nakasone would support one of three candidates, all of whom came from outside his own faction. He would choose the one who could guarantee him a prominent position in the international life of Japan — because he might, one day, want to return as prime minister. When the ordeal ended, Bob returned our government's tie and we ran for the nearest subway, a quick stop at the Foreign Press Center and the Tourist Office, then "home."

With Ted, we drank tea and watched sumo wrestling on television in our ryokan. The sumo tournament, called a *basho*, Ted explained, began formally in the eighth century as part of the Shinto seasonal festivals and now takes place five times a year. What you see on screen are two enormous men, dressed in loincloths resembling silk diapers, their hair in slick topknots. Before the match, they toss salt to purify the hard-packed earth ring, a circle about fifteen feet across. They also drink special water to purify themselves, bow to one another, touch the earth, clap their hands to summon the divine spirits, and stamp their legs to chase away evil spirits. This ritual regularly lasts longer than the match itself.

Managing the proceedings is a fully garbed referee, clad in a fourteenth-century kimono and carrying an iron fan like those used by feudal warriors. At a certain moment the wrestlers charge one another like bull elephants, pushing and heaving, until one poor chap loses his balance and falls, either in the ring or onto the fans. Touching the ground with anything but the soles of the feet represents defeat. Permitted moves include throws, lifts, tripping, shoving, and open-handed slaps to the upper torso. (Kicking and closed-fist punching are forbidden.) More bows, some mouth-rinsing and spitting, and the ring briefly empties, while the television audience watches replays from several angles. After fifteen days of this groaning and sweating, the wrestler who has tossed the greatest number of chaps out of the ring is the winner.

There are now fewer than a thousand sumo wrestlers, each of whom belongs to a stable run by a "boss," a former champion. There are six degrees of accomplishment, with *yokozuna* at the top. More than a sport, sumo is described as a "national skill." It attracts burly youth from poor rural areas of Japan, although there are now one or two professionals from other Asian cultures as far away as Tonga. As students, these hopefuls are assigned menial tasks, disciplined like monks, and stuffed like geese on a particularly rich stew (*chanko nabe*) until they reach a desirable weight, around three hundred pounds. The rewards for success are privilege rather than wealth: sumo wrestlers, like pop stars, have fan clubs of adoring young women who have acquired the taste. (Many wrestlers retire to run restaurants; most die young from obesity-related illnesses.)

When the matches were over for the day, we boarded yet another train and headed for Asakusa — an old working-class area of Tokyo that once held the Edo pleasure quarters. Asakusa still boasts the famously gaudy Kannon temple, dedicated to the thousand-armed Goddess of Mercy. This was the first temple we'd seen up close, and we approached it along a street lined with kitschy souvenir shops. The description supplied by Isabella Bird over a hundred years ago could still apply: "Every day is a festival day in Asakusa ... it is the most popular of religious resorts; and whether he be Buddhist, Shintoist or Christian, no strangers come to the capital without making a visit to its crowded courts or a purchase at its tempting booths."

As we walked away from the temple, Ted pointed to several rather shabby high-rise buildings distinguished by the absence of identifying signs. These were love hotels. "They're not really for prostitution," Ted explained. "It's just that the Japanese live in such close quarters that if couples want to be alone, this is where they go. Married couples go as well, for some privacy." There are four thousand love hotels in Tokyo, prices are reasonable, and management discreet to the point of invisibility: room selection and payment for a few uninterrupted hours can be handled entirely by machines. Rooms are notoriously outrageous and kinky — one can choose to make love in a Venetian gondola, a space shuttle, or a medieval torture chamber. All come equipped with vibrating beds, Jacuzzis, karaoke tape decks, that sort of thing. Frankly, I prefer our ryokan. Far more exotic.

Ted is over six feet tall, with a bald head, reddish curly beard, and Birkenstock lope. He's wonderfully at home in Japan, especially when he opens his mouth and pours out fluid, colloquial Japanese. He took us to a local restaurant that specialized in yakitori. That means grilled chicken, but may include anything from chicken pieces in salt or sauce to organ meats, all on skewers, cooked over charcoal. Sometimes they're snacks but we made a meal of them, adding mushrooms, onions, and who knows what. It was my first yakitori experience, and it was great fun.

As we entered the restaurant, the staff shouted out a welcome, or so I guessed. At one table near the door a young man was trying to impress two female companions. When he saw us come in, he yelled to the proprietor of this fairly humble joint, "Hey, your place is really becoming successful. Lots of international guests!" Ted replied with a joke — in Japanese. The young man's jaw dropped and he almost fell to the floor.

Donald Richie, in *A Lateral View*, his collection of pieces from *The Japan Times*, wrote that the Japanese believe their language is so difficult that no *gaijin* could possibly crack the code. When they hear someone who is fluent, their reaction is not to say, "Where did you learn to speak so well?" but rather to fall silent, as we might if we heard a monkey speaking English.

While we were eating and drinking, Ted passed on the following information: first, "A typhoon is expected tonight. Nothing to worry about though"; second, "Many people are predicting a big earthquake in Tokyo soon." Giant earthquakes occur every sixty years, approximately, and the last one that destroyed most of the city, the Great Kanto Quake, was in 1923 — sixty-four years ago. Thanks, Ted.

Every hotel or inn must provide its guests with an evacuation plan in English and Japanese, and a flashlight. Ted asked for ours at Seifuso. It showed the exit route and explained that we were to make our way to the Imperial Palace grounds. I'd like to see them, but not under those circumstances. Settling in for an uneasy sleep on our futons. Typhoon or earthquake? Earthquake or typhoon?

THURSDAY, SEPTEMBER 17

A quieter day. Today's breakfast, brought back to our room by Bob, consisted of white-bread sandwiches, one with an omelette filling, the other with some sort of cutlet, plus McDonald's coffee. Fortified, we took our bulging laundry bags to the neighbourhood laundry and dry cleaner. They're fast, but God only knows what the bill will be. That part of the negotiations was beyond our collective abilities. We'll assess the damage when we come on Saturday for pickup.

Then, off to Jimbocho and the Kanda book district. It was as remarkable as we had been told it would be — a huge street, Yasukuni-dori, one side almost exclusively devoted to bookstores, many with bins on the street. Some stores are small and specialized: Charles E. Tuttle,

the largest publisher of Japanese books in English, has its own outlet, and there's a large store with books devoted to philosophy in both Eastern and Western languages. Sanseido, a department store for books, is eight storeys high with English-language books well displayed and amply stocked. (Older buildings were never more than eight storeys because, until recently, that was the maximum height considered able to withstand the stress of a major quake.)

At lunchtime we picked up bento — a meal in a box — of sushi and dumplings, separated by a small piece of green plastic "fencing" and accompanied by little mounds of shredded pink ginger and wasabi (green horseradish), each in its own compartment, a tiny container of soy sauce, and disposable chopsticks. We headed to the Imperial Palace grounds (our neighbourhood evacuation site). It was blocked for an official function, so we wandered across the street until we stumbled into another park. We followed busloads of Japanese tourists into the grounds of a beautiful shrine and approached a small, intimate building. I took off my shoes and left them with the others at the door, smiled at the woman in charge, and was about to enter. She smiled back and said, "No, Japanese! No, Japanese!" She was forbidding me to enter. Quite a shock, or as the Japanese would say, "Shokku!"

We were, however, allowed into the adjacent military museum, where there were few signs in English. The space was empty, except for one or two Japanese women and old men who may have been Second World War veterans. We'd stumbled into the highly controversial Shinto shrine, Yasukuni, established to provide a home for the souls killed in the Meiji Restoration of 1868. The imposing concrete building, constructed in 1869, is one of the few to have survived both the Great Kanto Earthquake and Allied fire bombing. Here, the souls of 2.4 million Japanese soldiers, all killed in their emperor's service, are said to rest, transformed into guardian deities of the nation. (A half-century ago many Japanese soldiers were persuaded to die in order to assume this elevated status.) Separate areas are devoted to each imperial war — Sino-Japanese (1894–1895), Russo-Japanese (1904–1905), the invasion of Manchuria (1931), of China (1937), and the largest war, which began in 1941 with Pearl Harbor.

For me, the most compelling corner of the museum honours the contribution of the six thousand kamikaze fighter pilots and human torpedoes, men between the ages of seventeen and thirty who crashed in suicide missions near the war's end. Several of their photographs appear in glass cases — first, posed beside their apprehensive parents; then, arms around their comrades; and finally, waving goodbye. One inscription tells us that in their final moments they vowed to meet again when cherries blossomed at Yasukuni. Another recounts that some, as they plunged into their targets, were heard to shout, "Mother!" On an official plaque they are described as "martyrs to the new Japan ... Their devotion will remain in the hearts of the Japanese as an expression of patriotism in its noblest and purest form ... This spirit has laid the groundwork for the peace and prosperity of our nation in the future."

FRIDAY, SEPTEMBER 18

If yesterday was spent thinking about war, today was devoted to experiencing peace. We set off at about 9:30 a.m. for Kamakura, taking the Yokosuka line from Tokyo station. By mistake, we found ourselves on the Green Car, with reserved, first-class seats: we forked over about $20 each to stay put and avoid further embarrassment. I was surprised to discover that Yokohama is only minutes outside Tokyo, part of one giant metropolis.

Our first stop, after about an hour, was Kita-Kamakura. From there, it was only a few steps to our first temple, Engaku-ji, "one of the most celebrated Zen temples," belonging to the Rinzai sect — the "sound-of-one-hand-clapping" group. Bob was impressed by the temple's size — acres of woods, open spaces, and dozens of buildings. A remarkable sight awaited us just inside the gate: an ancient Zen master in *hakama* trousers, something like culottes, was instructing half a dozen extremely beautiful women in the intricacies of Zen archery. The most important lesson seemed to be the cultivation of a total lack of concern about hitting the target. Two roosters, understanding that they were in no danger, ambled in front of the target. The archers, stunning in crisp, white pants, clearly paid more attention to their costumes than to their technique. The instructor took his position and without looking, let fly his arrow. It sailed high over the heads of the roosters and well past the target.

In Kamakura there were few concessions to non-Japanese tourists. If there were foreign-language signs, they were in English only. Pity the poor French or German tourist. Distances from one temple to another are short, and we often followed the rail bed between Kita-Kamakura, Kamakura, and Hase. The weather was hot but not humid, perfect for touring. We reached our second temple about fifteen minutes later. It was in many ways the most charming, idiosyncratic, and peaceful — the Yoke-ji, or Divorce Temple, founded in 1285. It became a refuge for aristocratic women fleeing their husbands. If they stayed two years, they became Buddhist nuns and were automatically divorced. The temple remained a convent until the end of the Meiji era, ten years later, and the last abbess died in 1902.

We stopped several times along the way to buy drinks from the many vending machines featuring classics such as Pocari Sweat, which promised to replace our depleted electrolytes, or perform something equally beneficial. Coke is everywhere: "I feel Coke," the signs say. In several vending machines near our ryokan we can buy beer, sake, even large bottles of whisky and wine. We lack only Club Soda.

Our next temple, Kencho-ji (by this time I'm beginning to awaken to the idea that "-ji" means temple), is considered one of the five most important of the sixty-five Buddhist temples and nineteen Shinto shrines in Kamakura. Here, we encountered flocks of monks on the run, *geta* clattering. These flat wooden sandals have two crosspieces underneath to raise the sole and the wearer about two inches above the ground. (The Japanese never seem to walk or, God forbid, amble; they move purposefully, often at a trot or flat-out gallop, whether it's to the dining hall at a Zen temple, or to catch the last train out of Tokyo, or just to shop. Bob and I are rather poky by comparison.) Kencho-ji, although large, is only half the size of the original: much of it has been rebuilt several times after being destroyed by fire. Reconstruction always repeats the original, an idea that's completely foreign in the West where "progress" is a prime animating principle. Kencho-ji is also affiliated with the Rinzai sect, and we saw groups of people, gathered at the base of a giant tree, taking instruction.

After lunch in a small noodle bar, we walked through the huge Tsurugaoka Hachimangu temple, the most important Shinto shrine in the city, famous for its view of Yuigahama Beach. It was built in the twelfth century for the son of Yoritomo Minamoto, the ruling shogun, who was beheaded by a member of the rival Taira clan. This was only one of the many stories connected with the struggle for power in Kamakura — stories of love, betrayal, murder, and infanticide. A sadness permeates many of these buildings. They remain on their original sites, in something like their former configurations, a reminder of the 141 years when Kamakura was the first seat of Japan's shogunate.

Templed out for the moment, we ducked onto an attractive commercial street called Shopping Walk, where smartly dressed women moved in and out of hatbox-sized boutiques. We were drawn into one shop by the wafting smell of incense. I bought some for our daughter, Rachel, at the sort of astronomical price I'm coming to consider normal. The saleswoman, who spoke good English, gave me samples of the incense they were burning that day in the store. (I lit it when we got home and discovered it was more delicate, less irritating, than the Indian incense I'm more accustomed to.)

From Kamakura station we boarded a train to Hase and what I thought was the silliest Buddhist temple so far — Hasedera, where 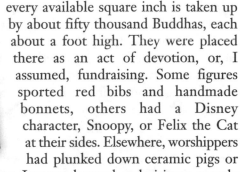 every available square inch is taken up by about fifty thousand Buddhas, each about a foot high. They were placed there as an act of devotion, or, I assumed, fundraising. Some figures sported red bibs and handmade bonnets, others had a Disney character, Snoopy, or Felix the Cat at their sides. Elsewhere, worshippers had plunked down ceramic pigs or stuffed cats. Incense burned and visitors, mostly women, laughed. Buddhists, I thought to myself, have more fun.

Here, as well, we stood in wonder at the eleven-headed Kannon, which stands thirty feet high, the largest wooden statue in Japan. This Goddess of Mercy was carved from a single piece of camphor wood in the eighth century. She has eleven faces, each turned in a different direction; her smiles are indeed full of mercy.

In a small tent, women knelt before tables, while other women wrote out their fortunes. We'd continued our walk when a fortune-teller came running after me, waving a piece of paper. "Japanese bible! Japanese bible!" she shouted, thrusting the paper into my hands. I smiled, bowed, and accepted it, without the slightest idea of what it said or what had provoked this gift. (Oddly, without understanding the significance of Hasedera, I lit a candle before the statue of Kannon and offered up a quick prayer for the safety of our children, on the principle that it could do no harm.)

Finally, we reached the Daibutsu, or Great Buddha, in the Kotoku-in temple, a bronze statue thirty-seven feet high sitting cross-legged and covered in flowing drapery. Now viewed against a backdrop of sky and trees, it originally sat at the centre of a wooden temple that was swept away in 1495 by a giant tidal wave. Neither the silly schoolgirls nor the tacky souvenir stands could distract from the majesty of the great iron Buddha. Bob and I agreed that our day in Kamakura had been sublime. Fears that we might not manage in such a strange country had evaporated.

Back in our room at the inn, I looked into a book on Kamakura and discovered how wrong my observations had been at Hasedera temple, or at least how incomplete. The little stone statues, looking to the uninitiated like lawn gnomes, represent Jizo Bosatu, the patron deity of travellers and children who have died. He is said to have come from India, an enlightened being whose name means "womb of the earth," appropriate since he's said to direct the souls of stillborn, aborted, and miscarried children. Temples dedicated to Jizo Bosatu are a growth industry, since about a million abortions are performed each year in Japan, the only industrialized nation left that considers the birth control pill unsafe. I think that I have just had my first — but I'm afraid not my last — lesson in cultural misreading.

SATURDAY, SEPTEMBER 19

It was wonderful to call home and speak to the girls and my mother today. All appears well. Otherwise a quiet day and somewhat frustrating. We wanted to walk in the Imperial Palace grounds but did not realize that this required advance permission. We did get into Kitanomaru Park at the northern tip of the Imperial estate, where we ate bento in the company of fat and insolent bees, protected no doubt by Imperial decree.

Then to the National Museum of Modern Art to see their permanent collection — two floors of highly derivative work in the schools of Degas, Cézanne, Picasso, Matisse. (Right masters, wrong pupils.) Of course, anyone coming to Canada to view our collection of painters of the same period — J.W. Morrice, for instance — might be left with the same impression. Knowing this didn't make the visit more interesting.

Japan is a statistician's heaven. Everything is measured, calibrated, and ranked. The main story today in Tokyo's four English-language dailies is not Nakasone's successor but Japanese education. Is it too strict? Does it create robots? Does pressure turn some young people into schoolyard bullies who publicly humiliate fellow students, and, on occasion, murder them? This old debate was reawakened not by a new incident but by a new survey: "The number of cases [of bullying] has gone from 55,729 to 136,476" in a few years. To improve their chances of getting into a good university, many students attend expensive cram schools in the evening. The papers reported that in one survey, 56 percent of parents said that cram schools were "a bad thing," but 82 percent of the complainers had enrolled their children. Regular school already occupies five and a half days a week: with inevitably long hours commuting, how do they find time to sleep?

I've been told that the "education debate" has been going on for decades — studies are commissioned, results published and debated. No consensus has been achieved on ways to improve the situation, so no political solutions have been reached. Everyone awaits the next survey.

Bob and I discussed these things as we walked around the Imperial Palace moat for what seemed like forever. Roland Barthes, the French critic and semiologist — a sifter of signs and symbols — described the emperor's palace as "the empty centre" of Tokyo. In *Empire of Signs* he wrote, "Daily, in their rapid, energetic, bullet-like trajectories, the taxis avoid this circle, whose low crest, the visible form of invisibility, hides the sacred 'nothing.'"

All I can say in defence of this sacred nothing is that the long sidewalk around the moat is pounded daily by joggers, and the public gardens provide green spaces that might help purify the air. These benefits are more than cancelled by the fact that no roads can go through the palace grounds, nor can subways be built beneath it. Overall, it probably causes more pollution than it eliminates.

Across the street, we were confronted by one grey concrete office building after another. They look exactly like the corporate headquarters that line University Avenue in Toronto, or Park Avenue in New York, buildings alive from nine to five but hollow and dull after dark. This is not a "recommended walk." We grabbed a cab, the first since our arrival, and headed back to Ginza.

We began with a bracing walk through Takashimaya department store, then popped into a Dunkin' Donuts for coffee and ice cream, and finally, a leisurely stroll through a record store. Compact discs are the big sellers, followed by vinyl, then cassettes that cost ¥2,800. Of the Top Nine (a Japanese variation on the Top Ten), five albums were Japanese. Number one was Michael Jackson's *Bad*.

The lack of security was impressive. Bin after bin of tapes, records, and CDs with no plastic tabs to set off alarms, no overhead mirrors, no niches for hidden cameras. No one, or almost no one, steals on a petty scale. Outside schools, subway stations, and office buildings, bicycles and baby carriages stand all day with no chains and no security guards. (Police regard the theft of a bicycle on their  turf as a personal insult, and hunt down bicycle thieves with Scotland Yard efficiency.)

Home for a rest, then into our lively neighbourhood for a comfort dinner of rice, noodles, and some morsels of protein. Lots of young people on the streets, boys and girls travelling in groups. Matching outfits signal members of special interest clubs? One way to meet future mates, I suppose, since high schools are generally single sex and not everyone goes to university.

Oh, yes. Picked up our first batch of laundry, beautifully wrapped, each shirt individually packaged and tied with a ribbon. Cost: ¥15,400 — over $150. It's true there was a pile of stuff, but it was mostly small items, like underwear and socks. Must find a better way to keep clean, or we'll be cleaned out.

SUNDAY, SEPTEMBER 20

Jill and David Bond of Ontario House met us, as planned, at Harajuku station at about 10 a.m. Kids detraining by the hundreds, not the usual gangs of students in school uniforms but  packs dressed in Tough Guy (and Gal) Leather, Tie-Dye Hippie, Pink-Haired Punk, Cool Preppy, and, most remarkable to me, American Frontier, complete with cowboy hats, boots, and fringes everywhere. They headed in droves for stalls lining the lane opposite the station exit. With David and Jill, we too wandered through several twisting streets where shops cater to the young, selling, among other things, clothing with hilarious

English: "Mercantile Ancient" on a boy's sweatshirt, "Grove Box" and "Official Proposal" on windbreakers, and "Light Menu" across the back of a girl's jacket. In context, if not literal sense, an inherent logic emerges from these logos, a groping toward coherence. I must go back next week and buy some as gifts.

Back aboard a train to Shinjuku, just up the road, but a journey I would never have attempted without the Bonds as guides. Shinjuku's the busiest rail station in the world — six train lines, four subway systems, and four department stores underground, a dozen skyscrapers on the west side, a lively entertainment district on the east. Getting out of the station was a major project. Jill, whose school is nearby, navigated through the tiled tunnels like a fish.

We headed for the Hanazono shrine and flea market, where about thirty vendors were selling everything from treasures to junk — silk, bamboo, paper, and steel crafted in the Edo (1603–1867) or Meiji (1868–1912) periods. People speaking French, German, and English were madly shopping, but I saw few Japanese customers. They prefer the new, and harbour residual fears of used items, especially clothing. They're also keenly aware of the distinction between the antique, for which they will pay top yen, and the merely second-hand, which they disdain. Household goods, such as teacups and sake glasses, must come in sets of five; if one is missing, the rest are of no value. Happily, I was not inhibited by superstition or exacting standards, only funds.

I bought a doll for one of my nieces, two hanging scrolls, one for my mother and one for us, four kimono, and ten old tinted postcards.

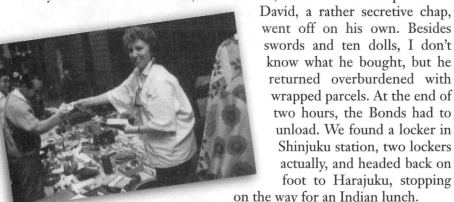

David, a rather secretive chap, went off on his own. Besides swords and ten dolls, I don't know what he bought, but he returned overburdened with wrapped parcels. At the end of two hours, the Bonds had to unload. We found a locker in Shinjuku station, two lockers actually, and headed back on foot to Harajuku, stopping on the way for an Indian lunch.

By this time Harajuku was jumping. The main street was closed to traffic and kids in organized "gangs" were dancing on the asphalt. Each group of between two and twenty kids had brought its own sound system, run off propane. As we walked down the street, one sound overlapped another.

We saw break-dancing on tatami mats, fifties rockers, and a highly styled and choreographed mock-traditional Japanese dance. The atmosphere was as relaxed as a private party. Despite the garish costumes, we were witnessing a tightly controlled rebellion. Jill said, "See all that orange and purple hair? It's sprayed on. By Monday morning, it'll be washed out and most of these kids will be back in school uniforms." Most of these young people follow an unwavering path, rarely taking any time off before university. If they drop out, it's practically impossible to drop back in; students they've been with since kindergarten have moved on, and they can never catch up with their cohort or join another peer group. In Japan, the kids you go to school with often become the people you work with; you may even end up marrying one of them. I think I would find these limitations unbearable, but in a culture where social rules are universally entrenched, perhaps they're more easily accepted.

More shopping followed in an open air market in Yoyogi Park, rather like a communal garage sale — everything from an elephant's foot ottoman to an exquisite traditional doll in a glass case for ¥1,000, or about $10. This was bargain hunting par excellence. The Bonds bought the doll and we headed off for the adjoining Meiji shrine, originally completed in 1920 by a hundred thousand volunteers to honour the emperor who died in 1912. That building was destroyed in the Second World War; what we saw was a beautifully proportioned 1950s reconstruction. It's located deep inside a wooded park, right beside the street dancers, the sort of urban mix that makes Tokyo so exciting. Every once in a while the sound of the street bubbled up through the shrine silence, but not enough to break the serenity. Just beside the main gate, we witnessed a Shinto priest blessing a newborn — the father in a dark business suit, the mother in a gorgeous kimono.

It is said that in Japan one is born Shinto and dies Buddhist. An anachronism among religions in modern societies, Shinto is characterized not by scriptures or hierarchy but by archaic tribal myths, a concern for purity and defilement, and a loose collection of shrines and rituals to promote survival — the need for protection from draughts, plagues, and one's enemies, not to mention safety on Japan's modern highways. Since the Meiji period, rites of passage have come increasingly under the aegis of Shinto priests, who preside over birth, coming of age, and marriage. Death is managed by Buddhism, a belief system that concentrates on individual enlightenment, compassion, and reincarnation, the bliss of Nirvana and the torment of hell.

Standing beside us in front of the offertory were the same costumed kids from down the road. They followed the prescribed procedure, clapped twice to gain the attention of the gods, then pressed their hands tightly together. It was hard to decide which activity was authentic — rock 'n' roll or praying to Shinto gods. Maybe neither. Perhaps both.

On the surface, Japanese life seems to be changing faster than the language. In one of the morning papers there was an article about honorifics — the way one person must assess another's social position compared to his own before speaking. The author, a doctor, argues that there can be no fundamental change in Japanese society without a major linguistic shift. Years ago, someone said something similar to me about the German language, about the psychological damage done while waiting for the verb to arrive at the end of the sentence. I understand that this is also a problem with Japanese.

We thanked the Bonds for a marvellous day. They were generous with their time and knowledge. I imagine they had fun watching our astonished faces. Tomorrow some official obligations which I hope will not be too tedious.

Monday, September 21

Hellish introduction to Japanese bureaucracy. First, in a minor way, trying to activate our JR passes. These passes, sold only outside Japan, will allow us to travel anywhere, at a rate fixed far below normal. Bob and I have two chits, each for one week, but must pick a date when we want our trip to begin. We'd decided to go to Kyoto for seven days, starting on October 4. From there we can make any side trips we like.

We were told to go to Tokyo station and the Travel Center there. Fortunately we'd left lots of room in the day for shilly-shallying — but almost not enough, as it turned out. After several false starts we arrived at the correct office, but oh lordy, it took the poor man about fifteen minutes to do the simplest job. There was no lineup. There rarely is, at least at the places we've been so far. Overstaffing is one of the benefits of "full employment." One would think this would result in speed. Not so.

There were three Swiss women, newly arrived — do I feel like an old-timer? — who spoke no Japanese and for whom English was a second or third language. You could almost hear them grinding their teeth as they waited in line ahead of us.

We finished and headed for the Foreign Press Center to meet with a Mr. Ueda, who was assigned to help us secure permission to see the Imperial estates in Kyoto. He was also going to introduce us to a Mr. Takashima, a friend of his, he said, a professor at Tokyo University, "someone who knows about the visual arts." Mr. Ueda must have been a handsome man once. Now in his late fifties or early sixties, after a thirty-year career at NHK, the national public broadcaster, he's assigned to shepherd foreign journalists through baroque institutions. Short and trim, under a crown of jet black hair favoured by older women and most businessmen and politicians from Nakasone down. Only the emperor, it seems, is allowed to go grey.

We talked briefly about the appointments he'd suggested we make: he was pleased we were seeing his kabuki man tomorrow, but unhappy we had not called his friend at NHK. I suggested that we thought it might be best to talk to Mr. Takashima, whom we were to meet at 5:30, since as well as being a person connected with the visual arts and Tokyo University, he was also a frequent guest on NHK. "Perhaps he could introduce us to specific people," I suggested.

"Well," said Mr. Ueda, "there are fifteen thousand people who work at NHK. Mr. Takashima is in the visual arts. The man I suggested would certainly know more." It became clear that he believed you talked to a theatre person about theatre, and a visual arts man about visual arts, period. His English was halting. He made no glaring errors, but every word was such an effort that he began to tremble and perspire.

Mr. Ueda accompanied us to the Otemon gate of the Imperial Palace. The Palace has been much in the news lately because eighty-six-year-old Hirohito has a bowel obstruction that is reported in the press in obsessive detail: "vomited on his holidays," "can't attend the sumo finals, a great favourite of the emperor." It was decided yesterday that an operation was needed, but the surgeons assured us that "the monarch is in fine condition for his age," and that "many older people do very well following surgery." One suspects he's sicker than we are being told.

Although I have little basis of comparison, the palace seemed excessively guarded: three or four riot trucks, which were really disguised tanks with huge hoses coiled on top, stood at every conceivable access point. I had been following the emperor's condition with ghoulish interest; his death would be followed by a national re-evaluation of his life, especially by leftists and ultra-nationalists. Questions would once again be raised about his actions in wartime — his role in the Manchuria Incident, the Rape of Nanking, and the Pacific War. Was Hirohito a dupe of his ministers, or a prime mover in Japan's Asian expansion? Did General Douglas MacArthur and the Americans make a mistake in allowing him to remain as a constitutional monarch? I wondered if we'd be in Japan during this historic transition.

It was a good thing that Mr. Ueda was with us. First our cab was stopped far outside the gate where we had to explain why we wanted to get to the security post, two hundred yards ahead. The post was guarded by a young woman sentry in a box and two older men standing nearby. One manned a thick, steel automatic gate that, in the Japanese style, slid across the pavement to the other side.

After animated negotiations, we were allowed to proceed to an office to fill out forms — name, nationality, passport number, Toronto and Tokyo addresses. Our passports were stamped, just as at a national border, and copies of the document we'd completed in triplicate were handed back. "Done," I thought. Not done. Actually, these forms gave us permission to fill out more forms. Security passes pinned to our clothes, we were led through the gate to an administration office further onto the site. A few cars passed and people went through the gate. Dozens of television vans were parked inside. According to Mr. Ueda they were awaiting "the emperor's death." (I was not the only one who discounted the upbeat medical reports.) He pointed to cameras with telescopic lenses mounted on several nearby buildings.

The hospital where the emperor's operation is to take place is on the palace grounds, close to the area we had just passed through, which could explain the extraordinary security. It could also, of course, be another example of "full employment." (Bob had made me promise not to talk about the emperor's impending death inside the palace walls. He thought my enthusiasm might be misunderstood by our hosts. But even he grimaced when I said, "How sad all the people will be when the emperor dies.")

Mr. Ueda, in discussing the age of the crown prince said, "Yes, he's in his late fifties. The age most others are retiring, and he hasn't even started his job yet." Then he chuckled.

"That's a good joke. Is it a Tokyo joke?" I asked.

"No. One of my own." This was the wittiest exchange we shared with Mr. Ueda in our three and a half hours together.

We were seated in the Imperial Palace office facing a perfect specimen of *Bureaucratis imperialum*. He took the papers we had just filled out and handed Mr. Ueda an enormous book of photographs of one of Kyoto's Imperial villas. With practised skill, Mr. Ueda turned every page, feigning interest, and commenting as he rushed along.

Each Kyoto site required its own permission slip. Each form asked for the same information as the last, including "occupation" and "age." Instructions were unilingual, so Mr. Ueda went over them quickly and retired to a sofa. Bob so absorbed the stultifying atmosphere of the place that he printed his address in the occupation slot. I thought the jig was up. After much discussion, and more time, a replacement form was found and we completed that stage of our business. (During the entire ten or fifteen minutes in the small office, one man sat in the corner at attention, vigorously stamping forms with a heavy metal implement.)

As we were finishing up, we were told that we would be allowed to go on a tour of the royal estate here in Tokyo if we wanted. From the writing on a map behind his desk I knew that this was a favour granted to everyone and that the tour clung to the inside wall of the moat. "Oh, yes, we'd love to." How do I know this isn't a trick question — say "no" and they cancel Kyoto. Anyway, they marked us down for Thursday morning.

It was now time to leave the Imperial whatnot and head over to the Tokyo Station Hotel, about a ten-minute walk. One of the few Meiji-era buildings still in use in Tokyo, the original Tokyo station is rather down at the heels but charming, and is occasionally used for rock concerts.

Mr. Takashima, we were told, was leaving one meeting and going to another and could therefore only spare us about a half hour. We checked the bar upstairs where Mr. Ueda thought we were to meet. It was closed. It was 5:00 p.m. a half hour before we were expected. We went to a nearby bar, ordered beer and "a typical Japanese snack," according to Mr. Ueda — soybeans boiled in their pods and salted. Just pop 'em in your mouth. Delicious, and good for you too.

To pass the time, Bob tried to engage Mr. Ueda in conversation. "What sort of art does Professor Takashima specialize in?"

"Oh, I do not know that," replied Mr. Ueda, "but he is a very important man. He studied for some time in Paris. I don't know him myself, although we went to the same middle school, but I do know his wife and his sister. They helped me to arrange this appointment."

"Ah!"

"Were you educated in Tokyo?"

"Yes, but I spent three and a half years at Stanford University, in California."

Bob told a story about a friend who taught Freud in Los Angeles to a class of university kids dressed in shorts and carrying skateboards. No response.

"And what did you study there?" Bob asked.

"Oh, not political relations. More like human relations. Ha, ha." Mr. Ueda had made his second joke, letting us know he'd been something of a lady's man. Meanwhile, he kept looking over his shoulder, out the door, for Professor Takashima. Recognizing him would be somewhat difficult, since they'd never met. We joked that he would certainly know who we were. Mr. Ueda, a chain-smoker, soon filled our ashtray. Bob and Mr. Ueda — we never did make it to first names — ordered second beers; I switched to coffee. A fresh ashtray arrived. This was shaping up to be a long wait.

"Perhaps we should move closer to the door so we could watch the stairs," suggested Mr. Ueda. These were the stairs leading to the bar that wasn't operating. We moved. At 5:40, to make sure he hadn't missed him, Mr. Ueda dashed out and up the stairs to see if, by some mistake, our fellow was waiting there. He was not.

"They know Professor Takashima well there. He comes quite often because he travels so much. In fact, he's going abroad tomorrow. That is why we must meet him today."

By this time, we were all a bit tense. Bob was being wonderfully jolly, telling the story of the time he and his publisher, at the urging of external affairs, took four Soviet writers to lunch at the revolving restaurant at the Harbour Castle Hotel in Toronto, thinking it would be a great treat. Once there, they discovered that their guests had eaten in revolving restaurants in Seattle, Calgary, Vancouver — *and* they had their own in Moscow. Tensions at our table eased temporarily.

Bob and Mr. Ueda had finished their second beers and my coffee was long gone. Mr. Ueda ordered the same again and ran upstairs a second time. When he returned alone, we questioned him about his life. He lives in Roppongi, a Tokyo neighbourhood favoured by foreigners, with his father. Taxes are extremely high. We asked if he was the eldest son. "No, but my brother doesn't want to live with our father." Mr. Ueda wore a wedding ring but never mentioned a wife, nor did we ask. He'd lived in England as well as the United States and worked there from 1964 to 1965 as an NHK correspondent. "I lived in South Kensington," he smiled ruefully. How odd. I'd been in England at the same time, living just up the road, off Kensington High Street.

I might have shared this information with Mr. Ueda but he didn't seem interested and asked no questions: a cultural thing, or just too edgy? Bob did give him a copy of the 100th Anniversary Issue of *Saturday Night*. He asked if Bob himself had written anything for it and Bob steered him to his article. Seconds later, we all looked up as an older man approached the door, peeked in, and left. Mr. Ueda stared at the man as he walked away, then, without comment, jumped up and ran down the long corridor after him. He returned, alone, and ordered a third round — and more beans. It was now 5:50.

To end the torture, Bob and I had agreed to say we had to be back at our ryokan for a phone call at seven, but how to raise the subject? Had Mr. Ueda been stood up or was he merely incompetent? (We must think hard before accepting official appointments that we don't arrange ourselves.)

"Do you have somewhere to go tonight?" asked Mr. Ueda. Yes, we told him in the gentlest way possible, and we offered the telephone story.

"It's been wonderful meeting you. The beans were delicious." I knew that I was blathering, but what else could I do? At 6:15, Mr. Ueda paid the bill and walked us to our train. "Just call me if there's anything else you need," he shouted after us.

Ended the day eating yakitori in Shinjuku in a dive with a jolly owner.

TUESDAY, SEPTEMBER 22

A day in search of art. Began with a 10:30 a.m. appointment at the National Theatre. Built about a decade ago, the National is home to two theatres — about 1,700 seats for kabuki and 630 for bunraku puppets. The man we were to meet, as arranged by Mr. Ueda, was actually there and waiting for us and spoke lovely English. Atsumi Karashima is in charge of the National Theatre's training program — noh, kabuki, and bunraku. He's a friend of Marty Gross of Toronto, a man so smitten with Japanese puppet theatre that he made a recent, much admired film about it. Karashima had interesting, and for a Japanese, quite candid things to say about the traditional arts.

Kabuki began in the early seventeenth century, about 250 years after noh, and it was, from the beginning, conceived of as lighter farc. It grew out of "shocking dances" performed by an all-female troupe led by Okuni, a priestess from Izumo shrine in Kyoto. At first she performed her disreputable dance in the dry riverbed of the Kamo, where jurisdiction was disputed. She called her act kabuki, a name she'd created from three Chinese characters — song, dance, and skill. As a result of her unique costume — she wore the pants of a Portuguese sailor — kabuki came to mean something stylish, eccentric, and wild. When her troupe played a command performance for the shogun in Edo, the audience fought over several cast members, male and female. As a result, women were banned from the stage: to this day women are not allowed in traditional kabuki.

There are about ten famous kabuki families who more or less own certain roles: to become a serious kabuki actor, you must apprentice with one of them. "About two-thirds of all kabuki parts are performed by members of these families," Mr. Karashima told us. "The remaining supporting actors come from the National School." When I asked if there was much competition for these parts, he laughed and said, rather sadly, "No. For one thing, the salary and the fame are nothing like that of a movie or TV star."

Both kabuki stages in Tokyo, the Kabuki-za and the National, are run by a single company, Shochiku; they abandoned bunraku some years ago as a money loser. Bunraku and noh are now entirely subsidized by the government. We did not discuss noh at great length, but I assume that if bunraku and kabuki are in trouble — he calls them "the vaudeville of Japanese theatre" — noh must be near death. To build audiences, they're doing what we do in Canada, trying to attract the young.

I asked if he'd heard of the successful New York and London performances of a kabuki *Medea*, but he hadn't. It seems that traditional Japanese theatre might have to adapt to survive. Not as easy as it sounds in a country with a deep, official respect for tradition, even if participation is declining. (Rather like attitudes toward established churches in Canada.) Mr. Karashima said that he'd try to get us tickets to kabuki. If he doesn't, we'll go on our own.

We were taken on a tour of the smaller, six-hundred-seat theatre where bunraku is performed, and the larger kabuki and noh stages, about twice that size. The backstage areas for both are huge and would be the envy of most North American theatres. On the bunraku stage there's an elevated section, about three feet high, behind which "actors" manipulate the puppets. (The audience can see them from about the knees up.) There are two shows daily; one at noon and the other at 5 p.m. We'd been given tickets for the second show.

It was now 11 a.m. and the backstage was coming to life. There was a crew of about twenty — ten musicians and about twelve puppeteers. Because bunraku puppets are about half to two-thirds life size, each major "character" is handled by three puppeteers. Two are dressed in black, their faces covered by a black hood. The chief puppeteer manipulates the puppet's head, eyes, mouth, right arm and hand, bringing the puppet to life. He dresses in white, face exposed. On a separate revolving dais, musicians perform on the shamisen, something like a banjo, seated beside chanters, who narrate the story.

Mr. Karashima asked if we would like to meet a master puppeteer. When we said yes, he ran down the hall, leaving us to take off our shoes and put on plastic slippers. (It seems that street shoes are okay where there's carpet but not on wood, even if the wood is dirty, as it was here.) We were asked to follow and there, in the equivalent of the green room — it really was painted green — sat a gamin-like man, Bunjaku Yoshida, a head like Oz — old, bald, and whimsical. He specializes in female puppets and is a member of the prominent Yoshida bunraku family. As in kabuki, puppet theatre is a family business and something of a closed shop — except that a performer may be adopted by a family that finds him worthy.

Yoshida-san scattered cushions on the tatami floor and, with Mr. Karashima translating, spoke a mile a minute about how each puppet was made, illustrating by taking real puppets apart — yanking their heads off their long necks. He showed us how, when you change a puppet's costume, wig, and makeup, its character changes. Once they're dressed in their elaborate Edo costumes, they weigh about twenty pounds.

Bunraku puppet theatre began about 150 years ago in Osaka when Uemura Bunrakken combined two ancient forms — puppetry and chanting. The greatest plays are historical epics written by the seventeenth-century playwright, Monzaemon Chikamatsu, often called Japan's Shakespeare. Although his work was commissioned for puppets, many of his plays were later adapted for kabuki.

Yoshida-san asked if we'd like to hold a puppet and try to manipulate it. Of course. We posed for pictures. Bob with puppet. Geraldine with puppet. Both with puppet master.

We left for lunch, and then our most harrowing subway ride so far — three transfers to Shinagawa and the Hara Museum, where a Michael Snow show is scheduled for next summer. After arriving at the station we hopped a cab and, using an English-only map, tried pointing and pronouncing Hara Museum every conceivable way. Finally something clicked for our driver. "Ah, Ha-ra Museum!" he said, using a marginally different pronunciation. The museum was just around the corner. (The humiliations that befall the unilingual traveller.)

The collection, housed in a lovely 1937 Bauhaus building that once belonged to the Hara family, was small and international — a Karl Appel, a Mark Rothko, a Robert Rauschenberg, a few French, Dutch, Finnish, and Latin American painters, and one Jean-Paul Riopelle. The part I liked best was the garden, where little grass grew but four old men worked steadily, raking mud, trimming trees, pruning excess branches, cutting them into equal foot-long pieces, tying them, and burning them in a pile. A smell from my childhood, memories of late autumn and a ritual now outlawed by overzealous and misguided concern for the environment.

Mr. Kanazawa, the head curator and the man putting together the Snow exhibit, was an amiable fellow but didn't inspire great confidence. Generally, he seemed to know more about the contemporary art world *inside* Japan. Most of it, he complained, was academic in style, resembling an update of ancient skills. This is the art that public galleries support. The private gallery system differs considerably from the West: any artist can rent space for the equivalent of $2,000 US for a six-day week. As well, the artist must pay for advertising, a reception, and the catalogue. Renting a studio is also terribly expensive, especially in Tokyo, where he knew of only three full-time artists who have what we would call a studio. The rest must supplement their art by teaching or work in advertising.

He told us that the visual arts in Japan lagged far behind technology, industry, and trade. There's only one other museum like his, a large one near Osaka. If he's to be believed, our quest for great contemporary art in Japan ended at the Hara Museum.

Unfortunately, he didn't seem to know much about Michael Snow and was stuck at the Walking Woman period of the 1960s. He hasn't settled yet on the size, scope, or focus of the show, which was unusual since advanced planning is needed for insurance and shipping. Doubly odd, since the Ontario government is picking up these costs. Mr. Kanazawa is going to Toronto next month. We exchanged cards.

Throughout our half-hour visit, high-pitched young women came in and out of his office bringing coffee, the mail, a package — their chattering created a more or less constant hum behind our conversation. No one paid any attention but they continued, undeterred.

We made our way back to the National Theatre in time for the second bunraku show. The house was about three-quarters full, mostly middle-aged, middle-class women. The food on sale in the lobby was delicious, and everyone seemed preoccupied with eating; perhaps bunraku was primarily an excuse for a sushi feast. People did an extraordinary amount of eating — before and during the show, and at intermission.

There were two separate plays on the program although we stayed for only one. It was so wonderful, I felt it couldn't possibly get better. I have never liked puppets, but these puppets shattered my prejudices. The puppeteers' costumes made them look like members of the Ku Klux Klan, complete with pointed hoods — but all in black. For about a minute I was conscious of their presence; then, magically, they faded and disappeared, leaving the illusion of the puppets, these wonderful actors, alone on the stage.

One of the most remarkable aspects of bunraku was the strength and talent of the various narrators. Dressed in wide *hakama* pants and a winged jacket, the narrator enacted all the voices in one section of the play from a kneeling position on the side stage. To increase his projection he would lean slightly forward, but otherwise was entirely motionless. We rented an earphone guide with an excellent English translation. It explained that to enhance his voice, a narrator ties a thirteen-yard cloth and a bag of pebbles around his waist, which he pulls tighter as the show progresses, to further strengthen his performance. He reads from a book resting on a short lectern in front of him, but our narrator did far more than "read": he wailed and pitched his voice to suit each character, using intonation that might once have been common but has long since disappeared from normal Japanese speech.

The proceedings began with the appearance on stage of a black-hooded man who announced the name of the play and the names of the succession of narrators and musicians. Everyone applauded. The play divided into three acts, each one building in length and emotional intensity. (There were three narrators, each better than the one before.) From the second act on, the chief puppeteer, Bunjaku Yoshida, in a white outfit, face, head, and hands exposed, stared intently at his puppet or at the ground, all carefully choreographed. He seemed to be manipulated more by the puppet than the other way around, as if he had to run to keep up to his puppet, by now a character in the play as much as any actor could be.

The story recalled the majesty of *King Lear*, the poignancy and inevitability of *Oedipus Rex*, the carnage of *Medea*. It raised the spectre of piety and filial loyalty, of personal sacrifice and the greater good, themes that occur and reoccur in Japanese life. The narrator in the last act was said, by our audio guide, to be the best interpreter of the play's climactic scene. Through his voice we came to feel the horror of a mother who found that her father had killed her adopted daughter and that her son-in-law was dead by his own hand — all to prevent a civil war between two rival princely households.

It's hard to explain but, in this brightly lit hall, when the bell tolled and the narrator said, "The ringing of the evening bell reminds us of life's transience," it was impossible not to cry. The old woman in front of me cried. So did I. Brecht saw bunraku in the 1930s and his work was deeply influenced, but no Brecht play I've ever seen has been as powerful.

WEDNESDAY, SEPTEMBER 23

Some of my best travel memories concern laundry. I remember a portable clothesline across a bidet in a rundown Paris hotel on my first trip abroad in 1961. Shortly after my father died in June 1978, I remember hanging clothes with wooden pegs on the line behind a friend's cottage in Clay Cove, Newfoundland — our daughters, Rachel and Sarah, six and four years old, running in circles around me, their long white nighties blowing in the sea breeze. And a year ago, my arms full of dripping clothes, I recall heading to a rope strung between a fig tree and an olive tree in a field of lavender behind a house we'd rented in Provence.

Today, I did my first Tokyo wash in a small machine at our ryokan. It sits, old and dented, under the tin roof on a miniature stone terrace. I hung each piece to dry on a plastic contraption with four arms. In keeping with Japanese aesthetics I arranged everything — Bob's underwear, his shirts, my things — attractively, mixing colours and shapes, while placing wetter things on the bottom, drier on top. I was incredibly happy.

Then, because it was a holiday, the autumn equinox, we did a holiday thing — a walk in Ueno Park, a visit to two museums there, a snack at the zoo, and a paper cup of sake on a park bench. The park is beautifully laid out, the vegetation overgrown and wilful, with acres of lotuses that have managed to survive in Shinobazu Pond since the Meiji era. The layout of the buildings and the meandering walkways are a treat, something that couldn't be said for either of the museums we visited.

The Tokyo National Museum is inspiring from the outside — a Japanese-style tiled roof on a concrete structure, a Meiji building of the late nineteenth century. The inside was a different story — dusty, neglected cases, poor air and humidity control, inadequate lighting, and confusing signage. They appear to hold their own collection in low esteem. The featured exhibit was on Thai art, but it was the Japanese art we'd come to see, particularly the ukiyo-e woodblock prints.

Ukiyo is an ancient Buddhist term for the impermanence of human life. During the lively and relatively peaceful Edo period, *ukiyo* assumed a new meaning based on the homonym of *uki*, meaning "floating." Even though life was fleeting, it was to be enjoyed. Licentious pleasure, however, was confined to teahouses, bathhouses, and theatres, licensed by the central government and restricted to specific urban areas designated as "pleasure quarters," where money, sex, and style reigned. Woodblock print artists became chroniclers of this "floating" world of kabuki actors, courtesans, geisha, and prostitutes. Was this the world I'd been trying to reproduce in my tentative adolescent rendering of a Japanese geisha? (Perhaps, since these prints have been widely admired abroad since the nineteenth century.) Unfortunately, the gallery where the National's print collection is normally displayed was closed until October.

The new Tokyo Metropolitan Museum of Art, built in 1975, was an even bigger disappointment, a large train station without the excitement of motion. On a sign at the end of the walkway, it was explained that due to height restrictions the architect had gone below ground to create the entrance. In the process much space seems to have been wasted. Inside, there was a central courtyard with people sitting at tables, smoking, and no art in sight. In each of four large rooms off the courtyard was a separate gallery to which we were invited to pay a nominal fee. Even that, however, seemed too much. A peek around the corner in each room discouraged us. We left as quickly as possible.

In the park I was impressed by how young the mothers seemed. Even given the youthful appearance of the Japanese, most of them had to be in their early twenties. They were certainly not North American Yuppie parents. If it's true that younger mothers produce "better" babies, these children had a head start. They seemed huge, happy, and responsive. The young mothers exuded a calm confidence I envied. There were no crying babies.

Back in our room, surrounded by piles of clean clothes, Bob received a call from a Mrs. Yamaoka, who asked to speak to "Dr. Fulford." She said that her company was setting up an International College in Canada and wanted to take "Dr. Fulford" for lunch. Bob roped me in and we're set for Monday. (That's also the day that the Ontario government is having a reception for us.) There was another invitation waiting, both names properly written, this one for a lunch at a French restaurant in honour of Canadians attending the Tokyo International Film Festival.

THURSDAY, SEPTEMBER 24

We'd arranged for a taxi to come to our ryokan at 9:30 a.m. to take us to the Imperial Palace for the tour of the grounds we'd been offered. From looking at the map in the Imperial Agency's office I could see that we could not expect to walk far from the wall. However, an Imperial request, even when issued by a stamp-crazed flunky, must be obeyed.

By the time we reached the second set of gates, we were part of a tour group that formed into two rows, like schoolchildren, and headed for the third gate. It was 9:50 a.m. We straggled into an indoctrination room — perhaps it was called the orientation room? — where we were seated in front of a giant map. Our tour guide, a middle-aged man in uniform, barked a few sentences in Japanese. Half the people marched out. Bob and I stared blankly at one another. Everyone else on the tour was Japanese, except for a group of five high-school girls under the large wing of a *gaijin* woman and a Japanese translator. I asked if they knew what was happening.

"Our interpreter said we were told that we could smoke in here but not on the rest of the tour and that there would be no sitting down." Great. I reported my findings to Bob, who recalled, in the words of our own regal personage, Prince Philip: "Never pass up a chance to pee." He left the room, smoking his pipe.

Our young English-speaking companions were from Auckland, in the last days of an exchange visit to a girls' school that was built by a manufacturing company for the exclusive use of employees' daughters. They'd slept in the company-owned dormitory and holidayed in the company-owned mountain resort. They were appalled by these arrangements and commented that the girls they'd met were totally unambitious and wanted only to get married.

When everyone reconvened, the guide began an interminable talk in front of a giant map of the palace grounds. I think he was pointing out spots of interest we wouldn't be seeing, but since he did not speak any English during the one and a quarter hours we were together, I can't be certain. The audience listened with mixed attention. Three Japanese school girls sat with knees together, feet on the ground, backs straight, hands clasped, eyes forward the entire time. The others, a ragtag assortment of lads looking a bit hung over, and a few older men, were as restless as we were. Some "exclusive" showing, I grumbled. Could we bolt now, or would it cause an international incident?

We toughed it out, and I do mean toughed. We trudged along asphalt roads, across parking lots, over a bridge, and back to the stamping building, where we watched at a great distance as men in morning coats bowed to an approaching car that stopped and unloaded one male passenger. I asked the interpreter with the foreign girls what was happening. "A man from the government is bringing very important papers for the emperor." So he didn't know either.

When the tour finally ended, we raced to Shibuya and the Tobu Hotel, where we were to pick up our press accreditation for the Tokyo

International Film Festival. It was our first time in this dense and lively area where everything seemed to be in a permanent state of becoming — roads, buildings, people. We wandered into one of the five Parco stores clustered together near the hotel. It was the most beautiful department store I'd ever seen. Built around a central escalator, it's like the new Holt Renfrew in Toronto but works better. There were about ten designer boutiques, not one with clothes in my size. Gulliver among the Lilliputians. For consolation, I ate a large lunch in the typical eighth-floor restaurant.

It's somewhat gratifying to discover that getting press accreditation for the Tokyo International Film Festival is just as nerve-wracking an experience as at the Toronto International Film Festival, except here there are twice as many young female helpers who are twice as nice. Since 163 movies are scheduled, we had to make drastic decisions: first to go, the Tribute to American Movies and the Fellini Retrospective. When in Tokyo, we decided, see only Japanese or other Asian movies. On last night's news we learned that the selection committee for the Grand Jury Prize was headed by "Gregory Pekku."

Across the street from the Tobu is a simple and charming museum, a tribute on four floors to two government monopolies for a pair of dangerous substances the Japanese use in excess — tobacco and salt. It was a fine example of museology — interesting displays, well-organized, clear, and fun — with cases that lit up as you approached them. Tobacco and salt appear as useful products, goods for barter, sale, and promoting international trade. No mention of cancer or hypertension. Home early and dinner (if one may call it that) at Lotteria, a version of McDonald's that made me long for the original.

FRIDAY, SEPTEMBER 25

The second Tokyo International Film Festival opened at the NHK Hall today. Our press kits warned that we should arrive early, as there were no reserved seats. We showed up at 10:28 a.m., two minutes before the doors were to open, or I should say "door" since although there were three, one was reserved for Distinguished Visitors, one for Guests, and one for Press. The hall has the charm of an airplane hangar with seats, but we had a wonderful view from the side of the front balcony.

On stage there were three folding chairs off to the left, two rather grander chairs behind a table slightly to the right, and three folding chairs at the right rear. These last three were filled by three unknowns, two men and a woman. The rest of the guests were introduced by a smooth bilingual fellow, a bit like the young Alex Trebek. They included the government minister in charge of international trade and industry, the powerful MITI. He spoke about "the international language of film." Then came the governor of Tokyo, who spoke about "the international language of film."

The centre two chairs were occupied by the tiny crown prince and princess, looking like figures on a wedding cake. She's fifty-three, and he's a year older. Her miniature, extremely stylish outfit probably cost as much as our entire trip. It was capped with a chapeau that sat forward on her head — combination stewardess and Shinto priest. His Almost-Imperial-Highness spoke about "the international language of film." They seemed genuinely pleased to be there (after having glimpsed the Royal Household staff, I could understand why), and far less remote than our own Royal Persons.

Formalities began at 11:40 as promised and ended at 12:30. This gave us a half hour to pick up a Japanese movie snack — a box of crustless white-bread sandwiches, one with a thin slice of ham, another with a scraping of cheese, and a third, a hint of tuna — all packaged with a disposable hand towel and a toothpick in a paper sleeve. Not much to eat, but lots to unpack. With coffee, about $10.

The movie started at one o'clock. It was called *The Princess from the Moon* and was a retelling of an eighth-century folk tale about the fall to earth of a moon child, her adoptive human parents, her lover, and her return to the moon via a spaceship. The producer's credits include Kurosawa's *Yojimbo* and *Kagemusha*; the director, Kon Ichikawa, has been making respected movies for forty-three years; Toshiro Mifune, *the* Japanese actor, played the father; the moon princess was discovered after a thirty-thousand-girl search; and the costumes were designed by Emi Wada, who did *Ran*. Despite all this, and a ¥100-million budget, the picture was a mess, at best a celluloid fashion show with outfits that seemed to walk out of a costume museum. When the movie ended, I thought I spotted June Allyson with Jack Valenti. (A certain amount of *that* sort of thing goes on at all festivals, but here it's rather low key.)

We headed back to Festival headquarters at the Tobu Hotel, and tried to arrange a mailbox for ourselves. This presents something of a problem for me since I'm listed as "Ms Geraldine S.P." This wasn't as crazy as it might seem in Canada, since Japanese family names are always given first. In the list of VIPs I'm there, in this form, a bit down from June Allyson (yes, she *is* here) and a bit above Diane Keaton (*she's* here too).

The choice for the evening was between a huge party at the ANA Hotel or the movie *The Man Who Assassinated Ryoma*, directed by Kosaku Yamashita. The movie won. It was the opening feature in a series of Japanese films, some vintage cinema, others more recent, like tonight's world premiere. They run as pairs, linked by subject matter — a new and an old film about the same subject, such as intergenerational conflict or aging. Donald Richie was one of the four selectors; the movies all sound intriguing; and they all have English subtitles.

Ryoma was to start at 7 p.m. after an introduction at 6:30. At 5:00, we set out from the Tobu, clutching the official schematic map showing all festival theatres as well as key stores and subways exits. An hour later we'd criss-crossed the district without success, even after about a dozen enquiries, a trip back to the hotel information desk, and stops at two movie houses, one of which seemed to be located right beside our goal, the Shibuya Shochiku Central. Finally, in desperation, we threw ourselves at one of the dozens of young people wearing festival jackets and begged him to actually walk us to the theatre.

Using our map, he retraced our steps exactly, and wound up at the Shibuya Palace movie house. The map was wrong. Three minutes later we were on the sixth floor of a large commercial building pleading to get into the screening. We did. Supper at our seats — more sandwiches, popcorn, and beer, a civilized addition to movie watching. The theatre was full, almost all Japanese. The movie was about the comin' of gunpowder and the dyin' of the old samurai ways. It was a triumph of cinematography but little else. It felt as if we'd stumbled into a genre film that's probably as well known in Japan as Westerns are in America. The worst part was the soundtrack — throbbing contemporary Western music over location shots of Kyoto. Do I detect the legacy of rock video?

A little tired in foot and eye, I looked forward to settling into a bath back at the ryokan. I do it the Japanese way now — soaping first on a little stool on the tiled floor of the bathroom, rinsing with a hand-held shower, then stepping into a deep, hot tub. It makes more sense than soaking in a pool of one's dirt. And it feels heavenly.

SATURDAY, SEPTEMBER 26

Left the ryokan in the morning for Shibuya and a second day of festival films. First, another in the Japanese retrospective, a 1985 movie called *And Then*, a story of love and disappointment in Japan in the 1920s, directed by a thirty-seven-year-old Yoshimitsu Morita. It was the mise en scène rather than the story that fascinated. I hadn't known how strong the Western influence was in Japan in the twenties — in music, fashion, literature, and thought. The story resembled a sprawling turn-of-the-century Russian novel about a brooding, self-absorbed aristocrat who realizes too late that he can't escape the consequences of his crime.

The afternoon film was its polar opposite, Shohei Imamura's *Intentions of Murder*, a 1964 black-and-white film noir set in poverty-stricken, post-war Japan. It was full of betrayal, rape, a miscarriage, two deaths, and, in the end, bravery by the unlikely impoverished heroine. I loved the domestic detail — poor lighting, knitting machines, vacuums. Seeing the film is a reminder of how depleted Japan was after the war, and how far the Japanese have come in such a short time.

We didn't leave the theatre until about 6:00, just enough time to check our press box at the Tobu Hotel and pick up the bumph that's issued daily, before meeting Ted Goossen and his friends at 7:00 at a designated subway track at Shinjuku. The mere thought of meeting someone in Shinjuku station would have caused waves of terror a couple of weeks ago, and now only raised a frisson of anxiety. If you avoid rush hour, Tokyo subways are safe, efficient, and user-friendly, quite an accomplishment in a city of about ten million.

We arrived a bit early and were joined shortly by Ted and Ms. Feng. She's a Japanese-language student from Beijing, one of the best in Tokyo University's comparative literature course taught by Koji Kawamoto. He was to meet us at a designated coffee shop but, because he was delayed, we moved to a nearby Korean barbecue. With Ted as interpreter, Feng told us something of her life.

She is twenty-nine, the middle child and only daughter of parents who were both journalists on the Beijing *People's Daily*. During the Cultural Revolution all her family were placed in separate labour camps — Feng for six years. There she worked in the fields and studied at night in bed. As she put it: "My sheets were covered in ink." Finally, when she was in her early twenties, the government conducted countrywide university entrance exams. Of the 275 girls in her camp, only three passed, Feng with top marks. After graduation, she worked as a tour guide for Japanese visitors, then wound up as a student in Tokyo.

One of her brothers remained in a forced labour camp for nine years. Now he, their parents, and a second brother are all newspaper journalists. Feng is away from China on a four-year student visa, which is difficult to obtain. She'd hoped to complete her course at Tokyo University, then travel to North America or Europe, but her mother has cancer and might need her at any time.

She is, by her own admission, very tough, highly critical of her own government but not blind to the faults she sees in Japanese society, especially when it comes to the status of women. Still, she knows that no other Asian country has as much to offer her. She often laughs aloud, one thing she says separates her from her Japanese contemporaries. She has tremendous self-confidence and only a little arrogance.

Ted left to fetch Professor Kawamoto, who'd been waiting in the coffee shop. He's a short, pockmarked man, rather standard issue in appearance but extraordinary in other ways. His wonderfully idiomatic English becomes increasingly animated when he eats or talks. (French, not English, is his second language: he did doctoral work in Paris.) An intellectual who was exposed to the Enlightenment, rationalism, and scepticism, he's a wonderful commentator on modern Japan. He recognizes that the Japanese educational system crushes many it touches, while at the same time admits that it worked well for him. "Now, as a teacher," he complained, "it's almost impossible to get my first-year students to do any work. Making it through high school and university entrance exams has completely exhausted them."

He'd just come from a meeting of a committee assigned to write and edit a new English-language textbook for middle schools — similar to our junior highs. Most young people, even after years of study, have little, if any, conversational English. To get into a good university, which is the ultimate educational goal, one needs to know conjugations, tenses, and vocabulary: comprehension and conversation are not required.

He grew up on the island of Shikoku, where the dialect differs sharply from the language of Tokyo. He's been to the English-speaking world infrequently — five days in Vancouver some years ago, and a recent trip to Princeton, where he lectured on the geisha in Japanese literature. From there he went to New York to see five operas, one of his many passions. Jazz is another.

After dinner, we set out to find a jazz club. The first we tried featured dissonant modern stuff, performed in a densely smoky atmosphere where patrons sat in rows at what looked like school desks. Fortunately, they were full. We finally found a bar that was perfect — the right mix of people, young and old, men and women, the right food, drink, staff, tables, and chairs. The band — trumpet, piano, and drums — were "very Chet Baker," according to Bob. They even began with one of his favourite tunes. The singer appeared later, cute and perky with a disconcerting habit of singing through her tiny nose tunes such as "Just in Time" and "What Kind of Fool Am I?" — in English, interspersed with Japanese patter.

There was a certain amount of translating going on at our table. Feng had never heard jazz before. "There is some in Beijing," she said, "but it's in hotels — for tourists." In China, disco belongs to the masses.

SUNDAY, SEPTEMBER 27

At 8:30 a.m. we were met at our ryokan by Hideo Tomiyasu, a town planner and architect, president of an urban development firm with offices in Tokyo, Osaka, and Fukuoka (on Kyushu, the southernmost of Japan's four main islands). The Canadian architecture professor, Fred Thompson, from the University of Waterloo, whom I don't know, is a friend and colleague of Larry Richards, head of the school of architecture there. I can't say that I really know Larry, but we spent a lovely day together last spring touring the site of the new National Arts Centre in Ottawa for *State of the Arts*, the CBC Radio series I produce. I liked him a lot. When I asked if he knew any Japanese architects, he said he did, and so did his friend, Fred Thompson.

On our behalf, Thompson wrote to Hideo Tomiyasu, whom he described as "a down-to-earth architect with a strong social conscience. He's easy to talk to, shockingly straightforward in his answers, and as close to an eccentric as a Japanese can be." He worked for a year in Toronto, and now creates large-scale housing projects. A man of enormous energy, Tomiyasu is the personification of the Japanese workaholic one hears about. (Everyone I know in Canada seems to work hard as well, but it's the concentration on details that appears to be different here.)

Mr. Tomiyasu spends two and a half days a week at his Tokyo office, two days in Osaka, and one in Fukuoka. His principal project for the last ten years, and into the next ten, is the creation of what will be the largest new town development in Japan, Kama New Town. When finished, it will house 400,000 people. There will be light industry, schools, and shops; a university will relocate there. An existing golf course, one of the oldest in Japan, has been incorporated into the plan. Two rail lines will join the town to Tokyo, where most of the residents will work. It will take about forty minutes to get to the city by train.

Mr. Tomiyasu had left his car in Kama New Town and come by rail to meet us early on Sunday morning, his one day off. He's fairly tall, between fifty-eight and sixty, I would guess, and appears to have cataracts, his one concession to old age. We had to run to keep up with him. He talked quickly, with perfect pronunciation but limited vocabulary. Out of practice, I imagine. He worked in Canada in the 1960s for Hancock and Associates, a firm I knew something about from studying town planning at the University of Toronto in the mid-sixties.

"My wife and I have fond memories of Canada," he said. At the time, Mr. Tomiyasu, his wife, and young daughter lived on the Hancocks' property in Cooksville. Mrs. Tomiyasu, who doesn't speak much English, broke her leg. It became badly infected, and she ended up in hospital for four months. Apparently, Canadians treated her well. They've kept in touch with their Canadian friends through visitors such as us and letters, and hope for a short return visit in two years. "When we went there twenty-five years ago, we were all young," he said. "Now, not so young."

On the train we talked a little about town planning, especially the housing shortage in Tokyo. There is an official plan, but a very loose one, with something like a green belt which is slowly, and predictably, eroding. Like many other planners, Mr. Tomiyasu paid obeisance to British models like Harlow New Town and Cumbernauld, both of which I had visited in the 1960s. Jokingly I said, "I hope you've avoided their mistakes." I soon learned he had not.

The rough concrete station looked older than its four years. They have certainly planned for a huge number of bicycles and motor bikes, which people are expected to drive to the station each morning. (About 60 percent of Tokyo residents own cars, far fewer in Kama New Town.) More facts: about 10 percent of the population here will be wealthy, mostly farmers who have sold all or part of their land to the Tokyo Municipal Government while retaining their homes, either as they were when the plan was approved (the planners simply worked around them) or in newly acquired lots set aside for large, free-standing single-family houses, built in traditional style. About 40 percent of the units are subsidized low-rent accommodations for the working poor who cannot afford to buy property. About half are condominiums in high-rise complexes called *danchi*: they will house about 150,000 of the expected population. Because land prices are so high in the greater Tokyo area, the average Japanese middle-class family of four expects to live in an apartment no larger than seventy square metres. It's impossible to think of employed North Americans settling for so little. There have been mutterings about moving the central government to Kyoto to ease land prices, but this seems unlikely.

Mr. Tomiyasu was involved with the first Japanese planned town near Osaka. Everyone moved in when they were young and now the town's population is considerably older than the national average. (Have I too become enamoured of statistics, or is this just planner talk?) No doubt the residents are reluctant to move because their rents are low and the living space is finally adequate.

We drove rather quickly through the half-finished townsite. It was hard to find anything positive to say; it was all so boring — apartment block beside apartment block beside shopping centre; no surprising laneways, corner stores, nothing one associates with vibrant urban life.

It was a relief to climb into Mr. Tomiyasu's Familia, a car Mazda considered too small to export, and head into the surrounding mountains, part of the same range as Mount Fuji (which we could have seen had it not been so hazy). The road turned from two paved lanes to one, then to a rutted, twisting mud track up hills covered by stands of bamboo, the first I'd ever seen. They looked like flutes stuck in the earth. At one turn we saw three men camping. One stood in waders, casting for trout in a clear-running stream. The other two huddled together in the quiet green forest, one playing a clarinet, the other a trumpet.

Why I ever agreed to be a back-seat passenger on this mountain trek, I'll never know. I get sick being a *front*-seat passenger. The only place I'm comfortable is behind the wheel, which is usually fine since Bob never learned to drive. Perhaps it's the "take charge" syndrome. Or, as a kind friend suggested, a sensitive inner ear. Who knows? But there I was, popping Gravol and praying that the nausea would disappear.

Happily, we soon stopped for coffee at a roadside diner.

"Did you know that Japan imports more coffee than any other country in the world?" Mr. T. asked. I did not, always thinking of the Japanese as tea drinkers. (I *had* noticed how good the coffee tasted here.) "The Japanese like expensive coffee," Mr. Tomiyasu said, "like Kona coffee from Hawaii."

The conversation turned to local agriculture, then to the Japanese way of doing things, the uniqueness of the Japanese, and how consensus builds. "It's all because of rice farming," declared Mr. Tomiyasu. Although wet rice farming was introduced into Japan from China, it's considered a key to understanding Japanese culture. Mr. Tomiyasu explained that rice grows on terraced hills with different families farming each tier. To produce a successful crop, sufficient to pay taxes to the local lord and still have enough left to eat, the whole community had to share the limited water supply. This created a collective purpose that overrode individual initiative. It also established distinctions between "them" and "us."

Rice came to be closely associated with the Japanese nation. During the Second World War, the military elite used rice to promote wartime patriotism, recommending "Rising Sun" lunches — white rice with a red plum in the centre, representing the Japanese flag. Near the end of the war, when food was scarce, they pushed the Japanese people to fight harder, holding out the promise of being able to eat pure white rice again. Mr. Tomiyasu told us that rice is sacred to the Japanese, and that it's been used as a form of currency in the past. I appreciate the sweep of Mr. Tomiyasu's theories, verifiable or not.

I gulped my last Gravol with the dregs of my coffee and somehow, miraculously, made it back to Kama New Town and Mr. Tomiyasu's apartment. (I'm ashamed to admit that it never occurred to me to ask if Mrs. Tomiyasu would be joining us for the country ride. Here wives stay home, end of story.)

Mr. Tomiyasu seemed proud to take us to the anonymous apartment block where he and his wife live, even proud of the elevator designed to stop on only three floors — 1, 4, and 7 (the top), presumably because any self-respecting resident can walk up or down a few flights. It's unusual for a designer to live in his own development, in an apartment like the others, albeit on the top floor and in a corner unit. Bob commented later that in Canadian terms it seemed "about right for graduate students."

We'd been told before leaving Toronto that Westerners are rarely invited to visit Japanese homes because the accommodations are so small and the Japanese are reluctant to risk their guests' judgment. Entertaining is usually done in a public setting — in bars or restaurants, so we were lucky to break the rule. Although my reactions were typical *gaijin*, I hope they didn't show.

There was a small kitchen, a combination living and dining room, a toilet room and separate bath, and two tiny bedrooms. Despite the fact that most Japanese women use a modern washing machine, they prefer to hang their clothes out to dry, even on the smallest balconies in the most congested parts of Tokyo, even overlooking railway tracks. The Tomiyasu apartment was traditional in many ways, but was crammed with ungainly Western-style pieces. The Western-style lunch we were served was a challenge — cream of corn soup from a can, cold ham, hard-boiled eggs, lettuce, mayonnaise, white bread, and store-bought pie. I would have assumed this was laid on for our benefit except that I often see stuff like this advertised in Japanese magazines and on television.

Mrs. Tomiyasu was sweet and understood more English than she was willing to speak. We mentioned the Canadian classic, *Anne of Green Gables*, said to be much loved by all Japanese women, but she appeared never to have heard of it. Undaunted, we pressed on: "Lucy Maud Montgomery? Prince Edward Island? *The Girl with the Red Hair*?" Finally she leapt to her feet. "Ah, *Anne of Red Hair*!" and disappeared, returning soon with her well-worn Japanese edition. Until that moment, she'd thought the author was American. In discussing why it was so popular, our hosts suggested that "the

Japanese very much admire imagination," and, more importantly, "its first edition, in 1952, was very well translated." Their daughter, a writer of stories for children, is also a big fan.

We said thank-you and goodbye to Mrs. T. at the apartment door and to Mr. T. at the station. Back in Tokyo, we returned to Harajuku, real and gritty Harajuku, where we bought a sweatshirt with eccentric English for Rachel — "Yours Cheerfully, Mama."

MONDAY, SEPTEMBER 28

Travelled to Shinjuku, exited on the west side, found the Narami Building, and zoomed up to the forty-ninth floor, only eight minutes late. We were met there by three representatives of the Canadian International College of Japan and Nelson, British Columbia. There were two NHK announcers, or former announcers — they call themselves "journalists" — Tsuneji Tsukagoshi and Koji Ito, accompanied by Yasuko Yamaoka, the woman who'd called Bob for lunch after learning about him from someone at the Canadian embassy. Bob wasn't exactly sure what they expected of him and was hoping to learn more over lunch.

We were ushered into an elegant private dining room in a traditional restaurant, a *ryotei* — tatami mats, shoji paper doors, waitresses on their knees. What followed was one of those meals you read and dream about — countless courses of tiny portions ending with rice and pickles, exquisitely presented on small lacquer plates, plentiful sake. This style of presentation is called *kaiseki*, and it was wonderful. For some dishes we used only a toothpick. There was raw smoked beef, crayfish, soup, two sorts of tea, and apple and kiwi for dessert.

During the meal, Bob and I were handed a three-page description of the Canadian International College, CIC. "The purpose of this first nongovernmental, international and educational project between Japan and Canada is to rear 'new internationalists' or 'new citizens of the world' by blending the East's soft and rich sensitivity with the West's logical and independent way of thought." Perhaps it was the meal, or the infectious enthusiasm of our hosts, or the sake, but I found myself thinking that, after all, everything in Japan seems geared to "internationalism," why not a school to promote it?

The intention was to open the school in 1988 on the former David Thompson campus in Nelson, BC. Teachers would come largely from Canada; the administrative head would be a Canadian now working on a doctorate at George Washington University. The students, all Japanese, would be high-school graduates who would enrol for a two-year program, which they would eventually expand to a four-year program to prepare graduates for North American universities.

The current BC minister of advanced education and training had written a rather muted letter of encouragement, which was part of the package Bob was given. The force behind the program is John Christianson, a former Manitoba minister and partner in a chain of private language schools in Japan. They felt that Japanese employers were more willing than ever to hire staff with foreign experience and a real knowledge of English, which as we've seen, is illusory. Bob was being rather quiet while I babbled on, my feeble attempt to be helpful. What could be wrong with private initiative, public discussion, and political approval? I felt I was watching the creation of a legendary Japanese consensus.

The lunch moved rather quickly and was clearly winding down at about two o'clock. At kiwi time, Mrs. Yamaoka pulled the rabbit out of the hat. "We would very much like it if Mr. Fulford (Bob had explained that he was merely an honorary doctor) could write an essay supporting our project." (I'm sure Mr. Fulford had seen this coming at about soup time.)

Bob remained extremely cool, frigid almost, and terribly Japanese. "I'll certainly think it over," he promised, nothing more. With that, the lunch, which must have cost at least $100 each, ended. I felt well rewarded for doing nothing. That night we were to be the guests of honour at a party given by Tim Armstrong, the Ontario agent general in Japan, and his wife, Betty. "Why don't we ask them, or someone at the party, what they think of this outfit?" I suggested. "Perhaps they'll have heard of the project."

It turned out to be a surprisingly fine evening. Both the Armstrongs were lovely. Tim's the same age as Bob, fifty-five, but seems a generation older. Jill and David Bond were there; Ben Fulford, a freelance journalist, one of the Belleville Fulfords who are, or were, the rich ones and not related to Bob; Ted Goossen; Bob Fairweather, a Canadian businessman living in Tokyo; and Stephen Heenley, from the embassy. There were other embassy people, and a charming three-person delegation from Quebec House who win the Most Loveable Civil Servants award hands down. Even Barry Steers, the ambassador, and his wife, Martha, came in dinner jacket and gown, dressed for their next event.

Halfway through the evening, Tim made a gracious welcoming address to Bob and me. At that moment Bob was in front of the crowd, while I was somewhere in the back. Tim read from Premier Peterson's letter, which appeared in the 100th anniversary issue of *Saturday Night*. (No mention of Bob's present non-relationship with said magazine — he'd resigned last summer, a few days after Conrad Black became the owner.) Bob made a gracious reply about how envious we were of all the people in the room whose stay in Tokyo would be so much longer than our own. Then I came forward and thanked the Asia Pacific Foundation for telling us not to work while we were here but to travel and experience the country.

Shortly afterwards, Betty and Tim took us aside and asked if we would mind briefly slipping away from the party. Two elderly retired teachers had been travelling in Japan on their way to China when one broke her ankle in Tokyo Station. After a stay in hospital, she was recuperating in one of the Armstrongs' spare bedrooms. They knew of Bob's work and wanted to meet him. They were frail and lively, in their early seventies, from Iona Station, birthplace of John Kenneth Galbraith, whom both women knew, or knew relatives of. That gave us something to talk about. It was sad to think that they'd come all this way and were now only hoping to be well enough to go home.

Since the party was a stand-around-and-nibble affair, a number of us headed off to a Chinese restaurant in Roppongi — Ted; Annie, a Chinese computer specialist; Gerald Utting, the *Toronto Star*'s man in Tokyo; and Hugette, whose last name I can't recall, from Quebec House. It was a long and happy and well-oiled evening, the end of yet another surprising and emotional day.

TUESDAY, SEPTEMBER 29

I suppose it had to happen that excessive drinking and gorging would catch up with me. Awoke with a smashing headache and queasy stomach. Began the day retching and vowing never to touch the damn stuff again. By eleven o'clock I'd pulled myself together sufficiently to dress for a luncheon at a French restaurant in Shibuya, hosted by our embassy for the film festival folks. After several false starts, we arrived about thirty-five minutes late, and had to catch up quickly on the first course and wine. Resolve, where did it go?

From above the crowd, I heard a familiar voice and discovered that it belonged to the Montreal film critic, Will Aitken, who'd been providing material for radio shows I'd produced but whom I'd never met. It was remarkable to be introduced to him here. Also met Kevin Sullivan and his wife Trudie Grant, in Japan selling nine hours of *Anne of Green Gables* to national television. We'd never met before but Bob explained to Kevin that we were *mishpocha* — Jewish for related, sort of; my brother's wife is his cousin.

Then on to two Japanese films, both about adultery. The first, made in 1986, was directed by Kinji Fukasaku and starred Ken Ogata, a familiar face on Japanese screens. *House on Fire* is based on a story by Kazuo Dan and is highly autobiographical — a womanizing writer, trapped by his past as an abandoned child, cannot remain faithful to his wife and their five children, or to his young mistress. It could have been more carefully edited for greater impact but it was fascinating for me to watch this modern man slip in and out of traditional clothes and religious practices as the occasion demanded. The second movie, *Wife, Be Like a Rose!* (1935), was the first great success of director Mikio Naruse. A rather common Japanese man abandons his wealthy, effete wife and no-nonsense office-worker daughter to prospect in a poor mountain region where he lives with Oyuki, a former geisha and their two children. When the daughter wants to marry, she drags her father back to town for the ceremony, but it's clear to everyone that he should return to his second family. It was fun to see the Tokyo of the past, and to watch our very Americanized heroine, played by an actress who later married the director.

Had dinner in a baked potato restaurant in Shibuya, now my favourite Tokyo district. It defies planning and logic, but offers unexpected delights at every turn. Will Aitken says he loves it too. He also loves some of the Canadian films we haven't seen as we relentlessly pursue Japanese film experience.

WEDNESDAY, SEPTEMBER 30

Here are some of the things I love about Tokyo: the wonderful sense of style everywhere. The highly idiosyncratic architecture that changes every forty feet. The vast expanses of neon. Acres of back-lit signs. The jumble of lettering from old Chinese characters to modern "Roman letters" (*romaji*). The garbled English. The stylish women, dressed, or overdressed, for every occasion, in designer frocks from around the world. The businessmen in their blue and grey uniforms, their crisp white shirts, and their hooded eyes. The babies with their young mothers, so relaxed, so unsuspecting. The schoolchildren in their sailor suits, straw hats, and Snoopy backpacks; their older counterparts, on the cusp of adulthood, roaming in groups, giggling, jostling one another. The old men dressed in yellow plastic who fish in all weather along a branch of the dammed-up Sumida River near Ichigaya.

I love department store elevator girls carolling out their welcome in falsetto voices, their white gloves and schoolgirl hats. The clicketty-clack of subway ticket punchers, soon to be replaced by machines. The food, everything from boiled root vegetables served in a four-stool restaurant where staff outnumber patrons, to shreds of raw tuna served in porcelain dishes in private dining rooms in the sky, where women in kimono kneel while men in business suits eat and drink too much.

These are some of the things that I love about Tokyo.

They are also some of the things I hate about Tokyo.

Saw two more films in the Japanese retrospective, both on the theme of death and burial. The first was *The Funeral*, by Juzo Itami, the same director who made *Tampopo*. It's the story of an acting couple and their two sons, a family like Itami's own. When the wife's father dies, the extended family gather to participate in a Buddhist funeral whose form and function they have forgotten, if they ever knew it. One hilarious scene shows the couple watching a matronly expert explain, on video, how to conduct oneself at a funeral, complete with properly dressed actors cast as grieving family and guests.

The second film was older, 1952, the work of the master, Akira Kurosawa, in a style somewhat like the Italian New Wave. *Ikiru* is a scathing exploration of the life of a small-time bureaucrat in a heartless society. For thirty years the hero of the story worked as the chief of the citizen's branch at city hall — doing nothing, offending no one. Then he finds out that he has less than a year to live, a fact that seems of little importance to his son and daughter-in-law. A stranger who befriends him in a bar and a young woman from work show him that there can be joy in life, even when one is close to death. He spends his last months battling his colleagues, his bosses, and local gangsters to help poor women in the district build a park on reclaimed land. After he dies, his family and co-workers come to appreciate his tenacity and dedication. Naturally, my eyes were hideously swollen. (Donald Richie wrote that in *Ikiru*, Kurosawa was fulfilling a desire he'd revealed the year before when accepting the Venice prize for *Rashomon*: "I would be happier getting it for having shown something of contemporary Japan.")

We returned to the Tobu department store to meet Susan Phillips, a fellow Asia Pacific Foundation fellowship winner and serious Japanophile. She was here first fifteen years ago and has spent much of the time since learning the language and working in the Pacific Rim section of Radio Canada International, broadcasting out of Vancouver.

She's an odd combination, an elitist left-winger: she prefers classical Japanese arts to popular culture while complaining bitterly about "regional disparities" between Tokyo and poorer areas such as Kyushu and Hokkaido. "The steel industry has suffered from the decline in shipbuilding, and fishing's so limited that people are forced to come to Tokyo in the summer to work in construction." She made it sound like a centralist plot. Typically perhaps, she did not see, or refused to acknowledge, that without the concentration of people, wealth, and talent in Tokyo, the arts she most admires could not survive.

She took us to "a typical worker's restaurant" — a dark hole-in-the-wall with room for four patrons to sit on stools squeezed between wooden beverage containers and a skinny countertop. (If I reached across, I could stir one of the boiling pots.) Here I encountered *oden*, the first Japanese food I couldn't stomach. I recognized none of the food being served, but Susan said the gummy ball I nearly choked on was *kamaboko*, a sort of fish sausage. Then there was *konnyaku*, gelatinous cubes of something appropriately named "devil's-tongue." Everything was boiled, grey, and nasty. Thank God the sake was good and plentiful.

For dessert, we went elsewhere, also excessively Japanese — ice cream with banana, kiwi, canned pineapple, peach and mandarin sections, topped with synthetic whipped cream.

THURSDAY, OCTOBER 1

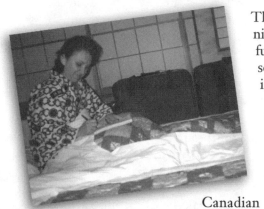

The seasons must have changed. Last night we were equipped with fall futons — thicker and warmer, and somewhat autumnal in hue. I was, in fact, beginning to feel chilly.

Bob spent some time on the telephone checking on the Canadian International College with Russell Mark, senior representative of the BC delegation in Japan, a Japanese-Canadian accountant. He was at the Armstrongs' party and seemed nice and smart. Since Nelson is in his territory, he was the best person to ask.

Generally, he feels that the Canadian end of the project is less impressive than the Japanese. The people involved at the Tokyo end also run something called Cheery, a sort of "Tupperware system for teaching English to Japanese housewives." They claim to have three thousand classrooms throughout Japan. Apparently they began the Canadian project three years ago, and have lost a considerable amount of money using the wrong chartered accountant in Canada. "Now," he reports, "they have the smartest CA in Vancouver on their case." And while they have "the political side of things" working, including the support of the Social Credit people in Nelson, they haven't convinced educational bureaucrats that this scheme is in their interest. However, Marks had just found out that Premier Van Der Zalm will be in Tokyo later this month and will attend a press conference the CIC group is holding when they go public with their scheme for the first time.

When Mrs. Yasuko Yamaoka called, Bob said he'd speak to her tomorrow morning. I believe he's decided to do his "essay," partly because the project has some merit and partly for the experience.

After breakfast we went to Harajuku to the Ota Memorial Museum of Ukiyo-e, the same sort of woodblock prints we tried to see at the National Museum. Described in *Tokyo Access* as "a jewel of a small private art museum," it most certainly is. Exhibitions rotate every month, showing some of the twelve thousand prints, fans, screens, and scrolls collected by one man, and reflecting a range of seventeenth-, eighteenth-, and nineteenth-century work once considered crude and déclassé. This particular show featured drawings of famous kabuki actors, about fifty on two floors. In the centre of the first floor was a rock garden. A wonderful place to visit, and the first museum where we had to check our shoes.

Before meeting Mr. Koji Ito — one of the principals in the CIC — for a tour of NHK, we ate bento in Yoyogi Park. The tour turned out to be exactly what I'd hoped for — a tramp through television and radio studios, newsrooms, the cafeteria, and best of all, the costume department, where kimono were stored for the many samurai dramas. They're like old American Westerns — corrupt leaders and incorruptible samurai, damsels in distress and samurai to the rescue, clashing swords and passionate glances, period costumes and modern values. (NHK's *Taiga* drama is said to be the most realistic period show, but the most popular is *Mito Koman*, on the air since 1969 and still going strong on the private TBS network.) Many NHK costume dramas have been fashioned for use on the new high-definition television, so you can imagine the exquisite detail in the costumes.

One music studio was the most beautiful I'd ever seen, all blond wood and plush carpet for great acoustics. The NHK Orchestra was preparing to record part of the score for a new TV drama. Besides us, there were thirteen people in the control room, with lots of space left over. The sound was luscious. I miss hearing classical music and my daughter Sarah practising her cello. On one monitor we listened to the Duke Ellington classic, "Take the A Train," which could be the theme song for the rail-crazed Japanese. Mr. Ito refrained from discussing the CIC project until the end of the tour, when he suggested that Bob call him when we get back from Kyoto.

I'm beginning to learn that although it's complicated and time-consuming to go from place to place in central Tokyo, once you set out on foot with a good map, you discover your destination is often no more than a twenty-minute walk away. And so we were able to go with ease from NHK to the Shibuya Shochiku theatre by 2:30, in time to see the first of two movies about fathers and sons, starting with this year's, *The River of Fireflies*, based on a novel by Teru Miyamoto and directed by Eizo Sugawa. Late in his life, a married man divorces the childless wife he loves, to live with his pregnant mistress, who bears him a son. When the father is close to death, he convinces his fourteen-year-old boy that if a heavy April snowfall is followed by a swarm of fireflies, any young couple who sees them is destined to marry. For the son and his girlfriend, searching for fireflies becomes an act of filial piety. Weird, but it might have worked had the director not sabotaged the mood by having the actors constantly shout, all except the wives who, as one might expect, are models of decorum.

The second theme film, *There Was a Father*, was a hit from 1942, directed by a master, Yasujiro Ozu. At every screening of a historical film in this series, a recorded announcement is played: "Because this movie was made long ago, the picture or the sound might not be perfect. We ask for your patience." So far no patience has been necessary, until this afternoon.

It was harder on the Japanese viewers since the sound was nearly inaudible; the image wasn't great either, but I could read the subtitles without much difficulty. It did have the look and feel of a silent film — black and white, *long*, long shots, a story about the struggle between independence and filial loyalty. A long-suffering father puts his son in boarding school while he goes off to Tokyo to make enough money to send the lad to university. The war hovers in the background until the end, when the father learns that his son is "A1" and must join the army. It's a brave film, considering it was made at the height of the war, after Ozu had done his time in the army. There's probably much here that was autobiographical.

A light touch for dinner — flaky tempura, lots of freshly fried fish and veggies, soup, rice, and drinks, all for ¥2,650 or about $25 Canadian. Who says Japan isn't a bargain?

FRIDAY, OCTOBER 2

Tonight, coming back to our ryokan later than usual, about eleven o'clock, was a shock. It was hard to remember that I was in one of the largest cities in the world. All around were private houses and small apartments lining narrow streets with no traffic, so quiet you could hear the crickets. Nothing had changed from other nights, except that we'd spent the day in the pressure cooker known as Japan at Work and Play.

The day began with Bob calling the CIC to say that he'd be happy to write the essay for them. We arranged a time to meet Mrs. Yamaoka at Seifuso; she would take us to the Cheery/CIC offices for lunch and

Bob's photo session. Just enough time to revisit the museum at Yasukuni shrine and check on my transcription of three English signs that had taken my breath away, especially the plaque marking Prime Minister Nakasone's controversial first official visit on December 8, 1985.

Yasukuni has become a lightning rod in the debate over the legislated separation of religion and government. The rekindling of pre-war state Shintoism began publicly in 1956, when the right-wing Bereaved Society of Japan insisted on the reinstitution of *eirei*, the glorious war dead. As a result, soldiers who died in Imperial service and post-war employees of civil defense units have been enshrined at Yasukuni and officially absorbed in the national polity. They are said no longer to belong to their families. This "elevated status" is particularly galling to Christians, to those who want to forget the past, and to the few who want to atone.

The controversy intensified in the 1970s, when the ashes of seven Class A wartime criminals, including Hideki Tojo, the general and wartime prime minister hanged by the US army, were enshrined here, and the urn containing Tojo's ashes was unofficially transported and housed in Yasukuni's inner sanctum, deceptively inscribed on site as Martyrs of the Showa Era. "By this act of burial," says the *Tokyo Baedeker*, "Tojo has acquired the status of *hotoke*, beings who are godlike." A plaque outside mentions the frequent visits made to Yasukuni by the present emperor, Hirohito, and the crown prince.

Then, back to Seifuso.

It was a relief to be doing something essentially silly, and for me, undemanding. Around noon, Mrs. Yamaoka escorted us to a medium-sized building on the outskirts of Shinjuku. The CIC office was dominated by a large table in the centre of the room, where about ten men (and a woman who took notes) sat and worked. The copy of *Saturday Night* they'd been given was part of a stack of papers piled in front of one worker, while different stacks of papers tetered in front of the others. No one appeared to have his own telephone. Noticeably absent as well were typewriters. Japanese script is so complicated that everything must be handwritten, then photocopied and transmitted by fax, if necessary. (No wonder Japan leads the world in fax production.) Today, the president was dislodged from his office by the photographers who'd come to take Bob's picture. I had the sense that he was happy to join the troops. It would be hard, perhaps impossible, for a North American to be productive in this atmosphere of enforced collegiality.

Whatever technique they use, on this occasion it worked: they handled Bob's endorsement beautifully. He'd written his statement on three sheets of steno paper. They asked for a little time to have it translated, read it over and, if necessary, make suggestions. While they did that, we went for lunch with Mrs. Yamaoka, who told us more about the project. The firm's president, Kazuyuki Takase, had wanted to be an NHK announcer and had "made it to the fifth level of auditions before losing out." He became an elementary school teacher and, although he doesn't speak English himself, he devised the Cheery teaching aids for housewives, the biggest consumers of continuing education in Japan. For the CIC project, he's chosen mostly announcers and former announcers as his front men. She spoke about the "news wars" that were going on between NHK and the private stations. News shows are being moved to prime time, and announcer-hosts are no longer old guys but attractive young men who have become television's new superstars, sharing the limelight with variety show hosts.

When we returned to the office they asked Bob to add to his essay a few points he'd made over our mega-lunch. (No one appeared to be taking notes then, but they must have been listening hard.) The photo crew arrived at exactly two o'clock and by three, after about fifty shots, we were out and on our way.

We left to catch part of our last film festival movie, *The Woman in the Dunes*, a rather creepy film about an entomologist who becomes the love-slave of a woman, trapped like a bug in a sand cave. I wasn't too sorry that we had to leave before the end; we were scheduled to meet Wendy Wortsman, the Toronto painter and illustrator, and her boyfriend, Tom Stolberg, an architect-turned-businessman.

Wendy had done work for *Saturday Night*, and a couple of days ago at the festival, she'd come up and asked, "Are you Robert Fulford?" She's been here about eight months; Tom, about three years. She's tall and lean, something of a whippet, wonderfully candid, smart, and funny. In a Japanese-language class she's attending, she met a Chinese man who acts as an agent for people who do her kind of work. He's the president of his own company, Creative Intelligence Association — CIA. "All he has to sell," she added, "is his taste." (After meeting him today, it was clear that his taste is considerable.) He'd been able to secure a commission for Wendy — four paintings for a Roppongi jazz bar, The Lounge, which opened tonight. Wendy invited us as her guests, and, following our unstated motto, Say No to

Nothing, we accepted.

The Lounge was stylish to the max, nothing but the finest wood and marble. As we approached the entrance, eight men, all in dark suits with orchid boutonnières, met us at the door. We deposited our business cards in a basket and climbed the stairs, both sides lined with garish floral arrangements sent, according to Tom, "by anyone you've ever done business with in your whole life." It's a sign of "good luck" to get flowers from the big boys, conglomerates like Mitsubishi, say, or Sony.

The place was packed. Dazzling women in kimono or miniskirts served drinks. Tables were crowded with fried chicken, liver-pâté tarts, cold meats, fish, breads, salad, but no forks, only chopsticks. Four of Wendy's paintings hung in the main room — two large canvases together, then one along each side — all with a jazz theme, all largely black, the chic colour at the moment in Japan. At first the crowd was middle-aged and largely male — mostly backers and representatives from the trades — tile company, roofers, kitchen equipment suppliers. They left early and were followed by a younger group, the intended patrons — guys in groovy suits and chicks in leather, lace, and diamonds. Someone had to run out to buy more wine to supplement the half-dozen brands of Scotch, evidence of changing Japanese drinking patterns, at least with this crowd.

Tom's a remarkable guy. He'd done some photography before going into architecture at Carleton University, in Ottawa. After graduating, he came to Tokyo for an extended vacation and picked up jobs as an audiovisual man for an impressive array of Japanese firms, starting with Nissan. He's about thirty-five, five feet ten inches, blond, balding, a high-energy hustler; he's smart enough to be at the right place at the right time and to know it.

For Tom, as for most foreigners in Japan, the main subject of conversation is The Japanese, frequently a variation on the "honesty story." Tom told us his favourite as we stood around gaping and eating.

It began the first night he arrived in Tokyo. "I'd gone into this little noodle shop near me, had a bowl of soup, and left." (Nothing unexpected there.) "Then," Tom continued, "about three weeks later — *three weeks!* — I went back. When the woman who'd waited on me saw me, she did this double take, ran to the kitchen, and dragged a guy out who must've been her husband.

"He stared at me, nodded at her, and slipped behind the counter. He opened the cash and pulled out a ¥5,000 note (about $50) and handed it to me. I was completely baffled. I knew about sixteen words of Japanese, they knew no English, so they had to act everything out." They pulled down a calendar, pointed to the date of Tom's arrival, and crawled around on the floor where he'd been sitting.

"I tried telling them that I hadn't missed any money, and sort of pushed it back, but they weren't having any. It was pretty clear that if I didn't take the money, they'd be insulted." Tom said he was certain that the bill he was given must have been the very one he'd dropped. We all chuckled, knowingly: another "Isn't-it-all-too-much?" Japan story.

We left this first opening led by Wendy's CIA agent and his company manager, a thirty-nine-year-old Japanese woman, Mari Kida. She was educated in England and despite her enormous charm and beauty, is regarded as unmarriageable because she's ambitious, independent, and over twenty-five. Women like this are called "Christmas cakes" — nobody wants them because their season has passed.

We were on our way to Seibu department store in Ginza and a second opening, this time an exhibition of British products featuring, among other things, the wacky postmodern furniture of Nigel Coates — chairs that look like buildings, that sort of thing. Altogether a remarkable scene, even, I think, by Tokyo standards. We entered past a row of young Japanese women on one side, and English-speaking boys and girls along the other. They checked our bags and handed us, in exchange, ten fake British pounds: "You can use them later to gamble." We took the escalator in this sparkling, modern retail emporium to the third floor. As we got off, we were greeted by waiters in white dinner jackets holding trays of drinks. Glass in hand, we wandered through a display of Nigel's work while a string quartet performed arrangements of Beatles songs. Other British exports, brand names of course, were present in great quantities — bone china, designer clothes, leather goods.

A row of chairs near one wall faced a bank of TV monitors, all showing the string quartet; all seats were occupied by Japanese guests who preferred the screen version to the real thing. Occasionally, the monitors switched to entertainment taking place elsewhere in the store — a spine-tingling violin and cello duet by young musicians playing Handel beside a rack of Burberry coats; a bawdy British busker on stilts joking among the Marks & Spencer canned goods, and on and on. The place was chock-a-block with beautiful people catching glimpses of themselves in mirrors or on glossy chrome surfaces. They were part of the entertainment and made the most of their roles.

Tom, who rattles away in a fast, flat, confident Japanese which he says probably sounds "like the English of a newly arrived Greek waiter on the Danforth," went up to five young Japanese standing behind a computer terminal before a bank of monitors. They turned out to be agents for designers and artists — the distinction seems blurred here. Tom pushed number 19 at random and on the screen a deep blue amorphous blob appeared. Should you desire a different motif for your home, hotel, or office, press other buttons and preview styles by dozens of artists this agency represents.

It was clear that Tom was impressed, asking if they could handle Wendy, or him, for that matter. (What about Mr. CIA hovering in the background?) Tom never stops working. Does he fit into Japanese business, I wonder, because this is his nature? Or has he revved himself up to make it in this intense commercial atmosphere? He did mention that he and Wendy plan to return to Canada in a year or so, but if tonight was typical, he'll find it hard to abandon this high-octane excitement.

We crossed over a fourth-floor walkway to a makeshift gambling casino. I played briefly at dice, won some, then lost the bundle, and shared the inexplicable thrill of playing a bit part in a drama of retail promotion. Tom said that even after three years, Tokyo still surprises and delights him.

All I can think of now is our wonderful inn with its garden, its country noises, a ten-minute subway ride from the rest of our evening. Japan is like a Rubik's cube: you can rearrange the pieces and think you've got it right, that it makes sense. Then, with the last move, all conclusions shatter, alignments fall out of whack, and you have to start again. Here's a game to last a lifetime.

SATURDAY, OCTOBER 3

I'm almost happy to report that not everything in Japan exceeds one's expectations. Some things are merely hype, while others are inaccessible to all but the most persistent *gaijin*. We spent the better part of the morning trying to organize our suitcases for phase 2 of our trip — Kyoto and Beyond, suitcases to be left at Seifuso for our return, as well as suitcases we plan to take with us.

That accomplished, we headed out at noon for Yoyogi Park and an event that certainly sounded interesting — a Tokyo Home Festival, said to feature a flea market and the best from many of Japan's forty-seven prefectures, including homemade items. The ad cordially invited us to "join in celebrating the 100th anniversary of local autonomy in Japan, hence from 1887." Inside the park, however, were the same crummy food vendors, second-hand clothes dealers, and kimono-clad, middle-aged Japanese women performing traditional dances to taped music in front of bored, middle-aged men. ("Prefecturism" bears an unhappy similarity to state-sanctioned multiculturalism. At least they didn't dress the children up and make *them* do the dancing.)

Next a long, pleasant walk from Yoyogi to Shibuya, taking a new route for us, down a wide boulevard lined with plane trees, which gives

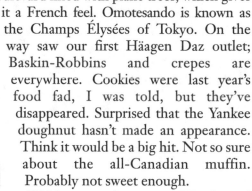

it a French feel. Omotesando is known as the Champs Élysées of Tokyo. On the way saw our first Häagen Daz outlet; Baskin-Robbins and crepes are everywhere. Cookies were last year's food fad, I was told, but they've disappeared. Surprised that the Yankee doughnut hasn't made an appearance. Think it would be a big hit. Not so sure about the all-Canadian muffin. Probably not sweet enough.

We'd arranged to meet Wendy and Tom at the Setagaya Art Museum for a noh play. Luckily, we were on the same train and met just as we were getting out. Tom led us to a local bus, our first, after he determined it went to Setagaya, a trick we could not have managed on our own. Together we followed a crowd into a lovely park, picked up squares of plastic to sit on, curry and rice in Styrofoam containers, and plastic cups of beer.

Tom had seen noh before and had wanted to stay home. After about three minutes, we knew why. He described it this way: "One man moves from one end of the stage to the other. That takes four and a half hours. Then, you go home." This was not an entertainment for the untutored. Quietly, or as quietly as people who are twice as big as everyone else can be, we slipped away. For a quiet chat.

Wendy and Tom described a wedding they'd been to in Tokyo, and from other reports it was typical, and quite different from what I'd expected. The ceremony was the least important part. Despite its traditional appearance, it's a fairly recent invention, a cobbled-together Shinto rite to which only a few family members are invited. (Pre-war weddings, if couples had a ceremony at all, usually involved little more than exchanging sake cups and a few toasts at home.) And although arranged marriages were standard in pre-war Japan, today they account for only about 15 percent of modern unions. (Most couples, like Tom and Wendy's friends, meet at work.)

What really mattered on their Big Day were the wedding outfits. First Traditional — for the bride, a multi-layered kimono, heavy wig, and white makeup, and for the groom, *montsuki hakama*, a short kimono marked with the family crest and subtly striped grey silk pants knotted at the waist. Because of the expense, Wendy says her friends rented their outfits, as most couples do. After formal pictures were taken, the wedding party received guests in a reception line and then disappeared for a change of costume while the guests were seated.

Soon the newlyweds entered the dining hall wearing traditional Western wedding outfits — long white gown and veil for her, morning coat for him, also rented. (In wedding ads that appear everywhere, the model is almost always Caucasian, and she's shown being assisted by a Japanese wedding organizer, a hired Super Mom.)

This particular wedding took place in a Wedding Palace, a thirteen-storey structure where, on auspicious days, one wedding follows another every two hours on every floor. Since a series of ever-changing rituals must be enacted quickly, the wedding party relied on the master of ceremonies. Dressed in tails and white gloves, he steered the couple into the dining hall, where they visited each table and lit a candle, then joined the head table. Various family members and appointed friends made formulaic speeches, to which the groom replied. He thanked his parents and her parents and his boss. The bride cried. She didn't have much time to eat, for a third change of outfit was required — an extravagant ball gown. Finally, bride and groom put on going-away outfits and left for their honeymoon week in Hawaii.

Each guest received an elaborate present, a set of wine glasses, which added to the already enormous cost. (The average wedding is about $65,000.) To defray expenses, guests are expected to give the couple cash — thousands of yen stuffed into specially marked envelopes.

The ceremony is always evolving, according to what is chic. Hotels are now considered cooler than wedding palaces, and marriage vows are occasionally re-enacted at other locations (for instance, the Anne of Green Gable house in PEI). Increasing numbers marry offshore, in Hawaii, for example. Even after transporting close friends and family, it's cheaper.

When the British historian Eric Hobsbawm coined the phrase, "the invention of tradition," he might well have had the Japanese wedding in mind. He noted that traditions can be manipulated and that many claiming to be old in origin are quite recent fabrications. This process, he suggested, is selective, a matter of choosing aspects of the past considered worthy of continuing in the present. The hybrid Japanese wedding has been created in just this way, with the easy assimilation of the best, or most luxurious, from the West, along with an imagined ideal from the mythical past.

The evening was still mild and the Setagaya Art Museum remained open until eight, so we dropped in. The building echoes Frank Lloyd Wright's organic architecture — concrete pergolas supported by upended triangles set on blocks — leaving graceful corridors and high, bright rooms, perfect for showing large-scale contemporary art. Unfortunately, they had a small-scale crafts exhibit and a thin permanent collection — Japanese artists "in the style of." We grabbed a cab to a restaurant on the main street. Tom insisted that Setagaya is one of Tokyo's wealthier suburbs. It looked as boring as Toronto's Willowdale.

We ate American-style food: Bob had the special, a mound of rice, two fried shrimp, spaghetti, Salisbury steak, salad, and a mound of yellow Jell-O — two little Mount Fujis on one plate. The rest of us ate variations of spaghetti. Tom wants to open Japan's first Jewish deli. Not sure how this would play, considering that the Japanese consume hefty amounts of anti-Semitic literature despite the fact that there are almost no Jews among them. Wendy remembered that today was Yom Kippur, the holiest day in the Jewish calendar, reserved for prayer and fasting. The three Jews in the group — Wendy, Tom, and me — looked somewhat uneasy. None of us is observant but somehow eating in a restaurant in Setagaya that night created a cultural dissonance. "Perhaps seeing a noh play," I suggested, "is a religious experience?" No one commented.

SUNDAY, OCTOBER 4

When a country contains rival cities, one often claims to be the spiritual or cultural centre while the other is regarded as a parvenu upstart, worshipping Mammon. Think of Jerusalem and Tel Aviv, Montreal and Toronto, San Francisco and Los Angeles. In Japan, it's Kyoto and Tokyo. On the Sunday we arrived, Kyoto seemed sleepy and self-satisfied, small and provincial, with a population around 1.5 million. Oddly, I feel more like a tourist here than in Tokyo, even though there are more bilingual signs, more people who speak English, and more racially mixed couples on the streets.

Getting here on the Shinkansen, the bullet train, was great fun. A cab arrived at Seifuso at 9:30 a.m. and dropped us in front of a porter at Tokyo station. He strapped our luggage on his shoulders and took us to the exact spot where we were to board our train — Track 15, car No. 12. Bob did a leisurely survey of waiting areas beside our track: you could buy beer, soft drinks, at least one English-language and countless Japanese newspapers, sandwiches and sushi — all beautifully wrapped, ready to take aboard — and much else besides. I hate to think what a Japanese tourist would find on a train platform in Toronto or Vancouver.

Our train pulled in at 10:45 exactly and left precisely fifteen minutes later. There's a digital clock at the front of each coach, as well as an electronic message machine that announces, in Japanese and precise English, the stops made on the way to Kyoto. The clock also notes the speed — we hit 224 kilometres per hour. We'd been advised to head immediately for the dining car. There was great variety but not great quality. Back in our seats, the bento boxes being unpacked around us looked much tastier.

As far as I was concerned, the trip was too short. I'd just settled in when we arrived in a station that seemed tranquil after Tokyo's. Our ryokan, The Three Sisters, had a building that catered exclusively to *gaijin*, which is both good and bad. Pleased to see the faintly obscene Japanese badger, or *tanuki*, in the outer courtyard. "Kay," one of the sisters, is helpful but rather aggressive, no doubt the result of dealing with so many of "us." There is further evidence of the Americanization of Kay in the booklet in our room. Beside the mandatory earthquake regulations, we are warned not to keep pets, not to cancel or shorten our booking, not to expect to have dinner in the inn if we ordered after four o'clock, and so on.

The room is adequate, smaller than our room in Tokyo, with a ¥100-per-hour pay television, a fluorescent overhead, and a doll's-size dresser. There's a small enclosed balcony overlooking a lovely garden, and a bathtub that was none too clean. I was a bit daunted by the used bar of soap with two unfamiliar black hairs attached.

We had time to tour our district. Bought a copy of *Kyoto Journal*, which is a remarkably good city magazine; *Eating Cheap in Japan: The Gaijin Gourmet's Guide to Ordering in Non-Japanese Restaurants*; and *Kyoto: A Contemplative Guide* by Gouveneur Mosher, written in 1978 and now in its twelfth printing. Mosher, not surprisingly, was furious about recent changes to his adopted town. Every writer, it seems, has an ideal Kyoto that is, or has been, or is about to be, ruined.

MONDAY, OCTOBER 5

In the morning, this being Kyoto, we should have gone to a temple, but started, as we did in Tokyo, with shopping. I bought my first pair of men's shoes. When one is travelling, shoes are hugely important. (Bob has holes in one of his three pairs, and my best walking shoes were, by now, soleless.) In Tokyo, I discovered that I measured 26, a large Japanese man's size. Bob, size 28, is a total misfit. Although the salesman managed to keep a straight face while I selected a lovely suede pair, I got quite giggly.

More fun later as we wandered up and down old manufacturing and retailing streets, starting from the Kyoto Hotel on Oike-dori and Kawaramachi-dori, then to the covered streets of Teramachi, Gokomachi, and Fuyacho. We had dinner nearby at Misoka-an Kawamichi-ya, a *soba* noodle restaurant run by the same family since the seventeenth century. They continue to provide noodles to pilgrims climbing Mount Hiei to pray at Enryaku-ji, a great Buddhist temple at the top. Each May 16, the birthday of the Emperor Kammu, and founder of Kyoto, Kawamichi-ya sets up a stall at the top of the holy mountain and serves *soba* to the faithful who have scaled the steep slopes to attend a memorial service. The restaurant was charming — a garden, then a few tables, then more garden, going back and back in the elongated Kyoto style.

Bob insists that the Japanese carry specialization further than any other people, and that this partly accounts for their commercial and industrial success. A tea shop doesn't sell cookies; an incense shop doesn't carry fans. There are few supermarkets. I might miss the convenience of "one-stop shopping" if I lived here and had to feed a family three times a day; for a tourist, it's great.

A stationery store we visited devoted about a quarter of its floor space to a small, private collection of old typewriters, pens, ink stones, moveable type, and ukiyo-e prints depicting scribes. One store sold nothing but a single type of mushroom, the *matsutake*, or "pine mushroom," now in season. This most treasured of Japanese mushrooms grows only in the wild, under red pine trees, and is available for just a few weeks in October. Here they were, arranged on beds of ferns, while down the road another store specialized in giant clams, split open and juicy. We were told that these male and female edibles should be consumed together to increase potency or fertility.

Phallic and fertility rituals are among the oldest known aspects of Shinto. Although they're disappearing, it's still possible to witness, or to participate in, public events dedicated to symbolic coitus. In Aichi prefecture each year at springtime, at Ogata shrine, a rousing festival concludes with a parade of portable shrines and carnival floats erected on "phallo-vulvar" themes. The centrepiece of this pageant is said to be a gigantic mechanical clamshell which opens and closes as it passes through the streets. A young girl, riding inside, tosses "propitious rice cakes" to the crowd.

In a nearby town, they stage an equally blunt event at the Tagata shrine honouring the most celebrated phallic deity in Japan. Here, a vermilion monster-organ leads the parade, which joins up with the neighbouring snapping clamshell. (It's hard to imagine that this country bans photos of pubic hair; but if Japan were easy to understand, where would the fun be?)

We wandered away from the shops, over to the Kamo River. Sadly, one of the city's great natural assets is a mess — garbage everywhere, walkways with no place to sit, but who would want to? Nothing, however, deters young boys and old men from fishing along its banks — catching what look like smelts. One hunched-over old fellow kept his creel on one side of the river while he fished the other. Every time he caught something, he climbed up the steep stone escarpment, crossed the river, and happily deposited his fish on the other side.

We saw bigger fish — and barrels of pickles, tofu, and seaweed — during a long and scent-filled walk through a crowded open market where housewives shopped for the evening meal. The covered street reminded me of the Mea Sharim market in Jerusalem — rough stone steps, a confusion of smells, voices shouting in a language I couldn't understand.

TUESDAY, OCTOBER 6

Today we hit our first royal palace and two temples. The Imperial Palace grounds, more beautiful than I could have imagined, were modelled on Chinese gardens — trees, moss, and lakes in exquisite relationship to one another. The day was cloudy, perfect for watching reflections on water. It had been some time since I'd been part of a mainly Western tour group, and it wasn't a pleasant experience. They were as nice as people gathered at random could be, but, unlike the Japanese, I don't enjoy being herded, especially by an officious guide with inept English. I used the time imagining the wonderful coronation ceremony that will take place here when the future emperor is crowned.

Then, unescorted, we visited two temples in the northwest of the city. Daitoku-ji, a complex of twenty-four separate temples, belongs to the Rinzai Zen sect. These buildings were erected in the seventeenth century, three hundred years after the originals. We were greeted and served green tea by a jolly monk selling autographed copies of his autobiography.

In Ryoan-ji, another Zen temple, the austere garden, made almost entirely of rocks and stones, is more famous than the building. There are fifteen large rocks, arranged in three groups — seven, five, and three — with raked gravel surrounding each group. (In the Buddhist world, the number fifteen denotes completeness.) We sat on the viewing porch and tried to count the large rocks, but it was impossible. No one can see more than fourteen from any single spot. A design to combat hubris? A three-dimensional proof that reality is beyond our field of vision?

After a few serene moments, we were surrounded by hordes of schoolchildren who seemed oblivious to the magic of the rocks and far more interested in Bob. At one point, as we were leaving, he was surrounded by eight teenagers from Hokkaido who wanted to exchange greetings and pose for pictures. An odd habit, this swarming of Westerners: Do these kids from the north island rarely see foreigners? Is it just a teenage thing? A dare? A lark? Turn it around and imagine eager North American teenagers besieging Asian tourists. I'm sure they'd feel threatened as well.

Ate two wonderful meals, one in a small Chinese restaurant in the northern suburbs where we happened to be; the other in Gion, once home to thousands of geisha. The word "geisha" originally meant "art person" — skilled in music, dance, and stroking the male ego. In the past, poor parents sold their young daughters into the trade. They were apprenticed to an experienced geisha, trained, licensed, and ranked by the central government according to their skills. Remarkably, there are almost twenty thousand today, but only a few hundred of the first rank.

Kyoto was spared by the American bombers, and parts of the celebrated entertainment quarter remain as they were a century ago — dark wooden buildings, red lanterns glowing along empty streets. In the silence one can imagine *geta* echoing on the cobblestones. There are few signs, almost none in English: these entertainment establishments are intended for wealthy and sophisticated Japanese businessmen.

Between meals we visited Nishijin, the silk district. (Not only are stores specialized, but sometimes entire districts are given over to a single product.) After touring a fairly routine silk museum, we went down the street to Komachi House, a well-known kimono shop run by a father and daughter with a small grandson in the wings. Antique silk kimono lay in neat piles on the floor or hung on racks in two large rooms. They were magnificent to see and touch, an inspired collaboration between worms and humans. I bought wonderful things, mostly gifts to bring home, black kimono jackets with a family crest on the back and a tasteful design on the lining.

WEDNESDAY, OCTOBER 7

October, contrary to what one reads, is a hot month, at least *this* October is. We began the day fairly early, leaving the ryokan to join the so-called "tour" of the royal playground, Katsura Imperial Villa, a seventeenth-century retreat built on the Katsura River, to the west of old Kyoto. On seventeen acres, various structures — palaces, pavilions, and one temple — are strategically placed among pools, islands, bridges, and artificial hills. Katsura Detached Palace, with its impeccable woodwork and moon-viewing platform, is the most celebrated example of traditional Japanese architecture. Our group — mostly Japanese, some Germans, a few English-speakers — was guided around the outskirts of the buildings at some considerable distance from anything that might have appeared beautiful up close. The sliding paper doors were closed, so we couldn't even peek in. I found it frustrating, and was happy when our brief visit ended and we rushed off by ourselves to a nearby temple.

The original Sanjusangendo was built in 1164, when it was believed that the world was entering a Dark Age and salvation was attainable only through the mercy of the Amida Buddha. (The temple was dedicated to Amida's agent in the world, the Bodhisattva Kannon, the Goddess of Mercy.) It burned in 1249 and was rebuilt in 1266. The most remarkable part of this reconstruction is the Main Hall. Along its length are thirty-three bays, each with a carved image of Kannon, and each of the thirty-three has been carved 1,001 times, and each of those extends, one behind the other, deep into one wing of the building — a total of 33,033 wooden sculptures. In the middle stands a six-foot-tall, thousand-handed Kannon wearing a crown of ten heads, the creation of Tankei, a sculptor of the Kamakura period (1192–1333). This awe-inspiring work slowly revealed itself as we walked along a ramp, burning candles and incense on the way. I offered a silent prayer at each station for people I knew. Votive candles of any faith turn me into a supplicant.

Then we crossed the street to the Kyoto National Museum and more larger-than-life sculptures from the ninth to the thirteenth centuries, pieces commissioned for surrounding temples and brought for safekeeping into the museum. Some, with their bulging eyes and grotesque musculature, are so terrifying one can hardly imagine an artist emerging sane after creating one.

After that, to the home of the poet and ceramist, Kawai Kanjiro (1890–1966), who, as an early supporter of the folk art movement, helped reintroduce traditional arts to post-war Japan. It's hard to believe that "typically Japanese" articles, perfected over centuries for use in the tea ceremony — pottery, lacquerware, textiles, bamboo —

have ever been in danger of becoming extinct, but in the headlong Meiji-era rush to modernize, these exemplars of restrained taste were eclipsed by gaudy mass production.

After a hiatus of about fifty years, at the beginning of the twentieth century, the folk art movement was rekindled by Soetsu Yanagi, a potter, who was soon joined by two others, one an Englishman, Bernard Leach, in establishing the Japan Folk Society. Kanjiro was an early supporter.

His house is a perfect example of the Kyoto "bedroom of eels" style — a long, narrow wooden house with room after room stretching back the length of the lot and interspersed with "pocket" gardens. The average house width is thirty feet and frequently ten times that long. None of these houses is more than 120 years old, but considering the high risk of fire, their age is to be marvelled at.

The residential landscape of old Kyoto developed like cells reproducing themselves and connecting. The smallest component, the tatami mat, is approximately six feet by three feet. Rooms are built around mats, houses built around rooms, and neighbourhoods built around forty-family units whose members usually share a trade or craft. The front room of a house became a shop or work space, and from that would flow a reception area and more private living quarters, all separated by sliding doors.

Kanjiro's house stands in the pottery area of modern Kyoto. Inside are two kilns, including a climbing oven (*noborigama*) with many chambers, able to generate temperatures of 2,600 degrees Fahrenheit. Nearby streets leading up the mountain to Kiyomizu Temple are lined with pottery shops. Kiyomizu itself is a clanging, shambling sort of place that I liked without admiring.

THURSDAY, OCTOBER 8

As if to protest Katsura, Bob and I boycotted our third and final Imperial residence and eased slowly into the day. (We're generally out and about by 9:30 and often not back until quite late.) We both woke this morning with the same idea — water. We needed to get on water. Tom had told us about a ride down the Hozu River from Kameoka to Arashiyama, in the westernmost part of Kyoto. "A bit choppy, but no danger." Perfect.

Our train arrived in Kameoka at noon. It was a fine trip, much of it overlooking the rapids we would later ride down. Bob looked up from his *Japan Times* and said, "We're not going down those are we? Not in a boat?"

"I think so," I replied, a bit nervous myself. Just then a large craft, followed by three or four more, passed below the train, happily bobbing along in the water.

Had lunch overlooking the docks in a prosperous tourist town while waiting for the next boat at 1:30. Bought our tickets for about $30 each and wide-brimmed straw hats for about $5 to protect us from the sun. (The weather was hot and breezy.) The twenty or so other passengers on our fibreglass boat were all Japanese. Although we were the last to board, they'd saved two seats for us in the first row. How to interpret such a gesture? Some might say we were being isolated from the others. (This would be madness.) I believed they wanted us to have a good time and to think well of them, which we did. We said "Arigato," and plunked ourselves down. Part of the pleasure of travelling in Japan is the generosity of strangers.

It's always been this way, even when *gaijin* were barred almost completely from contact with the Japanese. In 1690, a scientist with the Dutch East India Company, Englebert Kämpfer, lived in the foreign colony off Nagasaki and travelled annually by convoy to Edo. He wrote in his journal: "The behaviour of the Japanese, from the meanest countryman up to the greatest prince or lord, is such that the whole empire might be called a school of civility and good manners."

On our boat, with one guide at the tiller, another on the oars, and a third with a pole, we set off through shallow waters running between towering forested hills — train tracks on one side, a few bridges in the distance. The rapids were far less rapid than they had seemed from above, and we had an exciting hour and a half that included two agreeable commercial intrusions. As we turned a corner, one guide instructed everyone — or in our case, gestured — to look up: two men with cameras, perched on an outcropping of rock, took our picture, which we could buy when the boat docked. (We didn't.) Then, as we

entered the final shallow area, a boat came up beside us and attached itself to ours. It was a floating shop that sold snacks and drinks, including beer. They did a brisk business while motoring us to home base. Everyone seemed to have a grand time, keeping up a steady stream of banter that I wish I could have understood.

We were now in Arashiyama, a suburb in the northwest of Kyoto. It has a festive air, a place for short holidays, something like Niagara-on-the-Lake, with a magnificent natural setting — ringed by mountains and temples. It's said to be much the same as it was a thousand years ago, when it provided a tranquil escape for Kyoto aristocrats fleeing famine, riots, and political intrigue. We had time for only one temple, Tenryu-ji, a 1900 reconstruction, with a large pond filled with giant carp and wonderful vistas through open doors. Then the train to Kyoto station and a successful search for some reading material. We had run out, a potentially disastrous situation, since we had several days to go before returning to Tokyo.

At 7:00 we joined Kay of The Three Sisters in a sukiyaki supper for her guests. There was an American couple from Seattle, a Dutch physicist who asked me what a futon was, and a woman from Tennessee who'd done a lot of travelling but seemed vague about what she'd seen. Kay cooked but did not eat. It was a rather silent dinner during which we exchanged travel anecdotes. When it was over, Kay herded us into another room. There, at the request of the Seattle couple, she performed on the koto about as well as I play the piano. A small price to pay for an excellent meal.

FRIDAY, OCTOBER 9

I'm sitting alone in a Laundromat in a residential district about five blocks from our ryokan. There are four small automatic washing machines that use cold water; one large American Maytag that uses hot, two dry-cleaning machines; a machine that washes and dries sneakers; and two regular dryers. I imagine that the Japanese drag their wet laundry home to hang on their balconies or wherever. I love watching clothes spin. Haven't gone to a Laundromat since Bob and I got married in 1970 and a couple of relatives gave us a pair of indestructible Inglises that have lasted through two babies, Rachel and Sarah, and two stepchildren, James and Margaret.

Took most of the morning at the Japan Travel Bureau trying to arrange our trip to Takayama, a village in the Japanese Alps. We'll stay in Kyoto tomorrow, go to Nara on Sunday, leave for Takayama early Tuesday morning, where we'll stay for two nights. Then, back to Tokyo.

After making our arrangements, we boarded a rickety subway-style train for the forty-minute ride south to Uji. Nestled along the foggy banks of the Uji River, this region produces the finest tea in Japan. (It's rumoured that the secret of its success is the herring that's added to local fertilizer.) Japanese tea, said to have been brought from China by a Buddhist monk in 1191, was at first consumed only by royalty. Hundreds of years later, the privilege was extended to the upper classes, but not until the twentieth century, with improvement in production, did it became widely available.

Tea shops lined both sides of the street leading to the temple, selling dozens of tea varieties, most of which I'd never heard of — the powdered *matcha* used in the tea ceremony; *gyokuro*, a fragrant tea from the finest leaves of the best plants; and the more common *sencha*, a leaf tea from further down the plant. Tea, like wine, is the unique product of climate, soil, and history; it

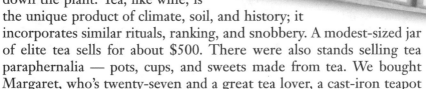

incorporates similar rituals, ranking, and snobbery. A modest-sized jar of elite tea sells for about $500. There were also stands selling tea paraphernalia — pots, cups, and sweets made from tea. We bought Margaret, who's twenty-seven and a great tea lover, a cast-iron teapot for loose leaves and an affordable leaf tea, beautifully wrapped.

Crossing the oldest stone bridge in Japan, we headed uphill for the beautiful Byodo-in, the only remaining temple from the graceful Heian period (794–1185). As we approached this eleventh-century wooden building, we could see the cantilevered wings spreading from the roof like a phoenix. At the temple a Japanese couple insisted we feed the carp with food they'd bought — something that looked like a Styrofoam baguette. Then they took our pictures as the fish engaged in a feeding frenzy. I rang my first temple bell, pulling a huge log out as far as I could, then letting go. The hollow echo of bronze resonated in my ears, and in my chest.

On the train coming home a group of young boys surrounded Bob and were aggressively bold — finding his height, his pipe, the colour of skin amusing. They managed to attract the attention of everyone in the car but no adult told them to behave. How will they ever be transformed into courteous adults, members of the "school of civility"?

After the Laundromat, we went for our first *shabu shabu* dinner — similar to sukiyaki but cooked in an aromatic broth. We were served in a small semiprivate room, our feet tucked under the low table, our backs resting on cushions against the wall. Romantic, except for the waitress, who insisted that I, not Bob, be the one to add things to the pot — meat, mushrooms, cabbage, whatever — each time saying "*Shabu shabu*. You, you!" We did our best to ignore her.

SATURDAY, OCTOBER 10

We called home first thing this morning and were reassured that everything was fine, except that Sarah's teachers were still on strike. Then we dressed, breakfasted, and set out to visit three museums close to our ryokan before a noon meeting with Ted, who, luckily for us, is now in Kyoto.

First, the contemporary museum, with its fine photography section, part of which was on display — early-twentieth-century work from around the world, including a marvellous shot of George Bernard Shaw looking both whimsical and virile. Then to the Kyoto Municipal Art Gallery, a fine Meiji building with three good shows. One featured the work of a group of modern calligraphy artists — bold, black strokes with range and depth. Bob talked about how the American painter Franz Kline was influenced by calligraphy and how these artists appear to have been influenced, in turn, by him. Then an extensive and moving show by a modern painter using old techniques on screens and scrolls to depict scenes from the early Meiji period, an era that was disappearing before his eyes in the drive to Westernize. At the end of the scroll there was a touching portrait of the old artist himself, Oukoku Konoshima, kneeling in front of his easel. In the third room, a group show again, contemporary clay sculpture.

But the most memorable of this trio was the Museum of Traditional Industry, where the emphasis was on selling things. The entire top floor was an outlet for bolts of silk and ready-made kimono for those willing to part with a small fortune. There, amid a confusion of grandmothers and mothers, everyone kneeling in an ocean of sumptuous fabric, young brides came to be fitted for what might turn out to be the only Japanese outfit they'll wear as adults, and likely the most expensive clothing they'll ever possess. Grandmothers rested material on their palms, turned it over, squinted, commented. Brides looked uncomfortable — draped in fabrics from their past while preparing for their future. Fathers tried not to appear too proud or too perturbed by the cost. I skulked around, pretending not to stare.

On the floor below, before we knew what was happening, a line of middle-aged women whisked us into an exhibition of ikebana, traditional flower arranging. Most of the innovation seemed to come from the variety of containers used — violent colours and bold design. Judging by this show, the Japanese like shocking juxtaposition and imbalance — flowers mixed with twigs and ribbons, nature in extreme, misshapen forms.

We joined Ted and wandered around the lobby of the Kyoto International Hotel, where eleven weddings were scheduled for the day. As we made our way through, the uniformity of dress among the guests and their single ethnicity made it look like one giant wedding — men in black double-breasted suits, white shirts, and white ties (quite Spanish), and women in kimono or afternoon dresses, most with garish bows or flowers in their hair (ingenue chic).

Nijo Castle, our next stop, was once a little-used home for the Tokugawa shogunate. Today it was too full of other visitors to be entirely enjoyable. This, despite the fact that, according to Ted, non-Japanese tourism is down from previous years. Not much remains of the six-hundred-year-old castle, built by Tokugawa Ieyasu to impress other feudal lords, as well as the emperor, with the chief daimyo's power and the virtue of the uneasy peace he'd brought to Japan after hundreds of years of civil war. The most interesting section is Ninomaru Palace, with its ornate reception halls and famous "nightingale floors" which squeak underfoot. If an enemy silently crossed the moat and scaled the walls, this singing floor would serve as a last-minute warning system.

Back to contemporary Kyoto and the arcades of Teramachi-dori. Ted popped in and out of second-hand bookstores, asking in Japanese for a particular book he wanted on Japanese prejudice. He recommended that we read the short story "Prize Stock" by Kenzaburo Oe to understand something of the Japanese ignorance of blacks. We bought an Oe novel, *A Personal Matter*, which is closely based on the birth of his brain-damaged son. Not sure I'm up to it now.

SUNDAY, OCTOBER 11

Last night we saw a temple by candlelight: if we'd done nothing else during our six weeks here, this alone would have made the trip worthwhile. We went in the morning to meet David and Jill Bond and their friend, Janette Dambrosky, on the outskirts of Nara. Janette was born in Philadelphia to a Ukrainian father and a French mother and studied anthropology at Ohio State University. She came to Japan fifteen years ago and settled for ten years on a remote island where she learned to speak Japanese. (She still cannot read, which must place her in an odd relation with the culture in which she lives.) For the last five years she's been teaching English in Nara. She's about five feet three inches tall, completely round, with almost no neck and short legs peeking out from under a billowing muumuu. Although she's been back to Cleveland three times for open heart surgery, she's spunky and great company.

Janette met us at the train station and took us to a nearby antique store where the Bonds were already deep into a trance-like state, practising the Zen of shopping, with obvious success — arms full of sake bottles, kimono, and dolls. I slipped into high acquisition mode myself and bought a lovely blue-and-white porcelain bowl for my mother-in-law, Frances. I was told that it was Arita ware from the southern island of Kyushu. There's something like a unicorn at the centre and I love it. We also bought sake bottles for various nieces and nephews and what I think is a wonderful short kimono — a sort of smoking jacket for a man, I think, but lined with a dramatic painting of a theatrical mask. It's for our daughter Rachel's sixteenth birthday, which is in a few days.

We crammed all the parcels and five people into Janette's Ford Escort and drove into the countryside to the home of the chief curator of the National Museum in Nara, Hiroyuki Matsumoto, who is also an artist. He lives in a modest, ramshackle house with his charming wife, three children, and several dogs. (I had assumed wrongly that Japanese hadn't adopted the unfortunate Western habit of keeping domestic pets.) The house itself, propped up on wooden supports, is surrounded by field grass and wildflowers, with exceptional stone sculpture scattered apparently at random over the property.

They welcomed us into their object-filled house, where Hiroyuki's work was on display everywhere, including a black-and-white shoji covered in his calligraphy. He'd used ink on paper but in every other way it was different from the work we'd seen at the Kyoto Municipal Art Gallery. Hiroyuki told us that the group showing there exhibited together because they share a teacher. He used to belong to such a group and participate in their shows, but stopped. "Who wants to keep repeating his teacher?" he commented, a radical notion in a country where pupils can repeat their sensei's style for a lifetime and not feel diminished by it. Hiroyuki is an artist cast in the more Romantic Western mould — greying hair, old clothes, a preoccupied air. His shining moment as a painter was a show in Paris in the late 1970s.

His wife, plump and dimpled, impressed me as a tough soul in a ruffled apron, which she wore during most of our visit. According to Janette, Mrs. Matsumoto doesn't drive, rarely leaves home, and is a relative prisoner in this isolated country house. She herself was quick to tell us, laughing, and in her husband's presence, "He never even lets me come to his exhibitions." I believe this is not a simple relationship (what marriage is?) and not a straightforward example of Japanese male chauvinism. Something I couldn't understand kept bubbling to the surface.

Lunch was served close to an open fire in the backyard. We sat around a large, square table on benches made from wood and cement, while their fourteen-year-old son barbecued sprats on a clay platter. It felt like a French movie, with wine brought by Janette to accompany scrumptious food beautifully served on short notice by a wife obviously used to such demands. There were pickled green peppers, marinated beef, sliced radishes with lemon, a hot *nabe* (a stew-like dish served in a large ceramic bowl featuring local vegetables in season), sweet potatoes dipped in a mustard sauce, soybeans and rice balls resting on flower petals in a basket.

We joked that in Canada a similar lunch would involve hot dogs and ketchup bottles. Like the artist-husband he is, our host grunted that he'd much prefer that. We went indoors for dessert, a cake brought by Jill and David, hot Indian tea served with milk and cinnamon, and cold weak coffee. Then Hiroyuki showed us photographs of his most recent work — painted, oddly enough, on paper lining the bottom of an otherwise empty swimming pool in Nagoya. "And where's the painting now?" I asked, assuming he had removed it to safety. With Buddhist fatalism he replied, "Probably turned into water!" Then he laughed.

I was told later that he destroys most of his art, which I thought particularly odd for a curator. Perhaps it's hard to have the riches of an art museum around you all day and then attempt to create on your own. On the other hand, it could be inspiring. Janette explained the reason was more commercial than aesthetic — his work doesn't sell.

After the usual photo session and gift-giving (posters from him to us), we said goodbye and headed to another extraordinary building further along the rough road — an artist's studio and shop belonging to a woman who works in stained glass and her designer husband, who built their house using 130 telephone poles for the outside walls. It resembled a Georgian Bay cottage, except that all the windows were stained glass, and when you looked out you could see tinted rice paddies. Across the length of the studio was an antique stained-glass window from Spain. Broken glass from around the world covered every surface, waiting to be transformed into windows or lampshades.

The couple were superb hosts and treated us to more coffee and dessert. He was stocky and tousle-haired, like a frightened peasant in a Kurosawa movie. We were joined by other guests — a dentist from Kyushu and her husband, a railway engineer from Osaka. We'd planned to pile into their van and Janette's car to visit a potter further along the road, but I had a fierce allergic reaction brought on by the Matsumotos' dog, and the stained-glass lady's nursing bitch and litter of four. Because the potter was also an animal lover, we revised our plans and headed straight for a local museum.

As the sun was setting, we parked the cars — there were now three — and walked in single file up a lane, past wooden farmhouses, towards a local government official's former house, now a museum. We looked like actors in an Antonioni film — definitely a day in the movies. The slightly pompous curator was willing to keep the museum open past five o'clock for our travelling troupe of nine. On display were several ghastly pieces of driftwood, some elegant swords and scrolls, and a lovely palanquin. We walked respectfully around the showcases, then gathered beneath a picture of a member of the Fujiwara clan, whose house this had been. The Fujiwaras (the name means Wisteria Fields) were a powerful clan for a thousand years, starting in the ninth century. We were about to expand our knowledge of the Fujiwaras, willing or not.

I should have been forewarned when an ancient woman who was either the curator's wife or his mother quietly retired from the room and the curator took centre stage. I offer this shortened version of The Curator's Tale, as it reached me, in translation and incomplete: to ensure obedience to the shogun, when a daimyo returned to his province, his wife and children had to remain in the capital, Edo. Thus, the Fujiwara heir was required to remain there from the time he was thirteen until he was seventeen. It happened that the Fujiwaras were renowned for their swordsmanship, and this particular young lord far outclassed the shogun's sons. For this offence he was asked to take the honourable way out — *seppuku*. At this point the stained-glass woman interrupted and announced that we must pose for the obligatory picture and be going.

Doubtless she'd heard the story many times before, but I was anxious to hear how it ended. Not happily, I suspected. In its bare bones it had all the ingredients of a classic kabuki play. It might well have *been* a kabuki play.

We marched back through the fields under borrowed plastic umbrellas as a thin rain began to fall. Then our small motorcade set off to a nearby temple, Enjo-ji, I think, which was somehow connected with one of Janette's pupils — I think she said that it "belonged" to him, which is possible since Buddhists are allowed to marry and their sons generally inherit the profession and the real estate. (All they have to do is spend a year as an acolyte, then write an exam.) We were to see a monk, a member of the Shingon sect of esoteric Buddhism, whose name, I believe, was Akira — bilingual conversations get a bit murky.

It was by now pitch black and wet — perfect for what was to follow. We parked just outside the main temple building while our new decorator friend went next door to rouse the priest. Minutes later he appeared, a withered, toothless, good-humoured old man, with a face we'd seen on countless ancient scrolls. He seemed delighted to let us in, and brought along his own flashlight. Someone in our party had also come equipped. As we entered the temple, beams of light flickered around the room and across the carved faces of dozens of Buddhas. Slowly, the place came to life, as if waking from the sleep of centuries.

We walked around the sides of the small, square wooden building. In one corner, a National Treasure, a small Heian Buddha draped in long robes that recalled Greek statues. Nearby, the light settled on a Buddha from the tenth century, inside which another Buddha, two hundred years older, was discovered. Next, a Kannon image painted on a lotus leaf backed by a leaf-shaped filigree fan, ornate and delicate. As we moved around the room, candles were lit, first in one area, then another. I returned to sit before the central Buddha, surrounded now by flickering light, glowing with holy fire like the biblical burning bush. Others joined me: we sat silently and watched.

Eventually, our Japanese guides began to stir. They handed the priest money for the upkeep of the temple and for his kindness. Then our small group of familiars trickled into the dark, wet night. I could not imagine a more perfect temple experience. In the car, I asked Janette how we might thank her friends for all they'd done. "Send them a note when you get back to Canada," she said. That seems woefully inadequate.

MONDAY, OCTOBER 12

Another enlightening day after Bob and I spent the morning sorting through, and shedding, some of our books, souvenirs, and other purchases, before packing. We met Ted at about 10:45 outside The

Three Sisters, then went with him to the Silver Pavilion, Ginkaku-ji, a National Treasure and one of his favourite places. It's compact and Spartan and, despite its name, was never covered with silver foil as intended. The Japanese, who appreciate the merely suggestive, have never felt the need. This lack of lamination, however, upset a Chinese tourist who arrived there, aged mother in tow. She passed the Silver Temple without noticing it and asked Ted, in English, where it was. He pointed.

"That?" she said, packing a ton of contempt into a single word. "And what about the Gold Temple? Not 'gold' I suppose?" It fell to Ted to inform her that the Gold Temple was indeed wrapped in gold leaf, but unfortunately it was closed for repairs. I thought that like Rumpelstiltskin she'd stamp her foot and descend into the earth.

Happily for us, there were few other visitors at the Silver Pavilion, and I saw why Ted loves it so. We sat quietly contemplating buildings, the mountains behind, and the white sand mounds in front — one raked to look like the sea, the other piled high, with the top flattened to resemble Mount Fuji. When we won our Asia Pacific fellowships, we were told: "Go and sit in a garden and look." Here we were, gratefully fulfilling our mandate.

While we sat, marvelling, I described our Nara experience to Ted. He explained that many old Buddhist temples fall into decay because people use them only on special occasions. Sons no longer want to go into the family business, temples are abandoned, and may even be bought by *gaijin*, who renovate them and move in, as if they were schoolhouses in the West. (The neighbours are usually accepting because they expect that their family ashes will continue to rest there securely.) Part of the cash flow problem in Buddhism is that priests are paid only for services rendered — funerals and prayers for special occasions. In a religion that promotes entrepreneurship, the more aggressive temple priests do well. The rest, like our toothless host, depend on the kindness of strangers.

Outside the temple grounds, we downed a bowl of noodle soup and headed south. Unlike Tokyo, Kyoto is laid out like a Chinese city — a grid pattern with major arterial roads pointing in four directions, with a few concessions to rivers and hills. Some of the excitement of aimless meandering is therefore lost, but strolling down Tetsugaku-no-michi — translated as the Path of Philosophy, or the Philosopher's Walk — was pure heaven. It follows the western curve of a canal and is lined with cherry trees on one side, and welcoming shops and coffee houses on the other. It's named in memory of a famous scholar, Ikutaro Nishida (1870–1945), who walked here daily. A professor at Kyoto University, Nishida attempted to fuse Western and Eastern philosophies: he was deeply interested in the works of Hegel, William James, and Henri Bergson; at the same time, he practised Zen meditation and was a lifelong friend of Daisetz Suzuki, the modern Zen philosopher who reached out to the West.

We stopped for coffee at a strange place that looked, at certain angles, like a temple, at others like a British tea house or an Alpine lodge. There were roosters wandering at will, carp doing the breast stroke, statues of Buddhas scattered around the yard like lawn gnomes in small-town Canada, paintings of Christ, and outbuildings filled with flowers, urns, ceramic pots, and animals. Here, at last, was the exception that proved the rule about Japanese specialization and taste.

When we sat down we were given tiny Danish pastries with our menus. The poor waitress nearly fainted when she saw Ted read and then heard him speak Japanese. I thought this explained our bill — less than half the listed price — ¥300 instead of ¥700. We couldn't leave without finding out more about this place, whether it was part of a temple or not. It wasn't. The owner is an actor, famous for his samurai roles. The clutter was the result of things he'd picked up in his travels, live animals excepted. "Foreigners are charged half price because he wants to promote world peace," our waitress reported. Vive l'internationalisation!

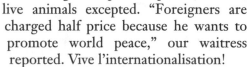

Continuing down Philosopher's Walk, Ted posed in front of a rack selling paper fortunes based on Chinese birth years and blood types. "Not unusual," he suggested. Near the end of our hike we stopped to gawk at the funeral of a financier — his profession was written on a sign outside the temple gate. Many people, mostly men, came to pay their respects. They wore the same black suits they wear to weddings, but with black ties rather than white. As wedding guests hand over envelopes containing substantial sums of money, similar envelopes are proffered to defray funeral costs. (One's relationship to the deceased dictates the appropriate amount, always equal to several hundred dollars.)

Off to our second temple of the day, Nanzen-ji, famous for its beautifully painted sliding doors from the Heian period, where we enjoyed a delicious vegetarian temple meal beside a carp pool. Then we hopped into a cab and back down to Kawaramachi-dori, to an English-language bookstore, where we loaded up with more books about Japan and novels by Japanese writers. The need to know more grows the longer I'm here. Back to the inn by eleven, settled the bill, and did our final packing for the next phase of our trip. Where did all this stuff come from?

TUESDAY, OCTOBER 13

Although we were at the station by 7:45 a.m., we almost missed our train at 8:44. We were on the correct track but at the wrong end. At 8:42 when a train pulled in far ahead of us, I had my doubts and left Bob with our bags. The conductor confirmed the worst — the train was ours. We'd travelled enough to know that trains in Japan run precisely on time. What we hadn't experienced was the short-train-on-a-long-track problem. The whistle was blowing when I signalled to Bob to run forward while I ran back. The trainman ran too, heaving our things into the last car. Because of us, this train departed several minutes late.

The trip itself was lovely, four and a half hours through the Hida Mountains, usually called the Japanese Alps, although they're more like foothills. In our car, middle-aged women on an outing didn't stop chattering except when they were eating. Food was available on the train, but these ladies were not having any. We watched them and waited. After the train pulled into one small station, they opened their windows, handed money to a trackside vendor, and brought on board lovely ceramic bowls with wooden tops, wrapped in rice paper and tied with string. Through hand gestures and the help of our fellow travellers, we too purchased these lovely lunches of cold rice and steaming hot vegetables.

Still watching out of the corner of my eye, I copied the ladies as they painstakingly untied the string, unwrapped the paper, and set it aside. When the meal ended, they picked up the paper and string, rewrapped each dish, and stored them neatly under their seats, knowing they'd be picked up at the end of the line. We copied them, move for move.

Our reservations in Takayama were at the Green Hotel, a modest business and tourist chain. Tonight, for the first time in Japan, we'll sleep on beds with feet, in the teeniest possible room, barely large enough for two of us to stand simultaneously. This was fine since we both have colds and want as much prone-time as possible. Bob coughs, I sneeze. After a nap, we ventured into the dining room. We were wearing street clothes while the other guests came in yukata, cotton kimono provided by the hotel, and plastic slippers. We grinned sheepishly at one another. I expected the food to reach Holiday Inn standards, but it was amazingly good — regional produce, beautifully served. I'm hoping we stage a miraculous recovery tomorrow. There's so much to see, starting with the farmer's market, open from 7 a.m. to noon.

WEDNESDAY, OCTOBER 14

Woke feeling somewhat better. Went for breakfast, which was prepaid, "Western Breakfast" it was called. From the buffet, Bob had juice, coffee, bacon, soupy scrambled eggs, and a roll; I had juice, coffee, noodles, tiny cutlets, and a salad — the East-West combo. We were out of the hotel by eight o'clock and headed for the farmer's market for which the town is justly famous. We started outside, where farm women sat behind rows of produce, including more fabled mushrooms at $35 to $40 for 100 grams. And there were pickles — tons of them — and tomatoes, radishes, cucumbers, and other goodies grown and preserved, many unfamiliar to me.

Near the market we visited a building full of historic drama. Once the seat of local government, it became a museum in 1968. It includes the storehouse that held rice collected as taxes for the shogun. And a wall-text described the three Ohara rebellions of the eighteenth century, all stemming from perceived tax injustice. Eventually the peasants won. In the same building, a room that was once a jail displayed instruments of torture.

We wandered through crowded streets lined with shops much like those in the Edo period — one of the great charms of this town. We explored stores selling lacquerware, woodwork, and culinary products, and followed a sweet, yeasty smell into a sake brewery that produces gourmet products for which Takayama is known. We found the lacquer sushi box our daughter, Sarah, had requested, under the influence of the Molly Ringwald character in John Hughes's film, *The Breakfast Club*.

Each year there are two major festivals in Takayama, the Sanno Matsuri in April, and the Yahata Matsuri in October — last week, in fact. More than two centuries ago, a plague came to Takayama. To placate the gods, elaborately carved floats were paraded through the streets and this became a twice yearly celebration. We visited the small museum that displays the huge, and alarming, floats — dragons in vibrant colours and puppets that move when the float is in motion.

By now, the combination of heat, inadequate shoes, and our colds got the better of us. Back to the hotel by about 3 p.m. for recuperation. We ate in for a second night, this time in the coffee shop where, as an experiment, I ordered the "fruit sandwich" — very white bread (no crust) cut in small shapes and covered with icing. Inside were thin slices of kiwi, peach, and banana. Ate some. Left some.

THURSDAY, OCTOBER 15

We checked out of our miniature room at about 9:30 a.m. and crammed our bags into several lockers at the station; accumulation seems to be getting out of hand, even though I'm abandoning worn-out clothes as we go. Off to Hida Takayama Folk Village, a sort of Upper Canada Village except that the four-hundred-year-old buildings are authentic, not reconstructions, beautifully spread over a series of hills. Roofs, understandably, are something of an obsession — keeping snow out and heat in. (Early builders relied on straw, about a foot thick.) We roamed the village at will, sharing the experience with busloads of Japanese tourists.

From there, back to Takayama to catch the train to Nagoya, then a quick track switch to grab the bullet train for Tokyo. As a reward for faultless execution of difficult travel moves, we headed immediately for the dining car. The couple with whom we shared our table was at least half male: a well-groomed salaryman-type and his partner, who was either a small, butchy woman in male clothes or a boy. The obvious male person ordered a beer; the other, geisha-like, poured for him but did not drink. The first received his enormous meat meal; the second, nothing. No words were exchanged. When the first was almost finished eating, he ordered another beer; then food arrived for his companion.

Many Japanese men, and women, are fascinated with effeminate boys. I've seen several on television, in magazines, and comic books. It's a common phenomenon, one that I suspect attracts gay and sexually confused *gaijin* to Japan. But I had never been so close to what most Westerners would regard as a highly unusual couple, and I caught myself staring. I yearned to ask, "Who are you? What is your relationship? How did you happen to be here, on this train, with us?"

Back in Tokyo, I feel as if I've come home. We're in a different room at Seifuso, down the hall from our original place. The waterfall sounds a bit different, but the rest is familiar — low table, TV on a wiggly metal stand, Thermos of hot water, toilet slippers. All the comforts of home.

FRIDAY, OCTOBER 16

Our first really rainy day, and not much fun. Dashed off to Ginza to catch an 11:30 a.m. performance of kabuki at the Kabuki-za, only to learn that no tickets were available. The building was lovely, very Meiji — winged tile roof and lots of vermilion. We had to settle for ¥10,000 ($100) tickets for Monday. Even then, it looked as if a tour company had purchased blocks of the best seats while we had to settle for the leftovers.

By cab to the Washington Shoe Store, which sells "larger than average shoes" — average for a Japanese, that is. This time we were looking for Bob, whose situation was desperate. Not a large selection in size 28, but a compromise between need and desire was reached. Then to a major department store for lunch and the last of our gift shopping, ignoring for the moment the thorny question of how the hell we're going to get all this stuff back home.

Returned to Seifuso to recuperate, then out again for Shinjuku and a 6:30 rendezvous with Ben Fulford before he leaves tomorrow for a holiday in China. We met, as did dozens of others, under the giant video screen opposite the exit. It was pouring. Water from our umbrellas trickled down our backs. As we left the inn, the owner smiled and said, "Maybe typhoon!"

Ben, an interesting guy, has been on his own for the last ten years and he's only twenty-six. His father's a diplomat, Dwight Fulford. When Dwight was transferred from Argentina to Saudi Arabia, Ben, the third of five children said, "No thanks," and headed either up — or down — the Amazon to imbibe a special hallucinogen with the local tribe. "We also ate a lot of nuts and maggots."

"Was the drug interesting?" I asked.

"Yes," he said, "but it did some organic damage to my brain. Probably not as much as marijuana did." Ben is a man of his time. He became interested in the East through drugs and mysticism and came to Sophia University in Tokyo where, after two and a half years, he was able to speak and write Japanese. (Clearly certain parts of his brain remain intact.) He forced himself to learn ten kanji a day as he travelled on the train to school. After classes he worked in a seedy bar where no English was spoken.

"At one point, six stark naked guys came in for drinks," Ben told us. "Once, another guy, deep into childhood regression, pulled down his pants and made ka-ka on the floor." In six months, Ben had a firm grasp of florid Japanese to go with his five other languages — English, French, Mandarin, Spanish, and Portuguese — although he's never been to Europe. He's written short stories, but hasn't published any, and dreams of writing a novel. Or else he'd like to return to Canada and enter politics. While in Japan, he's done TV ads dressed as a potato chip and made cameo appearances as a typical *gaijin*. Right now, he does financial reporting for a US newspaper chain, although he's never studied economics or business.

It became clear in our conversations — first in a screaming yakitori joint and later in a quieter coffee house — that Ben remains here largely because of the women. "Japanese women love foreign guys, and vice versa. They long for a cross-cultural marriage, to get away from all this." He has few Japanese male friends, but many female ones. "The men here are really nerds, believe me. Although in a lot of ways," he conceded, "they're smarter than Western guys."

This obsession with Japanese women has a long, sometimes honourable, occasionally shameful history, including *Madame Butterfly*. "Japanese women really know how to treat a man," is a cliché I've heard more than once from Western men in Japan. On his upcoming three-week holiday in China, Ben plans to visit Buddhist temples, and, I suspect, a few less spiritual haunts. He made me feel old.

SATURDAY, OCTOBER 17

In our regular phone call home, we found out that our daughter, Sarah, while waiting out the strike, now entering its fifth week, had gone to Montreal to stay with Margaret, her half-sister. Rachel sounded generally happy and pleased with life. I'm feeling rather homesick. Six weeks is the most I can imagine being without them, but one day, not long from now, they'll be gone forever, my chickens. How do parents survive?

Off again for Yasukuni shrine in the midst of a typhoonette. The weather was like summer again, but with a heavy, impending-storm feeling. On the way to the shrine, as we walked past an unused building, a large sheet of plate glass blew out of a window and fell four storeys to the ground, crash landing just ahead of us. What if our phone call had been seconds shorter?

At the shrine we were expecting to see a demonstration of martial arts and a messenger, dressed in Heian garb, deliver a letter from the present emperor. Perhaps because the emperor was suffering from anemia, or because we read the newspapers incorrectly, no messenger appeared and the martial arts were neither military nor artistic. Japanese members of the audience seemed as disappointed as we were. There was a rather shabby show of chrysanthemums. Definitely not worth risking one's life for.

Ted joined us later in the morning at the Tuttle bookstore in Kanda. With his help, Bob interviewed two or three bookstore owners for his column in *The Toronto Star*. I bought two books Ted had recommended: *The Anatomy of Dependence* by a psychiatrist, Takeo Doi, and Chie Nakane's *Japanese Society*. I'm committed to lifetime study.

On our own again, we went to see *Robinson's Garden*, a film that won several awards for its young Japanese director, Masashi Yamamoto, including one at the 1987 Berlin film festival. It's the story of a young woman drug addict living in Tokyo, and I'm afraid it added to the day's disappointments. For dinner we picked up bento and beer on the way home and retired early to watch TV — another samurai drama; then Charles Dutoit conducting a Japanese orchestra; and, to round out the evening, a group of uniformly dressed cool guys lip-syncing to some godawful pop tune while the audience went bananas.

SUNDAY, OCTOBER 18

Back from a trip to Nikko that I know I'll find humorous one day. It's said that "He who has not seen Nikko must not use the word *kekko,*" which means that anyone who has not visited Nikko cannot be satisfied with life. Perhaps, but the trip itself was a traveller's comedy of errors.

The misadventure began when I misread the brochure and thought that "a celebrated procession of 1,000 people" was taking place today, not yesterday. Unintentionally, however, we joined our own procession — a cavalcade of thousands. We'd reserved tickets but not specific seats on the Tobu train line leaving from Asakusa station. Our car was full, only the odd single seat available when we got on, but three young women moved so that we could sit together. They were holidaying in a way that's common — one or two days tacked onto a weekend so that their mandatory two weeks of vacation time would disappear unobtrusively without disturbing the company work schedule. They'd come from Nagoya to Tokyo, where they'd seen the Japanese road show of *Little Shop of Horrors.* Now they were going to Nikko, to "the very famous hotel" run for more than a hundred years by the Kanaya family. (Isabella Bird stayed there in 1878 and described it as "a Japanese idyll.") By Tuesday they'd be home.

Like the British, the Japanese are mad for railway schedules. The conductor handed them out on the train, and our three travel mates spent much of their time studying them. The group next to us came equipped to party away the hour-and-a-half trip on this baby bullet train (small bottles of Suntory whisky, lots of beer and food). There seemed to be about twice as many staff as were necessary, including a "stewardess" in a bright pink uniform with matching gloves and hat. Her job was to take our tickets — and immediately hand them to the conductor.

From the Nikko station we walked to the first cluster of Shinto shrines and Buddhist temples. I like crowds — love them, in fact — but this was too much. Large tour buses disgorged more and more tourists. Every time we entered another part of whatever complex we wanted to see, we had to line up and fork over another ¥350. Everywhere priests and their helpers were hawking religious baubles. For the first time in Japan, the blatant commercialism of men of the cloth bothered me.

We visited the garish shrine-mausoleum consecrated to Tokugawa Ieyasu. Fosco Mariani wrote about it in *Meeting with Japan*: "You ask yourself whether it is a joke, or a nightmare, or a huge wedding cake, a masterpiece of sugar icing made for some extravagant prince with a perverse, rococo taste." I vote for "nightmare." Carved on the side of the only unpainted structure in the complex are the well-known monkeys: "See no evil. Hear no evil. Speak no evil." (An admonishment I refuse to take seriously.)

Since it was a truly magnificent day and the Nikko scenery was some of the most dramatic we'd seen, we decided to spend the three hours before our train was to depart taking the bus to Lake Chuzenji, said to be a twenty- to thirty-minute trip. That would leave us forty minutes for the boat tour at the top. With the help of kindly Japanese tourists, we found the correct bus and grabbed the last two seats at the back. We were set. Or so we thought.

We started to climb the hairpin-turn road into the mountains, through forests sparkling with red and gold leaves. But it appeared that every mobile Japanese for miles around had decided that today was the day to see Nikko's autumn colours and enjoy one of the rare nice days on Lake Chuzenji. No Japanese person on our bus objected to the inordinately long climb, but I suspect that they didn't have return tickets for later that afternoon. They chattered, undeterred by a recorded female voice which announced, in English as well as Japanese, "Soon we will be approaching ...," and thirty minutes later we would arrive.

The whole event became increasingly absurd: what were we, Canadians born and bred, witnesses each year to maple trees changing colour, doing on this particular sightseeing expedition? I had a giggling fit. Out of politeness, I'm sure, I was joined by a group of Japanese women who had wisely brought tons of food, which they munched when they weren't nodding off.

The trip lasted two and a half hours, until 5:40: the last train to Tokyo left at 7:30. As soon as we reached the summit, we ran to catch the return bus for a downhill trip, which took a mere thirty minutes. At the station we traded our now useless reserved tickets for the last two seats in the last train. It turned out to be a subway car impersonating a long-distance passenger train. I think I fell asleep as we jolted our way home. Perhaps I'm becoming Japanese.

MONDAY, OCTOBER 19

We finally saw kabuki — a program of three plays, each representing a different style and theatrical tradition. The first, *Kumagai's Battle Camp*, was originally staged in 1751 using bunraku puppets. We were told in our rented audioguide that before the curtain moved aside, the warrior hero, forced to repay old debts, had killed two people he loved — the courtesan who made it possible for him to marry, and his own son in place of the son of the emperor. In much Japanese history, and history-inspired kabuki, dramatic tension usually grows out of the conflict between duty (*giri*) and human feelings (*ninjo*). When today's action begins, Kumagai has decided to enter a monastery. Needless to say, he hasn't consulted his wife.

The actors moved as if they were imitating puppets. The narrator sometimes spoke in unison with the character; at other times, he described actions mimed by the character. Quite often, he expressed the character's inner feelings. Costumes and sets were brilliant, but I might have preferred to see this play performed by puppets, still further from naturalism.

There were moments in all three plays when the audience cried out — either the actor's stage name on his initial appearance, or phrases of recognition or approval as an actor struck a particularly dramatic pose, or *mie*. "This is what I've been waiting for!" The calls came mostly from the third balcony, where true kabuki lovers traditionally sit. It occurred to me that some shouters might be paid, because how could the management rely on a modern audience to know what was expected.

The earphone guide had alerted us to one *mie* that occurs in this play, at the moment Kumagai places a wooden placard firmly on the step below (hinting that the young prince should be spared) and stands cross-eyed and still as a post. This, we were told, was one of the most famous *mie* in all kabuki. To show emotional pain, an actor might cross his eyes, grimace, or stick out his tongue. The audience, prepared to believe in these intense emotions, apparently never laughs.

To outsiders, it's remarkable that the usually restrained and polite Japanese seem to forget their manners at kabuki. They come and go during the performance, often with crinkly shopping bags and they eat food at their seats from beginning to end. No one seems to mind. Explanations for this behaviour are rooted, as one might expect, in the past: as Mr. Karashima of the National Theatre told us, in Edo times, a kabuki performance lasted the whole day, so eating was expected and audiences treated the theatre as a home away from home. It was the people's art, much like opera in Italy. Even though common speech had changed over the years, making much of the language of kabuki as archaic as Shakespearean English, the stories were so well known that audiences could easily follow the action. The mass appeal of kabuki continued into the twentieth century, until movies, then television, pushed it to the margins. Now, sadly (I think) kabuki requires, as one observer put it, "scholarly determination," and some government assistance.

After the first third of the day's program ended at 1:30, we made our way to the theatre basement for the lunch we'd ordered and paid for earlier: I had grilled eel (*unagi*) and rice, served in separate compartments inside a large lacquer box. I'd read that this was the most appropriate dish to order, since a version of it was first served in the most popular kabuki theatre of the Edo period, and eating eel in summer was said to make the heat more bearable. (I love eel and will always associate its oily taste with Japan — my madeleine.) Bob stuck to raw fish and rice, a radical choice for him that, I think, surprises both of us.

We ate at a long table in a room that resembled a Chinese restaurant or fancy church basement. Lunches were already waiting in front of name cards in holders so we knew where to sit. I kept a close eye on the woman beside me who approached the art of eating with the precision of an eye surgeon. Following her example, I lifted the rice box out and placed it closer to me and the eel box further away. I took half of one strip of eel and placed it on the rice and went on from there. When the meal was finished, I recovered and restacked the boxes and returned the chopsticks to their paper wrapper. I nodded in the general direction of my table companions and left. The second part of the performance was about to begin.

It was called *Kanjincho* and in it we rejoined one of the characters encountered in the first play — Yoshitsune, who was escaping with five of his retainers from the wrath of his brother, the shogun Yoritomo. This play, first performed in 1840, is "one of Japan's most popular dance dramas." There was a full orchestra stretched out across the stage on their knees the entire time — drums and other percussion, flutes, shamisen, as well as a choir, wonderful to watch as well as to listen to.

Again, the theme is loyalty to one's superior, a subject still close to Japanese hearts. This time, a trusted servant of the shogun was so impressed by the daring, devotion, and wit of one of the retainers, Benkei, that he pretended to be fooled into letting the group cross a bridge to safety. The cost? His own life, of course. The lead, Benkei, was brilliantly played by Tomijuro V, a huge-faced, short-limbed actor who dominated the stage with his impersonation of a *yamabushi*, a wandering religious ascetic. He's truly a great actor and would dominate any performance anywhere.

In kabuki families, when an heir replaces his father, he takes the family name and, like a monarch, adds the number of his succession, such as Ichikawa Danjuro XII. An actor like Tomijuro repeats, with minor changes only, the role as it has been performed for generations. In kabuki, only the greatest actors earn the right to modify a role with which they're closely identified. As the Japanese say, "a great actor enters the mould, and then destroys it."

This was theatre as it lived a century and a half ago and continues to live today. As the critic Donald Richie wrote, each historic period "petrifies, retaining its own characteristics, frozen apparently forever yet still alive since each style is studied, performed, and retains its audience. It's as though one went to Rome and found there theatres specializing in Plautus done in Latin in the original style; playhouses where the commedia dell'arte was retained in its perfection, and halls where Pirandello is performed in the manner of 1925." In the West we endlessly update the classics, modifying them for the times, making them "relevant" for contemporary audiences. What would happen if Laurence Olivier's son precisely imitated the master in Hamlet's soliloquy? This runs against every Stanislavsky-inspired notion about bringing oneself into a role but that doesn't mean it's not worthwhile.

The third play, *Double Murder on Mount Toribe*, written in 1915 and said to be the most frequently performed piece of modern kabuki, is set in the Gion geisha district of Kyoto. To me, it was the least successful. It did offer, however, a remarkable piece of casting: the young actor in the starring samurai role often shared the stage with his geisha love,

Osome. Offstage, Osome is the samurai actor's father. To their credit, their gender and relationship in no way detracted from the strength of their portrayals. Male actors who play women, *onnagata*, develop an abstract version of femininity based on gesture, costume, makeup, and past interpretations of a particular role. At one time, *onnagata* continued their roles offstage as well as on. While watching this performance I began to understand why *onnagata* appeal to women — they represent the perfect, unattainable self. (If I lived here I would come often to kabuki and learn more.)

We ended the day at Sophia University, at a lecture Bob saw advertised in *The Japan Times*. The subject: "Canada's Place in the World." We entered the campus through a main gate off a busy street, and stood there, unable to figure out which way to go. A young English-speaking *gaijin* sitting on a nearby bench offered to help us. "It's okay. I was just waiting for a friend," she said. "I'll leave my purse here so she'll know I'll be back."

"But won't someone take it?" I protested. It seemed a crazy idea, even in Japan.

"Oh, I've done stuff like this before," she explained. "No one's ever taken anything." Once again, I was overwhelmed by the evidence of public honesty.

The lecture, by a retired Canadian history professor to students in their newly combined Institute of American and Canadian Studies, turned out to be extremely boring; on the other hand, the questions from the audience, about forty Japanese students, mostly women, were

impressive — well-reasoned and clearly presented in excellent English. The university seemed filled with *bon ami* and bustle.

We had dinner along a charming laneway nearby, in a fish restaurant with an inflated, laminated, poisonous blowfish (*fugu*) hanging on a hook near the door. While we carefully picked our way through potentially lethal fish bones, we discussed the possibility of Bob coming back to Sophia to lecture. Perhaps I would join him. We might come for longer, an academic term. Something to dream about.

TUESDAY, OCTOBER 20

Hideous news in all the papers about "carnage on the stock market." Yesterday was reported to be the worst single day's loss for the Dow Jones, breaking records set in 1929. The bottom has also fallen out of the Nikkei, the Japanese stock market, and the press is warning about global recession. This economic disaster will surely spread to everyone. Like most people around the world, I feel helpless. Diversion is called for, so we went again to the Tokyo National Museum in Ueno to see the ukiyo-e woodblocks we were unable to see in September. At that time they told us to come in October: this time they said to return in November. Alas, we'll no longer be in Tokyo.

We wandered south a bit to the National Museum of Western Art, built in 1959 to house the collection of one man, Kojiro Matsukata (1895–1950). He lived in Paris during the 1920s and collected work by well-known artists such as Monet (truly lovely examples) and Renoir (a mixed bag) and lesser lights. Alas again, his eight-thousand-piece ukiyo-e collection is housed in the National Museum. There are Rodin sculptures in the surrounding garden. He's a huge favourite throughout Japan. Perhaps the over-muscled, powerful Rodin men appeal to Japanese males as the Western ideal.

We strolled into the noisy Ueno market, towards Asakusa, through a commercial district devoted almost entirely to selling religious objects — ten-foot-high Buddhas and high-gloss lacquer ancestral shrines. On the shopping street leading up to Asakusa Kannon Temple, we bought a Buddhist Christmas tree decoration for our own ecumenical household. (No one here seemed to have heard about "the crash," or to care.)

Exhausted, we climbed into a boat for a ride on the Sumida River, which runs through the city and was once an important means of transport in Edo. We spent forty minutes gawking at waterfront construction on both sides of the river. Even this banal sight filled me with nostalgia as I imagined not being here.

Getting off the boat, we were approached by a middle-aged couple from Detroit who asked for directions. "Two days on our own in

Tokyo," the wife said, a catch in her throat. They were finding it daunting. "It'll be a lot easier when the rest of our tour gets here and we go off to Bangkok, Hong Kong, and one day in China."

She asked where we were from and I said Toronto. "Joe has just been saying," she responded, "that we should've gone to Toronto instead. We always have a real good time in Toronto. And our money would have gone further, that's for sure." I agreed with them.

We took the train to Roppongi, where, I confess, to satisfy my urge for meat, we ate at Tony Roma's Ribs. The place was dark, informal, loaded with plants, Hallowe'en decorations, and a clientele pretty evenly divided between *gaijin* and Japanese. When my steak arrived, falling off the ends of the platter, it seemed an alarming quantity of meat. As if to overcome a sense of dislocation, we discussed Japanese politics. Nakasone had named Takeshita the new leader of the Liberal Democratic Party and hence the new prime minister. The orgy of endless, boring speculation was over. The fact that Mr. Takeshita is a known tax-evader did not make one whit of difference. When I glanced down at my plate, every ounce of beef had vanished.

WEDNESDAY, OCTOBER 21

As he promised, Mr. Karashima invited us to kabuki at the National Theatre. Before picking up our tickets at 11:30 a.m. for the noon show, we visited Kanda one last time to buy extra reading matter for our return trip across the Pacific — two copies of *The New Yorker* at $12 each.

Then to watch two acts of two different kabuki plays, a custom I still find rather strange. (The program told us what had happened before the act we were about to see, and after it.) I found the first offering, *Gappo and His Daughter*, jarring and unsuccessful. Written in 1772, the play was, like another we'd seen, first performed by bunraku puppets. The program told us that the theme, a young wife's love for her stepson, was originally considered improper. It wasn't adapted to kabuki until 1834, and was performed only once, in a 1910 revival, then again in 1937 before it was banned again. It remained popular since its last revival in 1947.

Alas, we joined the action in Act 3, at passion's hottest moment — rather like catching Oedipus when he learns that his wife is also his mother. (Again there was a suicide to satisfy social obligations.) One role was performed by a Living Cultural Treasure, an eighty-four-year-old actor, Kataoka Nizaemon XIII, who played Gappo opposite another treasure of equal rank, Nakamura Utaemon VI, described as "the greatest living *onnagata*." This performer had been playing the same part since 1947 — forty years refining a complex role that demands abrupt personality shifts. First, she's the licentious stepmother lusting after her stepson; then, a mother who makes the ultimate sacrifice to save her son; and finally, a Buddhist saint who escapes to the Western Paradise, leaving behind a fundraising program to build a temple where nuns will praise her forever. Unfortunately, this particular *onnagata* bore an uncanny resemblance to Lily Tomlin.

The second performance — two acts of a six-act play, *Sukeroku and Paper Kimono* — was receiving its first Tokyo production in thirty-three years. While the main actor, Kataoka Nizaemon, was listed as "supervisor" of the production, these plays seemed to be largely director-less. Our audioguide told us that this work is rarely performed here because Tokyo audiences prefer samurai tragedies, and these "lighter" dramas (forget that it ends in the double suicide of doomed lovers) are not so popular.

Walking home, we agreed we'll miss Japan. Without doubt, *Ich bin eine Tokyoite*.

Thursday, October 22

After organizing our packing and calling the airport to confirm our flight, we went to the BC government office to have lunch with Russell Mark, their senior representative. He arranged for a friend of his to join us — Tony McArthur, a lawyer who speaks Japanese and is married to a Japanese woman. We took them to a French restaurant around the corner.

Tony's been involved in the Japanese government's plan to encourage old people to move out of the country. Word of this project was leaked to the press in 1986, with a predictable outcry from many citizens. (Perhaps this was the purpose behind the "leak," which may well have been the government's doing.) Proportionately, Japan has the world's largest aging population, with more than 10 percent over sixty today. Of these, about half live with their children. The greying of the society is expected to proceed more rapidly in Japan than any country in the world: by 2025 more than 25 percent will be old. Because pensions are modest and health care is state funded, the next working generation could face an unbearable economic burden.

As the story appeared, MITI, the powerful ministry of international trade and industry, was proposing that Japan take advantage of the yen's foreign buying power and encourage old people to settle overseas, in colonies. Tony represents Canada on a committee of foreign delegates, many of whom are eager to provide space for aging Japanese, hoping to redress, slightly, the uneven balance of trade. The most enthusiastic are the Australians. But how would the Japanese feel about these foreign old-age ghettos? Generational tensions arise in Japan, where busy children have aging parents. That tension is increased because corporations often demand family-style allegiance, which leads to conflicted loyalties. It seems unlikely there will be a simple solution to this complicated problem, or that overseas colonies will be acceptable.

Lunch was followed by a visit to the fashion emporium of the designer, Hanae Mori, where her exquisite taste and name are stamped on every product — chocolates, shoes, kimono, children's toys, and of course, women's clothing. Later to the Suntory Art Museum. Suntory, the beer-and-other-things conglomerate, is the current favourite employer for recent university graduates. They take care to associate themselves with everything good, from golf tournaments to art exhibitions. On the eleventh floor of a graceful office tower is an attractive exhibition space, this month featuring a show curated by a Tokyo University art scholar. His thesis: the strange and exotic in Japanese art is not fictive but based on observing nature. Grotesque paintings of people, animals, and plants filled the show. I was more attracted to the poster in the lobby showing Mickey Rourke snuggling Suntory Draft. I asked if I could buy one but was told it was "not possible."

Took the subway to meet Wendy Wortsman and her two recently arrived friends from Canada — husband and wife architects. The five of us walked to the house Tom and Wendy rent in Akasaka. It's large, well laid out, and smack dab in the heart of Tokyo. She and Tom are still on probation with the landlady, a once-glamorous lady-about-town favoured by black musicians passing through in the 1920s. We could see her staring out the front window. Wendy was right when she told us she fit the part — all shawls, fringes, layers of beads.

Although it was wonderful seeing Wendy again, meeting this new couple was not. They spent all our time together criticizing everything they'd seen so far, with the possible exception of Japanese street life, which they granted was "interesting."

Tom joined us at a nearby Indian restaurant. He'd been working night and day on a huge audiovisual presentation to accompany a sales pitch Nissan's making to distributors from around the world. They needed a new image. They don't want to be seen as manufacturers of Dinky cars but as one of the big boys, ready to take on executive-class European automobiles. Tom thought that they might have blown this one. "It's been too little too late," he groaned. He looked tired and thin, but seeing him again was like running into an old friend.

Travelling seems to compress the amount of time between introduction and affection. Wendy promised to write at least once to wean me off my Japan high. I told her that one of the nicest things about our trip had been meeting them. Her friends looked embarrassed. I hope *she* wasn't, because I meant it. We had to leave early because Bob was feeling, as he said, "a bit logy." Hope it doesn't last. One more day before we leave.

FRIDAY, OCTOBER 23

Spent a restless night with Bob suffering from a cough, diarrhea, and fever. We set the alarm for 5:50 a.m. so we could go with Ted to the famous Tokyo fish market, Tsukiji. Bob insisted we all go, regardless, so we met beside the first car at the Kojimachi subway stop on the Yurakucho line, as planned. It was a ten-minute walk from our exit to the largest, most bustling fish market I could imagine — 1,200 wholesale shops on 54 acres providing about 90 percent of the fish consumed in Tokyo, and that's a lot. Tsukiji means "reclaimed land," and that's what it is — a block of land, drained and filled,

that extends from present-day Ginza to the bay. It became Tokyo's fish capital after the Kanto earthquake destroyed the old market at Nihonbashi.

Unfortunately we arrived too late to watch the unloading and most of the auctioning, but we walked for miles peering into bins at fish, crustaceans, bivalves, fresh and frozen tuna, eels, mussels, lobster, clams, crab, roe, *fugu*, mackerel, dolphin, whale, shark, and other creatures beyond my knowledge. Ted had warned us that the men who work here were rough, and they were — understandable since we were in their way. It was important to keep an eye out for handcarts, motorized trucks, dollies, and wagons barrelling over the slick floor. We stopped and had a modest breakfast, followed by a visit to a pharmacy before hurrying home. Bob wasn't well. Had to cancel a lunch with Betty and Tim Armstrong. Then I foraged for bananas, apples, apple juice, Coke — all the recommended ingredients.

At 4:30 I called Ted to cancel the rock opera I'd booked earlier in the week at the Ginza Saison. The ad had said that it starred "Japan's Mick Jagger" and was based on the arrival of Portuguese Catholics in Japan in the sixteenth century. I will resist saying, "How Japanese!" but I am truly sorry to miss it.

SATURDAY, OCTOBER 24

On our way to the airport now. It's hard to say a final farewell to Tokyo when we can't see more than a few inches in any direction because of the rain and the steamed-up windows. Bob had a miserable night. His fever seems to have broken, and the cough is somewhat improved, but he's still feeling wretched. He sits stoically reading a crummy novel he picked up at the Tokyo City Air Terminal, where we'd arrived on our first night and where we caught our bus today.

Ted came to the ryokan at noon to take me to lunch. Then all three of us left in the two taxis it took to transport our bags. I knew from experience that the best thing I could do for Bob was to let him read — on the bus and when we arrived at the CP lounge, where I turned my attention to Bloody Marys and re-entry preparations.

Among the many things I've learned on this trip are some rules on "How to be a good tourist." Travel makes demands on guests in the same way that parties do: when entering someone's country, or home, each person is obliged to participate, to engage, never to sit back and merely observe, or even worse, judge. Although I often fail to live up to these ideals, at least I've learned to be suspicious of instant opinions, especially those that find fault.

When I think of Bad Tourists, I think of the newly arrived architects we met yesterday, and this particular example: when Jill Bond first told us about the importance of blood type in Japanese hiring practices, Bob and I were curious and wanted to know more, to compare this classification system with those we're more familiar with, such as astrological signs or birth order. But when I passed on this bit of anthropological lore, the other couple immediately said they were "appalled." Not surprised or intrigued. Appalled. With that single word, they closed an avenue of understanding, of the Japanese and of themselves.

To borrow from quantum physics, travellers, like scientists, alter everything they observe. All conclusions, especially those reached on the spot, are therefore suspect. Over time I must ruminate on all I've seen and reconsider all I've learned.

TUESDAY, SEPTEMBER 30 TO WEDNESDAY, OCTOBER 1, 1997

It's almost exactly ten years since our last major trip into the land of small people and large pleasures. I no longer work at CBC Radio but, to my surprise and delight, have become something of a writer — book reviews, magazine articles, and short stories, always on subjects I care about. I cherish my freelancer's freedom and the time I have to spend with friends. Bob has flourished without editorial responsibilities at *Saturday Night* — some teaching, lots of magazine articles, a couple of books, as well as a weekly column for *The Globe and Mail*. We spent last June in Jerusalem, thanks to the Halbert Centre for Canadian Studies at the Hebrew University. That trip and this one seemed impossible six months ago.

Last December Bob fell down the back stairs and ruptured his quadriceps tendon, a nasty business with an operation, weeks bedridden, a cast for more weeks, a walker, in physio — unpleasant and painful for him, trying and tiring for me. But we survived and here we are. Unfortunately there have been more serious fractures in some family relationships, which is sad, and rekindling of others, which is good. Some friends and family have died, new friendships have started, and babies have come into our lives — all normal, all bittersweet. Now, in a Canadian Airlines jet somewhere over the Pacific, halfway between Canada and Japan, after one Bloody Mary and a small bottle of wine I grow maudlin.

Inside my carry-on bag is a small Toshiba 110CT with an Intel Pentium chip. In the hold of the plane, safe I hope, is our Okipage 4W printer and an ergonomically correct keyboard, new toys in our lives without which we cannot function. The Luddites have surrendered and now I hope we can set up to connect with the *Globe*, so Bob can file his column and with e-mail we can keep in touch with friends and family. Who would have thought?

Ten years ago we promised one another we'd come back, that we'd stay in a house or apartment so we could shop and cook and experience Domestic Tokyo. Bob and many others worked hard for the Japan Foundation grant that allows us two months of apartment living in Tokyo and travel in one of the world's most expensive countries. Bob will have some sort of relationship with Meiji University. After all this effort, I'm disappointed that I don't feel more enthusiastic.

I think that ten years ago I did not consider that I would be fifty-six, a robust fifty-six, but still not forty-six, and that Bob would have become a senior citizen with a gimp leg. Nor did I imagine that I'd feel so discombobulated because we don't yet have a place to live. Until about a week ago it looked as if we could stay in a guest suite at the Canadian embassy, one of the loveliest residences in Tokyo. Bob and I made a brief visit to Tokyo in 1991, when the new embassy opened. At that time we met our ambassador du jour and his wife, the wonderful Cy and Mary Taylor. They now live in Ottawa and lobbied on our behalf with the outgoing ambassador, Donald Campbell. The residence was empty but we were told that the staff was in place. I had visions beyond my station. Just before we left came news that because the embassy windows were being replaced, we couldn't stay there. So we're booked for two weeks at International House while we look for more suitable long-term accommodation.

Our reliance on technology is also making me edgy. The entire time we were in Israel we couldn't get our e-mail to work effectively. It seemed like a seismic catastrophe. I've come to rely on the low-cost, instantaneous, and frequent conversations with friends that e-mail allows. I don't want to be out of touch again. We'll be here for almost nine weeks and I miss friends and family already and wish they were with us so that we could show them our Tokyo.

Before we left, people asked, "What are you going to do there for two months?" Where to begin? In the past ten years I've read more books on Japan, reviewed a few, written a couple of travel pieces about the country, and bored stiff anyone who'd stay still, talking about the wonders of Japan. Because I have a deep desire to share this trip, I've decided to restart the journal I kept a decade ago.

Still, a few nagging fears: will I love the place as much as I did in 1987? Will I be able to observe and not judge? To absorb and not reject? Do I have the patience I once had? And how has Japan changed? At a recent dinner friends talked about how Japan was once called Number One by popular economists, (Ezra Vogel comes to mind), but now it seems to have fallen into the economic dumps. Between 1990 and 1995 the bubble burst — stock prices, property values, and corporate profits tumbled. Banks staggered under trillions of dollars of debt they're unlikely to collect.

These marketplace disasters were followed in 1995 by the Hanshin Earthquake, the great eruption everyone had been anticipating but not for the Kobe area. In its wake, there were six thousand dead, twenty-five thousand injured, and three hundred thousand homeless; Japan's once-proud belief in its "earthquake readiness" was shattered. Only months later, a fanatic sect, the Aum Shinrikyo, released toxic sarin gas in the Tokyo subways, killing twelve and injuring six thousand, and in a single act destroying Japan's image as a crime-free society.

Today, the Nikkei is still down and Little Tigers are springing up throughout the Far East, unencumbered by Japanese bureaucracy, which once bolstered trade and now weighs it down. Adding insult to injury, there have been no recent Japanese Nobel Prize winners, and they really care about that.

Katherine Ashenburg, another journalist and friend, once with me at the CBC and now at *The Globe and Mail*, recently won an Asia Pacific Foundation grant and stayed at International House. She says it's pleasant, the staff obliging, and the library excellent. But I want to fast forward this hunt for accommodations. Reading various faxes that have gone back and forth has me white-knuckled — key money you don't get back, security deposits, several months' rent in advance. My dentist, a spirited Czech refugee, said that I should look at it all as a grand adventure. I wish I could.

Thursday, October 2

Takenori Egawa of Meiji University was waiting for us at the airport. He'd visited Toronto earlier in the year and met Bob then. At a lunch with Masamichi Sugihara, head of the Japan Foundation in Toronto, there had been an inordinate amount of discussion concerning the size of the vehicle picking us up: Would it have enough room for our luggage? Would there be room for Mr. Egawa as well? He had come, in fact, with a unilingual driver from the Foundation and after general greetings, he handed us our itinerary — a single-spaced typed sheet called Temporary Schedule, passing it over, as one does in Japan, with two hands as if it were made of delicate papyrus. Bob received it, properly, with two hands, and immediately began to study it as if it were an update of the Ten Commandments signed by God.

It stated that today is unscheduled (assuming jet lag and the fact that the Japan Foundation is closed for the anniversary of its founding). Friday, tomorrow, Bob is to meet Hyon Ko, co-ordinator, academic programs at Meiji University, who will take him (us?) to the Japan Foundation offices to meet Naomi Iino, program co-ordinator responsible for "stipends and orientation during stay in Japan." There Bob will receive close to ¥2 million, or roughly $20,000 for two months — more or less the amount we had ten years ago. We'll see how it stretches in 1997.

Bob's visit to Meiji is scheduled for noon. Even though Japan is notoriously safe, it would be nice to deposit some of the cash in a bank before we get on the subway. I have no idea what ¥2 million looks like.

The weekend is open; Monday, October 6, Bob is to meet the board of directors for the international programs and later that day we're to talk about housing with Professor James Bowers. Tuesday, October 7, it says we are to "find suitable housing accommodation."

After surveying our two carts full of luggage, Mr. Egawa concluded that there would be no room for him in the car. He looked somewhat relieved that his part of the reception was over and left us with the efficient but silent driver. It's incredible to me that on our last visit we managed to get to our ryokan without a guide.

International House, in Roppongi, the *gaijin* area of Tokyo, is quite wonderful in the openness and optimism of its design, rather Frank Lloyd Wrightish. Our room is compact, twin beds, small dresser in a small closet, small bathroom with small shower, and a lovely small balcony overlooking a mature, terraced garden with carp pool. At first glance it appears ideal for a single person who does not have to write. The staff is friendly and competent. Breakfast is ample and hot, if somewhat limited — egg or cereal, a single slice of bacon and one of toast made from what Katherine Ashenburg calls "pillow bread," thickly cut, white, and fluffy. The weather was warm and sunny and we had coffee on the terrace overlooking the garden.

I'd forgotten the joy that comes from looking at carp bump into one another in murky water — carp viewing, if you like. It was worth scrambling up the rocks to a promontory with a view, listening all the while to the crickets who made themselves audible above the traffic.

I'd also forgotten that when we travel unexpected invitations arrive from people in high places, generally a great treat. At 9 a.m. back in our room, Bruce Barnett, cultural officer for the Canadian embassy, called to invite us to join the Canada-Japan Friendship Society on Saturday for a day at the races, followed by dinner with a few embassy staff in the country. We are to meet at 8:45 a.m., go by bus from the embassy to the track and by train to dinner. I'll adore sitting back and not making a single decision. I promise never to laugh again as troops of Japanese tourists de-bus at the CN Tower.

And Joseph Caron, the embassy's political minister and the highest-ranking bureaucrat in lieu of a sitting ambassador, wants to have a dinner for us "sooner rather than later." We shall oblige. Before retiring to the garden to read and write, I picked up a message at the front desk: M. Caron would like to help us find an apartment or house. I'm somewhat reassured. Bruce also invited us to two embassy receptions: one for P.E. Trudeau, who has just returned from leading a trade delegation to China, and the other for various players from the National Hockey League who staged an exhibition game here. I left it to Bob to decline without revealing a mutual lack of enthusiasm for either PET or the NHL.

Later in the afternoon we wandered through local banks looking for an Access Plus outlet so we could grab money from the wall to use for a one-month subway pass that costs ¥16,000 (about $190) and will probably provide considerable savings. After much searching, we managed to take about ¥10,000 ($120) from Bob's Toronto account. At first glance, the buying power of the yen seems much as it did ten years ago, although the value of our poor currency seems to have shrunk. Must not dwell on these things.

Decided to look for the Japan National Tourist office near Hibiya subway station and wound up walking all the way to Tokyo station with its ghastly memories of Mr. Ueda from the Foreign Press Centre and all those soybeans consumed while waiting in vain for his friend the professor. But, as I remember, walks in Tokyo are never boring. On our way we travelled through a cluster of restaurants tucked under the JR Yurakucho railway station, some as modern as yesterday, others apparently a century old and covered in tar paper and soot. We walked down the lane beside one of them and peeked in: there, an antique woman, a bucket of red meat in front of her, was slipping chunks on skewers for yakitori. How many sticks a day? For how many days? Over how many years?

Finally, on our return to Hibiya we entered the science fiction–like building, new home to the JNT organization. It's tucked away inside what looks like a monolithic structure of curved steel on the outside: inside the courtyard it's all struts and glass pods. This is the barely uncrated Tokyo International Forum, designed by Rafael Vinoly. Neither Bob nor I had heard of him but I later read that there'd been an international competition for the 144,000-square-metre space intended for theatres, museums, and other arts-related spaces. Judges included Kenzo Tange and Fumihiko Maki, two prominent Japanese architects, and the international superstar I.M. Pei. The winner, Mr. Vinoly, is a New York–based, Uruguayan-born architect who "narrowly pushed aside British RIBA Gold Medallist, James Stirling." It's hard to tell what the battleship-with-four-satellite buildings will look like when fully occupied, but it's an exciting tangle of structures and empty spaces at the moment.

On the way home, I noticed new intruders on the scene. Crows, with the wingspan of eagles, seem to dominate the Tokyo airspace. They're so noisy they drown out the traffic. They rip fruit off trees, then drop picked-over cherries and mandarins everywhere. One day they'll make off with a baby and ways will be found to eradicate them.

At the International House, referred to by the cognoscenti as IH, I overheard Bob try to impress someone from the embassy that "we really do need a place to live." He then gave his ideal expectations and what he'd be willing to settle for, which I suspect will change as the days go by. Then a nap, followed by a light supper of chicken soup and a tuna sandwich on pillow bread. Must fight off a developing cold as public appearances begin tomorrow.

FRIDAY, OCTOBER 3

Outside the coffee shop at International House there's a framed calligraphy scroll, written and presented to IH by the late prime minister Shigeru Yoshida when the building was completed, with Rockefeller money, in 1955. Underneath, the English translation reads: "The sentence is from the opening chapter of *The Analects of Confucius* and reads in Legge's translation, 'Is it not delightful to have friends coming from distant countries.'" No question mark, no room for ambiguity.

Today we met two of those in charge of our lives — Ms. Iino and Mr. Ko. At 11 a.m., "stipends and orientation day" began when Mr. Ko met us and we cabbed together to the Japan Foundation offices in the ARK Mori building. There we met Ms. Iino of the Foundation's receiving division, exchange of persons department. She speaks almost no English nor does Mr. Ko. We were deposited in a tiny boardroom, served chalky green tea, and handed a cheque for ¥2.5 million which included airfare. Ms. Iino explained that after "orientation" we would go to the Fuji Bank downstairs where they would cash Bob's cheque, if we were lucky, and then we would go across the hall in the same building, to the Sakura Bank, where they either would, or would not, open an account in Bob's name. No one explained why we couldn't simply stay with Fuji, and I was not prepared to ask since it was beginning to seem that even with piles of yen, banking was considered a privilege, not a right, for foreigners.

"How do they decide whether or not you can open an account?" Bob asked.

"It depends who serves you," Ms. Iino answered.

"Ah," we replied in unison, as if we understood.

We were joined by Hiroshi Nirasawa, managing director, exchange of persons department, and Fumitomo Horiuchi, director, receiving division, exchange of persons department. They came in and asked if we had "any more questions about orientation?" Any *more*? Mr. Managing Director looked at Bob's file, which included photocopies of articles by and about Bob and said, "So, the University of Toronto?" It's true that Bob was, for one year, the Barker Fairley Distinguished Visitor in Canadian Culture, has an honorary degree from U of T, and is a Fellow of Massey College, but since he's also a high-school dropout his university connection is not his most distinguishing characteristic. Being a smart fellow, Bob adopted the "Don't-say-anything-that-will-further-befuddle-them" approach, and answered, "Yes."

Then we turned to the Housing Issue. The Foundation folks suggested that this might be Meiji's responsibility. Mr. Ko, representing Meiji, said something in Japanese that I gathered meant "That's not our job," because Ms. Iino disappeared and returned with information on a small place in Kito for about ¥250,000 (about $3,000 a month) a mere twenty minutes from Meiji. There followed much reading of the description of the place, and the revelation that it belonged to Mr. Nirasawa's friend, which is how we were being allowed to see it and rent it so cheaply. I can't remember how the conversation ended, except abruptly: Messrs. Nirasawa and Horiuchi leapt up, greatly relieved, and announced, "Orientation is over," before racing from the room.

Mr. Ko, who'd earlier informed us that he had "a very busy day," kept looking at his watch. To regain his attention, I asked him if he was a graduate of Meiji University. "Yes," he answered. "Last year."

"And what did you study?"

"Law," he replied. Poor bloke. Assigned to this thankless task, bottom man on the totem pole.

While waiting for the elevator on our way to the bank, a man approached us. "Mr. Fulford?" It was Osamu Honda, who had worked at the Japan Foundation in Toronto. We were both thrilled to see someone for whom we were not simply a burden.

At the Fuji Bank things went smoothly. Bob was handed thousands of yen in the identical pink plastic baskets I remember banks using ten years ago. He stuffed his swag into two large envelopes and then Iino, Ko, Fulford, and Sherman proceeded, without police escort, across the lobby to the Sakura Bank. There we were greeted by a friendly young woman wearing a Felix the Cat watch with a wide plastic band that read "How Are You," no question mark.

There was much paper signing, passport viewing, and document passing in ubiquitous pink plastic baskets, with nary an objection that Bob's foreigner status made it impossible for them to take his almost two million yen. In a week's time he was to be issued a bank card along with cheques to be delivered via Ms. Iino. When the deposit was completed, Ms. Iino confided to us that the last time she'd engaged in a similar transaction with a *gaijin*, the bank had rejected them.

After leaving the ARK Mori building, we toured the bowels of the subway system looking for the office that issued monthly travel passes. More forms, but we left eventually with passes in hand and bid adieu to Mr. Ko. For dinner, in part to initiate our new subway passes, we headed for Ginza and were astounded at the facelift the rather tired area had received. It positively sparkled with metallic and glass cladding and glowing neon. We strolled down the wide streets, happy to be away from the noise of the overhead arterial roads that criss-cross Roppongi and make walking unpleasant. We dined on the eighth floor of a concave building at the main intersection overlooking Chuo-dori, in a Chinese restaurant we'd glimpsed from the street. At first, the maître d' seemed reluctant to admit us. "This is a Chinese restaurant," he said, as if we had been elevated eight floors by mistake. Eventually we were ushered in and given the perfect window table. The Chinese meal, served one small dish after another, was delicious. All unkind thoughts about Japanese banking vanished.

SATURDAY, OCTOBER 4

Today we joined Bruce Barnett and members of the Canada-Japan Friendship Society for a day at the massive Tokyo Racetrack with the world's largest grandstand. As we walked through debris-strewn Roppongi on our way to Aoyomi-dori and the embassy, we searched in vain for a cash machine, only to discover that they don't open until 9 a.m. Bank rich, wallet poor, we hailed a taxi and arrived just in time to board the waiting bus already full of elderly Japanese, mostly couples, a few widows, in chic Western clothes, perhaps reflecting time spent abroad. A grey-haired man and his wife were granted the front seat. He's a former Japanese ambassador to Canada. "She's from an old samurai family," whispered Bruce.

The only other foreigners besides Bruce were John Sloan, a financial officer at the embassy, and his wife, Martine Sloan, a sad-looking French-Canadian in her late forties. We were handed name tags; I corrected mine from Mrs. Fulford to Ms. Sherman. Standing at the front of the bus and speaking what sounded like fluent Japanese, Bruce introduced us and invited all of Canada's Japanese friends to speak with us.

We travelled for about half an hour through an urban sprawl called Setagaya, a place we'd visited with Tom Stolberg and Wendy

Wortsman ten years ago. "It's twinned with Winnipeg," we were proudly informed. Then we de-bused at the entrance to the Tokyo Racetrack, which is also a sort of equine theme park — a racing museum, a cinema-in-the-round, a racing video library where you can watch endless reruns of favourite races, the grave of local racing legend Koremasa Ida, and a playground for children with dozens of horse-related rides. The grandstand accommodates two hundred thousand, the capacity crowd that usually attends the Tokyo Cup, all of whom would have no difficulty simultaneously placing bets at the numerous and accessible wickets.

Our exclusive box on the top floor was like a hotel dining room with a long buffet table, five large individual tables, and eight television screens, without which it would have been almost impossible to see the horses. The moment our group entered the box, out came the tout sheets, calculators, and cigarettes. Except for betting and eating, our Japanese friends maintained this tense tableau through eleven races lasting seven hours. A lunch buffet appeared at about 10:45 a.m. — sandwiches, noodles, cold meat, smoked salmon, casseroles of rice and shrimp, coffee, tea, and juice (alcoholic beverages could be purchased at numerous bars in the hallway). The leftovers stayed out for hours, curling in the heat and smoke. Petits fours and packaged cakes arrived at about 3 p.m. and were quickly devoured.

We ate and watched for a while and I wandered off to inspect the six public levels where the hoi polloi were eating, drinking, smoking, and betting in a gloomy atmosphere of desperation, not helped by the grey, wet weather. Although the grandstand looked fairly empty, we were told there were about forty thousand people in attendance, a drop in the bucket.

Soon one racetrack manager, then another of a slightly higher rank, approached Bob, urged on by the embassy staff. Bruce had slipped away to give them Bob's bona fides, exaggerating, no doubt. Because they thought Bob was deeply interested in sports, they whisked us away to their cinema-in-the-round for an exclusive showing of *A Day at Newmarket*, an orgy of Anglophilia that made a day seem like a week. Then our exclusively *gaijin* group pushed aside paying visitors for a personal tour of the museum led by one of dozens of high-fashion Girl Guides identically dressed in purple and mauve, topped by snappy little hats. With its meticulously researched genealogies — from the first Arabian horse to the best Japan has to offer — it was clear that horse breeding was the prototypical exercise in genetic engineering. I tried desperately to think of something pleasant to say. Anything, actually.

"Ah yes," I struggled, "there's our own Native Dancer, a Canadian horse. We know the owner ... " One becomes manic in an attempt to display interest. Pity the Royal Family. This is how they live — though the Tokyo Racetrack might be one of the few places where they could express genuine interest.

Besides the huge facilities, there were acres of unused space — at how much a square metre? One hates to think of the extent of the gambling that sustains this complex. Just as I thought our tour was grinding to a close, we were ushered into a boardroom and settled into overstuffed leather chairs designed by some unemployed Soviet maker-of-official-furniture-for-functionaries. More green tea.

"Do you have any questions?" they asked. Yes, I thought. When can we go back to our box? Still, I tried.

"Who designed the various buildings?" I asked. Much chatter in Japanese up and down the hierarchy.

"They have people who do this," came the answer. Others tried to start a conversation but failed. Bruce later informed us that all the late-middle-aged men we had met that day were most likely recipients of the "golden landing," a well-cushioned, low-stress way to ease a senior businessman or bureaucrat out of serious money-making or decision-making and into a functionary's position. This way they earn hefty salaries and retain the trappings of significance. It also postpones the day they stay home full-time and get in the way. Some particularly disgruntled women refer to their retired husbands as "oversize garbage." Japanese working men thus confront two equally unpalatable alternatives: *karoshi* (death from overwork) or the newer post-retirement ailment, *kyofu no washi zoku* ("take-me-with-you-terrors"). For women who've managed on their own all their married lives, a full-time husband can spoil the fun.

At last it was gift-giving time. We were given a fan decorated with horse-racing scenes, literature about the track in English, and a bag to schlep them home in.

No sooner had we returned to our seats in front of the giant screen than Tomoaki Endo and his wife marched over to sit beside us. He's the director of the Paper Museum, a charming man we'd met on the bus. He passed on the sad news that his museum, one I was looking forward to visiting, was closed until spring 1998, when it would move to a new building. (He was once an executive with a multinational paper company and lived for two years in British Columbia.) It seemed they were combining the museum's reopening with an advertising campaign and a new image. "Would you mind reading these and tell me which 'logo' you like best?" He handed me a list of six short mission statements to be given to English-speaking visitors entering the museum. I did not ask how he came to have it in his pocket, or what Bruce had said my qualifications were for this job.

"Really, I'm not the one you should ask. Bob, my husband, he's one of Canada's finest editors ... " (I know this was unenlightened and cowardly.)

Bob quickly took out his blue pen. He chose the shortest, simplest explanation, a decision that baffled Mr. Endo since he'd favoured the most florid. "This one is simpler," I explained. "More elegant."

"Simpler. More elegant," Endo-san repeated, as if memorizing the words he would repeat to his board. He said he was grateful and promised to send us an invitation to the museum's re-opening. His wife handed me her personal calling card before departing. "May Peace Prevail on Earth — Etsuko Endo." Who could argue? By the end of the eleventh race, the Canada-Japan Friendship Society rose as one and headed back to the bus for the trip home, but we did not join them.

Bruce had booked us, along with John and Martine Sloan, for dinner in Okutakao, a small hill town about half an hour away, in a restaurant called Ukai-Toriyama. Here I had one of the most memorable meals of my life. After a train ride into increasingly rugged countryside, a bus, travelling quickly around hairpin turns on the narrow mountain road, took us to our restaurant. Because it had been raining all day there was a heavy mist, almost a fog, hanging over the entire area. For the last fifty metres or so, on restaurant property, we were surrounded by flickering lamps in the middle of a landscaped garden. Kimonoed hostesses with colourful umbrellas guided us over stone bridges, across rivulets full of bright carp, through woods and waterfalls, under bonsai trees, over moss, up stone steps and around at least a dozen small pavilions, each a separate dining room far from the main kitchen.

We were ushered into our room, nine tatami in size, a large table over a sunken floor with two charcoal braziers in the centre and sliding paper doors. We removed our shoes and left them on a canopied rock at the front door. To bring our food, the hostess had to travel back and forth carrying trays and an umbrella, always managing a smile. We started with beer, fruit juice, sake, and water; an appetizer of chestnut and mustard tofu; barbecued whole fish that resembled smelts, the head consumed by the more intrepid — or insensitive — including me; and finally, chicken yakitori with okra and onion dipped in a delicious sauce. The meal ended, traditionally, with rice and sweet potatoes, in honour of the season.

We drifted into a conversation I regard as the Japan-China conundrum. Ten years ago the talk seemed to be all about the United States and Japan, and who was, is, or will be the world economic leader. Now, similar conversations with Japanese and others inevitably lead to debate about who will dominate Asia — Japan or China? John and Martine Sloan, who'd spent some time in a Beijing posting, ventured some comparisons: the Chinese, they said, were more easygoing, natural, ebullient, in other words, more Western. I think that they would have pressed their point had they not sensed that in Bob and me, and certainly in Bruce, they had hard-line Japanophiles. John did report one of those unverifiable facts that clarifies everything and nothing: "If every Chinese person received an egg a day, just one egg, it would require all the world's grain resources."

While we ate we could see umbrellas and kimono going and coming from other dining areas, disappearing into the fog or behind paper screens, the forest glowing in gaslight. Occasionally laughter drifted our way from nearby pavilions. We might have been in Edo more than a hundred years ago, but in fact this restaurant is fairly new, modelled either on something that once existed or on someone's idea of something ancient. The feeling, if not the reality, was authentic and I felt privileged to be there.

The only sour note: Bruce, who is usually tactful as befits someone in the foreign service, attacked David and Linda Frum. It seems that he had met their parents, Barbara and Murray Frum, during their 1986 visit when he was posted to Japan the first time. He'd read the *Elm Street* article by Naomi Klein in which she accused the children of rewriting their mother's liberal political beliefs to bolster their own conservative ideology. Klein's reading of Linda's memoir of her mother coloured all future discussions of that book. I tried to keep cool while telling them that Barbara had been a close friend (Murray still is) and that the book, which Bruce hadn't read, was far more nuanced than he imagined. Bob chimed in, saying that Barbara's politics had been more fluid than indicated in the *Elm Street* article.

"In fact," Bob said, "she certainly, at various times in her life, held both socialist and liberal beliefs. On the other hand, if you think that someone who is against affirmative action, which she was, is necessarily a conservative, then she was that too." There was chill in the air and the conversation never again equalled the food.

Back by train to Shinjuku and home by cab in a downpour. Is there ever, I wonder, an "ordinary day" in Japan?

SUNDAY, OCTOBER 5

Today we visited the elegantly named Palais Royale, an apartment hotel Bruce heard had some vacancies. After many misadventures, including a long walk around Hie shrine — there are at least two Palais Royales in Tokyo — we arrived in a wonderful neighbourhood close to the Akasaka subway station. My heart soared. The building was red brick, no more than ten years old, with balconies visible from the street. The lobby was pleasant if cluttered. Then we were taken upstairs for a viewing. The corridors were the first tip off — grey fluorescent lights, narrow hallways with doors flush to the wall, my idea of death row in an Alabama jail. We'd been warned that Japanese apartments were small compared to those in the West, that we couldn't expect much for ¥300,000 (about $3,500) a month in downtown Tokyo. Size, however, was not the main problem. Sure, there was one tiny kitchen, one tiny bedroom, one tiny living/dining area, one tiny toilet/shower, but what gave me the willies was the dismal light, the filthy stove, the absence of closets and drawers, and the sad presence of two spoons, two knives, and two coffee cups. "Palais Royale" was neither Palais nor Royale.

Spirits rose slightly with a visit to Shibuya, one of the hipper shopping areas. It seemed that the crowds were thicker and more unruly than I remembered. This might be simply because I am ten years older — a scary thought. A sort of magical street radar still prevents anyone being trampled on the densely packed sidewalks and bicycles from crashing into pedestrians.

Had lunch in the Bunkamura wing of the flagship Tokyo department store, in the chain owned by the Tokyu Corporation, developers of the Tokyu rail line. Bunkamura means "Culture Village" and this modern steel and glass structure contains a 2,150-seat symphony hall, Theatre Cocoon, for plays or film; another 747-seat multipurpose space; and a large non-commercial art gallery. The film festival will be held here later this month.

In the gallery, we saw a wonderful exhibit of photographs, 1905 to 1997, from the Centre Georges Pompidou in Paris. (Last time we were here there was a show of Man Ray photographs.) Bunkamura is France-obsessed, which is fine by me. This time there were works by Atget, Brancusi (something of a surprise and more exciting than many of his signature sculptures), and Kertész, as well as several women artists I'd never seen before.

A mid-afternoon nap and a walk in the general direction of the Tokyo Tower, a grimy also-ran compared to our CN Tower. In keeping with the day's French theme, we ate in a Japanese version of a bistro — good baguette and cheese.

MONDAY, OCTOBER 6

According to schedule: "1400 hours: Visit Meiji University and meet the Board of Directors of International Programs including Professor Bowers, host of Mr. Fulford. (Talk about housing arrangements.)"

If all trips have a rhythm, and I suspect they do, today was as close to the bottom as I'd care to get. We waited around IH, hoping for the miracle phone call: "We've found just the place for you ... " It did not come. Then we set out for Meiji, neurotically early, fearful of getting lost, of being late. We had in our possession a hopelessly inadequate English-only map. From it we did learn one Life Lesson: always use a bilingual map; otherwise, don't ask for directions.

With the help of two English-speaking Meiji students, we found the International Studies Building. Once inside, Bob remarked, "It's half as good as Ryerson in its worse days." That was generous. Dark corridors, dim fluorescents, everything grungy and antiquated.

The office of Professor Shigehiko Arai, the director of international programs, had as its centrepiece a low Arborite coffee table covered with ashtrays and papers and surrounded by mismatched brown Naugahyde chairs. It became painfully clear that they had no idea how to make use of Bob. There's no office for him, no computer, no teaching responsibilities other than one formal lecture for the journalism students. Professor Arai, who appeared to speak no English, was dead keen to show us his scrapbook filled with eight-by-ten glossies of Jean and Aline Chrétien, and Oscar Peterson at a Markham Street restaurant in Toronto. The Toronto academic connection is with York University, a program set up by the redoubtable John Saywell that allows for student exchange for language learning.

Professor James Bowers, rumoured to be a former spook who served in Vietnam, had oily, wavy hair and wore a slick blue suit with bell-bottom pants. When he and Bob tried to tap into Bob's Toronto e-mail account, it was evident that he knew how to make a computer work even if he was unable to make actual images appear on the screen. Bob was to return at four the next day to try and break through Telnet and into his e-mail. Meiji's computers are below primitive. Their journalism students, they say, work for the most part "independently," or "theoretically," whatever that means. I suspect it confirms rumours about Japanese university education as pretty much a time-waster, a chance to recover from the rigours of admission exams.

About housing, the Japan Foundation and Meiji University share a close relationship with a rental organization, the Tokyo Housing Bureau. This same company had contacted us when we were still in Canada, trying to interest us in taking an unfurnished house for eight weeks in Kamakura, a lovely place but about an hour outside Tokyo. Bob explained over the telephone that since we spoke no Japanese, acquiring furniture and looking after any repairs that might be necessary would be well beyond our capabilities. This message needed to be repeated at today's meeting when the same suggestion was made.

We were told again that a friend of Professor Arai had an apartment for rent, one room with bedroom, cooking, and bathing possibilities in Kiba ("very historic") on the Tozai line and we were "lucky" because he would make it available to us for only ¥140,000 for the rest of the month of October, and ¥320,000 for November. Who were we to say no, even though the floor plan made it look weenie? (We're large people, even by *gaijin* standards.)

Once again we were on the move with Mr. Ko acting as mother duck, showing great concern over Bob's rusty leg, slowing down on the stairs, that sort of thing. We set out at about 4 p.m., had a fifteen-minute walk from the subway exit through a working-class area built on reclaimed land where, in Edo times, lumbering was the chief activity. Now there's nary a tree in sight; this was the centre of the 1923 Kanto earthquake as well as the fire bombing in the Second World War. It was an area far removed, both physically and psychologically, from Roppongi, and for that we were grateful.

The apartment? Another story. Mr. Ko described it, cautiously, as "too small." No, again that wasn't the main problem. There was a tatami sitting room, a bedroom with twin beds (musty odour, no closet, no chest of drawers), few dishes or utensils in the kitchen, and wretched lighting (again!), dismal lobby where even the pop machine was broken. It resembled a military barracks, or a halfway house for convicts.

Coming back I asked Mr. Ko where he lived. "About an hour outside Tokyo," he said. "Also very small." He described the single room for which he pays ¥65,000 (about $700) a month. He gets up at six to be at work for nine. He finishes at 7 p.m. five days a week, and at 1 p.m. on Saturdays, and after drinking with the boys doesn't arrive home until about 11 p.m., when he makes dinner — no doubt a bowl of instant ramen noodles — and falls into bed.

"It's very hard," he said, and I believed him. We parted at our respective transfer points completely dejected. Returned briefly to IH before taking ourselves out for an Indian nosh, always a comfort.

TUESDAY, OCTOBER 7

This morning Bob misplaced his wedding ring: we found it in the wastepaper basket. I tried not to read too much into this unfortunate accident. Over breakfast I went through *The Japan Times* looking for accommodations and later called about ten agencies, each one claiming to have dozens of short-term rentals. Unbelievably, each one sent us back to the Palais Royale! Is this the only place available in the world's largest city? Despair set in. I did casually mention to Bob that perhaps we should consider going home.

I had arranged for us to meet a Mr. Fujiwara of the AKI rental agency to see an apartment in a building called Elite Hills. On the phone it sounded not bad. I imagine that Mr. Fujiwara, now in his seventies, once held a better job. He was dressed in a stylish Ultrasuede jacket when he met us, as arranged, at a nearby Roppongi intersection. We walked together past the Self Defense Forces headquarters and into neighbouring Akasaka.

The apartment building, located on a charming laneway, looked as if it had seen better days. "Elite" was not a word that sprang readily to mind. There was a four-storey climb, no elevator. Once inside the apartment, I was afraid to touch anything — it all looked sticky. Even Mr. Fujiwara was embarrassed. We said goodbye and Bob and I headed for a coffee shop.

There, a young man sitting beside us leaned over and said, "Mr. Fulford?" He was a Canadian who'd lived in Tokyo for six and a half years and had once heard Bob lecture at Trent University. We were grateful to talk about something other than apartments, although that subject inevitably came up as well. The young Canadian spoke highly of Humber College's Asian business course, which had given him the background for the work he's doing. He and his Australian partner, a big chap he was lunching with, hope to set up entertainment theme parks in Japan with about US$25 million in investment capital; there's even some buoyant talk of going public. He reminded me of the young Tom Stolberg, alive to the entrepreneurial possibilities in Japan, bubble or no bubble.

Then to the thorny question of apartments and spirited recollections of spaces so small that the principal decor was suitcases, regularly rotated for effect, and about infestations of various kinds. "What you must ask, the key question," said the Australian fellow, "is 'How old is the building?' Anything more than ten years here is a write-off."

Bob toddled off to Meiji, where he and Bowers brought forth out of Internet ether some business mail and two personal notes, from Margaret Fulford, my stepdaughter, and Joy Crysdale, a friend. They're like gold when one is far away. Meanwhile, I found a wonderful liquor store on my walk home, where I bought sake and Perrier, which still seems hard to find and more expensive than wine. There were divine-looking French crus at little cost, and twenty-six ounces of Stoly vodka for a mere ¥1,700.

Felt fine entering IH. Then, while I was moving a few suitcases around to retrieve some clothing, it hit me. Nausea. Sweat. In short order I'd thrown up four times. Sinuses ached. Undressed and turned the air conditioner on full blast. Both Stephane Jobin and Bruce Barnett from the embassy called and I was not at my best. Body rebelled. All too much. Couldn't even get the television to work.

Bruce offered us the spare room in his apartment for one week. Nice, but no solution. When Bob returned, we discussed, in earnest, the possibility of going home. He was solicitous and somewhat relieved, I think. Because I wasn't up to eating, Bob dined solo in the IH café. At 1 a.m. he put through an SOS call to the Japan Foundation office in Toronto. I felt like a dishrag but somewhat happier now that the alarm had been sounded. Unusual times, unusual measures.

WEDNESDAY, OCTOBER 8

Woke up hungry. A good sign. Made a list of all the individuals or agencies I'd already contacted about housing and it came to eighteen! Bob inquired how long we could stay at IH: Answer? Until October 16, one week from today. Not a lot of cushion.

Escaped to Shinjuku to explore the station — the busiest railway terminal in the world where an estimated four million people a day burrow their way through the underground maze. A few hundred homeless stay there at night in decorated packing crates filled with garbage pickings. We saw mock-leather office chairs, plastic clotheslines, colourful quilts, kettles, and hot plates. The scene put our "homeless" situation in perspective.

On the way back to IH, I looked at a map of Japan and realized how much I wanted to visit the Inland Sea that I'd heard and read so much about. And Hiroshima, Miyajima, Okayama, Shikoku. Would I ever have another chance? Bob called Canadian Airlines and learned there was a direct flight from Tokyo to Toronto Saturday to Wednesday, with openings most days.

I remember thinking ten years ago how frustrating it must be for foreign visitors to Japan who do not speak English and must cope with English-only translations. This was illustrated, once again tonight, when we attended the Deutsches Institut für Japanstudien to hear the renowned expert on Japanese literature, Donald Keene, who has been famous for so long I was surprised he was still alive. We went by taxi and showed our driver a rather poor map faxed to us from the Institut.

After a hair-raising trip with reflex turns down tiny alleys we stopped in front of a nondescript building with no meaningful sign in any language outside. (The only name in evidence was Evance, which turned out to be a dressmaker on the ground floor.) To make sure that he was not dropping us far from our destination, our driver leapt out of his cab, raced into the building and over to the tenant listings. He ran back and said with a smile, "Hai. Secondo floor." Amazingly he'd found it. No tip given because in Japan, none is expected.

Although the lecture was free we had to call in advance and there, with legendary German efficiency, were our names, sort of: Fulford and Fulford. The mock classroom was hot and crowded, about fifty people, mostly young Japanese women. The blonde buttermilk Frau of the Institut executive who introduced Keene was forced to use English, the new global lingua franca, and Keene spoke entirely in English, though he probably knows some German along with his Japanese, Chinese, and Korean.

His talk was listed as something like "Japan in the Pre- and Post-war Periods," but it was pure autobiography. Since his adult life and the life of his adopted country, Japan, are so closely linked it didn't matter. Nor did the fact that much of his address had been published previously in his 1994 autobiography *On Familiar Terms: A Journey Across Cultures*, a book I'd borrowed from the IH library.

Born in 1922, he's now seventy-five, a sprightly man with the New York accent of a Columbia University intellectual. He's on the editorial board of the *Asahi Daily News*, the English-language daily that has traditionally been slightly critical of the reigning Liberal Democratic government. He spends three months teaching at the Donald Keene Center at Columbia, the rest of the time in Kyoto.

He acknowledged how astonishing it was that his career and what he called "the Japan boom" didn't simply coincide chronologically but were interdependent to an astounding degree. Speaking with apparent modesty that in retrospect rings false, he told us how opportunities presented themselves to him — and he of course had the wit to take advantage of them. In 1941, just in time for Pearl Harbor, he switched from the study of Chinese to Japanese at Columbia, one of the few places it was taught. The American Navy recruited him and intensified his language training so that he could translate documents and interview prisoners of war. He said, "I was given the intellectuals to interrogate and I confess that I spent much of the time questioning them about the novels they'd read." He was given these particular prisoners, he implied, because he was so much smarter than his colleagues, some of whom were Japanese newspapermen who disagreed with their government and chose to stay in the United States. (I had wondered if there were any Japanese war resisters; we hear so much about European dissenters.) Keene remained friends after the war with some of the men he'd interrogated.

"When the war ended," he recalled, "people predicted that it would take fifty years for Japan to recover but in fact the Japan boom began in 1955." He talked about the scarcity of translated Japanese literature at that time and how he set out to correct the deficiency in three volumes: the beginning to 1603; 1603 to 1868; and 1868 to the present.

"I *found* myself in Japan," he said. I suspect that in his case, as in the case of many of the American post-war generation of experts, what he found here was a sexual freedom not then available at home.

Throughout the talk the audience behaved most peculiarly: one woman couldn't find the ringing cell phone in her enormous handbag and had to dash out of the room to turn it off; another rather large *gaijin* female stood alone in one corner, exercising — knee bends, stretches, rotations. I don't think she was visible from the stage but the audience had a hard time ignoring her.

As I've observed on other occasions, the questions from the Japanese were articulate and polite. Keene is now working on a biography of Emperor Meiji. He was asked if there was much first-hand material available. Did Meiji have any real power? (I suspected that this question had as much to do with Hirohito as with his grandfather.) Keene answered that yes, there was a lot of material, including an imperial log where all activities were noted, and yes, Meiji had more power than is generally assumed and gave some specific examples.

A young Russian woman asked, "I'm just beginning to study the Japanese. Do you think that anyone can ever hope to understand them?" (Much knowing laughter from the audience.) Keene replied, "I think that question really should be, Can the Japanese understand the Japanese?" (More knowing laughter.) He gave as an example the special ceremony that's supposed to occur on the third anniversary of a death but actually takes place on the second. "I've asked many Japanese friends why this is so and they have no explanation. It just *is* that way."

Still, he offered this advice to the student, one that could apply equally to tourists: "You must allow yourself to participate in Japanese life. You must step inside the culture and not be fooled when you see all those Kentucky Fried Chicken outlets. And you must learn to obey their rules and not your own."

"The Japanese," he continued, "tend to think that foreigners can never understand them, while Americans think that all educated people speak English and understand American culture." He did admit that this was the natural outcome of America as a receiving nation for immigrants who must be "Americanized" as quickly as possible. "The Japanese still have invisible, intricate screens to protect themselves from scrutiny."

Bob later observed that Keene mentioned only one other contemporary scholar of Japan: Edwin O. Reischauer, who was born in Japan, served as American ambassador to Japan, taught at Harvard, and wrote several books including the classic, *The Japanese*. Of those who had inspired Keene, only George Sansom, his teacher, received any credit. Perhaps he does have the field to himself. Certainly the shelf of books he's written on Japanese literature and the honours he's received place him in the top half-dozen *gaijin* scholars who came to Japan after the war and stayed to explain the nation they loved to the rest of the world. I was thrilled to have had the chance to hear him.

It was a beautiful, breezy night when we emerged from the lecture, high on thought, so we wandered off, got lost, as one so often does in Tokyo, and wound up by chance in our old neighbourhood, Iidabashi. The police box in front of the subway was still there, as was the McDonald's where Bob foraged for morning coffee. We spotted the tobacco store where the owner, a little old lady, swept the road in front of her shop every day, and the sake shop where I would make a nightly purchase. We found ourselves walking up the lane to Seifuso, our old ryokan, but alas, in its place was a smart white-brick apartment building four storeys high with two expensive black sedans parked in front. Did "our" family still live there, rich from the new development? Or had they been forced to sell? We walked alongside the building and glimpsed what I think was our lovely rock garden, the one we could see from our bedroom. It, at least, had been preserved.

Everything else in the area was tarted up, the result of the rise of property values until the early 1990s. There were still droves of students in the same 1930s German naval academy uniforms and many of the same single-family traditional houses. We were misty-eyed with nostalgia.

THURSDAY, OCTOBER 9

Woke up feeling queasy again. Some mischief in the sinus area, no doubt related to stress. Spent the post-breakfast period writing postcards, reading, and waiting in the lobby. At about 11 a.m. Bob was called to the telephone. It was Mr. Sugihara of the Japan Foundation in Toronto. Le shit had hit le fan. He was, he said, "most upset" at our situation, that he would tell the people in the Tokyo office that "this is a most important Canadian," etc., etc. (He'd already spoken with Mr. Horiuchi, who said that he could do nothing today. "I find that frightening," was Mr. Sugihara's comment.)

Somewhat bucked up by having a heavy-hitter in our corner, we set out for the Sakura Bank in the Foundation's building where we met Ms. Iino, transferred some Japanese money to Canadian accounts, and acquired the blessed plastic bank card. Then to the thirty-seventh floor of the ARK Mori building to visit Xsitehill, "a new design center." (Noted on the way up that Goldman Sachs occupies six floors, ready to provide the Japanese with the private investment savvy they lack.) The Xsitehill lobby contains a huge terra cotta clay mound that could be a Joseph Beuys sculpture or a burial site for ancient Mayans. There are clay pillars with twigs sticking out (a Japanese improvement on the tree?) and on the far side, a stone wall of traditional design.

We walked up and over the mound into a long hall that ran the length of the building. There was a restaurant, exhibition spaces, a garden and design library, and benches at either end from which one can see the Tokyo Tower and Tokyo Bay at one end, Shinjuku at the other. We'd heard of a recent, well-received exhibition of toilets that had been mounted here. Now their attention was focused on "designing aesthetically pleasing spaces." (It wasn't until much later in the day that I discovered that the INEX corporation, which rents the space and controls the exhibits, is the Japanese equivalent of American Standard. A clue was discovered in the washroom, where space-age sinks and toilets discreetly displayed astronomical price tags.)

The Japanese washroom is a subject so serious it was the starting point of Junichiro Tanizaki's wondrous little book on aesthetics, *In Praise of Shadows*, in which he extolled the beauties of the dark, wooden Japanese toilet room. However, when the author designed his own dream house, he installed gleaming white porcelain Western-style fixtures — another Japanese paradox. In this country even porcelain toilets are somewhat different from those in North America: instead of a flat tank cover, there's a small basin built into the top with a tiny curved faucet and a drain leading into the water storage unit. This allows users to rinse their fingers in clean water, soon to be recycled in the toilet. Many owners decorate this small basin with coloured marbles or floating plastic flowers.

Ultramodern public toilet seats often are heated, and are, on occasion, almost searing. Others have a button one can press before sitting that moves a plastic seat-cover a full rotation, guaranteeing that no bottom will ever actually make seat-contact. The goofiest, faux-polite invention is built into the side wall of public cubicles and looks, at first, like a toilet paper dispenser. However, when you touch it, as I did accidentally, it activates a tape that makes the sound of rushing water, lasting just long enough to mask the sounds of the functions for which toilets were invented.

INEX displays an almost mystical approach to materials and motherland in the creation of toilets and other products such as home interiors and patio tiles. These are made from "a full selection of regionally distinctive soil and sand, brick and tile gathered throughout the country." We saw samples as we walked — recessed into the floor were soil samples under Plexiglas from all the regions of Japan, Hokkaido to Okinawa.

Ate lunch in the charming Garden Café, sort of French bistro food, with a fine view of the Tokyo skyline. From there we could see lovely landscaped rooftop gardens, a site denied mere pedestrians. I looked with envy at all the wonderful housing. "Make it mine. Make it mine. Make it mine!"

We ended up at a bookstore in the building where I replenished my stock of Japanese literature and non-fiction. Reading about Japan while I'm here is the best education in the world. Spent the night curled up in bed, reading and imagining a place of our own. It could be small, 2 rms w vu would do.

FRIDAY, OCTOBER 10

Today is Yom Kippur, and I've given it little thought and less planning. I couldn't bear the idea of asking anyone to find me a synagogue or Jewish home to go to. I felt I was already asking too many people for too many favours. Bob and I went instead to visit Nihon Minka-en, "Japan's Open-Air Folk House Museum," one of the architectural parks scattered across the country — a convenient way to preserve the past from the wrecker's ball by carting representative buildings from a single era to a central location where locals and foreigners can glimpse how things were.

At first I had thought of sticking closer to home and going to Arai Yakushi-ji, a temple where I'd read there was to be a flea market. I asked the clerk at the front desk to call and see if it was in fact open. "Yes," she said, "it is. But not for a sale. It's for a ... " and then she wrote the word in Japanese and checked her dictionary. "For an exorcism!" I assume that this meant a ritual cleansing of the temple but decided against venturing beyond my depth.

Getting to Nihon Minka-en was not half the fun. We headed for Kanagawa City from Shinjuku on the Odakyu line to Noborito. From there, it was a long hot trek up a hill on a tawdry street. Along the way we bothered about half a dozen people for directions: they kept pointing straight ahead. (I have become acutely aware of the pointing style adopted here: one never uses a finger but the whole hand, palm up, thumb tucked in.)

Katherine Ashenburg, the architecture maven, recommended this day trip and she was, as usual, correct. There were twenty fifteenth- to seventeenth-century houses, as well as a waterwheel, a kabuki stage, and a shrine, most from Kanagawa Prefecture but some from as far away as Iwate Prefecture in the northern part of Honshu, the main island. They bear the weight of various finely graded assessments of their worth — "An important cultural property designated by Kanagawa Prefecture," or, "An important cultural property designated by the Japanese Government," and a few with no special commendation beyond their age, and in most cases, elegance, even when the floors are part mud. There were lit braziers in some of the houses, stoked by ladies from the local historical society. One wonders how people survived in these smoke-filled inner rooms. Some original residents shared space with horses; attics often housed silkworms; and, in one home, they manufactured gunpowder and stored it under the floorboards!

We lunched cross-legged in the Yamashita House (early nineteenth century), dining on soba noodles, cold for me, hot for Bob. I wondered why more tourists weren't there. Despite the fact that it was a national holiday, I saw no buses at the gate, no tours inside, and few *gaijin*. As we travelled at a careful pace through the lovely wooded grounds, I noticed that the Japanese we encountered along the way seemed sophisticated and keenly interested in what they were seeing, walking at their own speed. Not a tour guide toting power-pack microphone in sight.

Under the thickest straw roof, a group of young people, probably in their early twenties, were clustered together, standing stalk still, then moving at a snail's pace, following the lead of a young woman. Suddenly, they fell to the ground, eyes closed. Then, some minutes later, their eyes popped open. All this was being intensely observed by a group of slightly older adults who laughed, took photographs, and chatted. I assumed they were drama students. Bob asked a young man at the fringe of the group who said that they were in fact students of architecture from a nearby university. They were "experiencing the building."

After arriving home, I decided that the subtext of the trip so far is Home: the homeless in crates in Shinjuku; the material from which homes are built in the INEX display; the preserved homes of Edo at Nihon Minka-en. As the good Dr. Freud remarked, there are no accidents.

SATURDAY, OCTOBER 11

A day of tranquillity and productivity. Bruce Barnett called last night and again this morning. When I told him what we'd done, he seemed surprised we'd seen so much. Do we seem that incompetent? Or sulky? I hope not. He suggested we meet the following day at 4 p.m. at the embassy and go for an early supper.

Received a five-page fax from Professor Arai telling us that Meiji has "an arrangement" with the Fairmont Hotel, near Yasukuni shrine, where we could have a twin or double room for ¥16,000 a day instead of the usual ¥20,000. It did include "a beautiful breakfast," but was still more than we'd budgeted for accommodation. However, we are nothing if not flexible. Decided to forego one shrine sale to visit the area and inspect the room before replying to the professor.

Earlier, in an attempt at lateral thinking, Bob suggested that we find out whether IH has larger rooms (I thought I spotted one when the maids were cleaning down the hall) and if one might be available for our whole stay. I also called the AKI agency again. In today's paper their company advertised for rent about a half dozen apartments that sounded sort of right. Mr. Fujiwara picked up the phone. I began to suspect that the AKI agency was a cell phone in Mr. F's briefcase.

"What about these places you list in Roppongi?" I asked, "and Shibuya, Shinjuku, Ueno, Akasaka? Are any available now?"

"For long term only," he replied.

"All long term? Even those in apartment hotels?"

"They're not available. They're *sometimes* available."

"So you mean to say that you're running these ads every week, when you don't really have the apartments available? What *do* you have available?"

"Well, there's Elite Hills ... "

"Where we've been?"

"Yes."

"Thank you very much."

Masao Kunihiro, a former parliamentarian, wrote that the Japanese had perfected "an esthetics of silence," which makes reticence a virtue and open expression of one's thoughts vulgar. My dealings with Mr. Fujiwara were doomed to fail.

Whenever I feel like throwing in the towel, Bob seems optimistic. Then we switch roles. It would be no fun doing this alone.

Happily, the library at IH seems never to close. Reading and waiting.

Spent much of the afternoon in the company of the two Donalds, Keene and Richie. Both are American by birth, both arrived after the war, both are committed Japanophiles. There the similarities end. They seem to represent two dominant *gaijin* attitudes towards the Japanese. Keene is a traditionalist who yearns for pre-contact, pre-Meiji Japan. He comes to Japan through its ancient and early modern literature, is exclusively homosexual, I assume, and an elitist. Richie is deeply into the modern — films, street life, architecture, social mores. He's as concerned with pachinko (pinball) as with Bushido, and looks to the future more than the past. From his writing I gather he's sexually omnivorous. Each has written about his fraught relationship with Yukio Mishima, who seems to have imposed himself everywhere in Japanese life, even more so after his vainglorious suicide in 1970.

I think I'd treated Mishima rather too lightly in my mind, as a poseur and egomaniac, a view reinforced by Paul Schrader's indulgent film about him. He was no doubt both of those things but something more: he managed to captivate, in entirely different ways, the two Donalds. Keene thought Mishima the only "true genius" he ever knew. "A genius," Keene wrote, "is someone who can perform with little or no effort actions that are impossible for ordinary people." Although Richie appreciated many of Mishima's charms, he was more critical of his writing and thought *Confessions of a Mask* was his only adequate book.

In many ways, the two Donalds parallel the two Japanese experts I learned so much from — Ken Richard of the East Asian Studies, University of Toronto, and Ted Goossen, East Asian Studies, York University. Both were born in the United States and both have translated works of major contemporary writers. We became friends working on a radio series about Japan. Ken once played the shamisen in our sunroom and Ted was in Japan at the same time we were ten years ago and is here today. Richard resembles Keene; Goossen is more Richie.

Another "companion" on this trip has been the writer Junichiro Tanizaki (1886–1965), an acquaintance of both Donalds when he was alive. Long ago I'd been given his most famous novel, *The Makioka Sisters*, written during and immediately after the war and translated into English in 1957. I started it and put it down: now it's the constant reference point for this trip. Where can I find the delicate sea bream, so beloved of the sisters? Do arranged marriages still occur? Donald Keene has written that the Makiokas were his travelling companions on his first trip to Japan — read no doubt in the original. And we now know that Tanizaki's wife was the model for Sakiko, the second of the four sisters in this once prominent Osaka family.

There are sections of the book that should be read by anyone negotiating with the Japanese for everything from an apartment to a multinational trade agreement. In the internal monologues we "overhear" the agonizing that goes into making even the simplest decision — "simple" only from a Western point of view. We witness the imaginary role-playing of the "what-would-she-think-if-she-knew-that?" sort, the constant ruminations on consequence, not only for one or two people but for everyone in the family and their retainers. The novel is full of *tatemae*, expressions that run contrary to a character's feelings but are considered to be the proper response to a given situation. In the West, this might seem like duplicity or at least being "out of touch with one's feelings." In Japan, where it's crucial to avoid offending anyone, *tatemae* is a great social lubricant. *The Makioka Sisters* is a textbook on Japanese behaviour as well as an irresistible story.

In the late afternoon we went to inspect the Fairmont Hotel. Bruce mentioned it was the place preferred by Karen Kain and Frank Augustyn when they came to Tokyo but that was years ago. The closest subway stop is Kudanshita on the Tozai line in the heart of the dead, formalist part of Tokyo that includes Kitonomaru Park and endless office towers where salarymen busy themselves on weekdays. On weekends, it's deserted.

The Fairmont appears to be a middle-class family hotel for Japanese guests. We were shown a typical double bedroom that was dark but respectable, larger than our room at IH — a coffee table, two chairs, desk, large chest of drawers, television, small refrigerator and bath. (Amazing that we're even considering this place after our plans to live and work in "a typical Japanese neighbourhood.")

Other negatives: almost no place around to eat but the hotel dining room. There are also notices up everywhere in the hotel apologizing for the noise and inconvenience of the renovation being done until November 30. Could this explain the discounted rate? Still, I think if it comes down to the Fairmont or leaving Japan, we'd probably take the Fairmont.

SUNDAY, OCTOBER 12

Overheard at breakfast at IH: two men, one Japanese, the other American, professors sharing a table and talking in the easy manner of colleagues. The Japanese said, "Let me ask you, How do you find Japan?" It sounded like the sort of question a visiting surgeon might ask a team of interns standing at a patient's bedside. It stems from the anxiety I sense on this visit about the health of the nation. It's different in tone and intent from questions commonly asked visitors ten years ago: "Is this your first trip here?" "How do you like it?" "Are you having a good time?" Those questions were full of optimism and anticipated approval. Today's questions reflect, I think, a national insecurity, internal anxieties that linger after "the bubble burst" — the excuse one hears constantly to explain everything from stagnation to corporate crime.

Went to a shrine sale at Hanazono near Shinjuku-sanchome. It turned out to be the same place Jill and David Bond had taken us on our first Sunday in Japan, ten years ago. The kimono stall to the right of the entrance where I bought gifts was still there, as were silk kimono for ¥1,000. I must go back before we leave; there were lovely pieces of pottery, lacquerware, scrolls, and postcards as well. I did buy a scroll for ¥8,000, probably too expensive, but it was already framed in silk and pictured a "typical" mountain scene that reminded me of the restaurant we went to with Bruce. Also bought postcards and old photographs for ¥3,000.

One vendor showed us four matching postcard books collected by one person in the early decades of the century, many featuring the young Hirohito and his bride. They were museum quality, and selling for ¥150,000. For the right person, a collector or dealer, they were a steal at $2,000 Canadian.

For lunch we stopped for bento in a department store basement and ate on the steps of the shrine. At 2 p.m. it started to rain and everyone scurried for cover. Bob and I bought two clear plastic umbrellas, which are cheap and promote safety (you can see the person with whom you are about to collide). Then home to change, meet Bruce at the embassy, and go to Meiji Jingu, a popular wedding locale.

Bruce had booked a table for 4:30 p.m. to give us a chance to overlook bridal festivities on the grass outside the restaurant. The food was wonderful and he was clearly a frequent guest, well known to the horse-faced hostess with gold front teeth who showered us with attention. (Bruce is a friend of the shrine's Shinto priest.) Afterward, under the watchful eye of the Mama-san, we were shown the empty wedding chapel and allowed to try out the seats reserved for the bride and groom, seats covered in red and white paper with a small lectern in front. There were similar chairs along both sides, two rows deep, for guests, no more than 120. In one corner was an ancient multistringed instrument on a raised platform beside a "special tree." According to the Mama-san, "it is usually not real, but this is real."

Beside it stood a complex electronic system for taped music and for plugging in video cameras; all but two moments in the ceremony can be taped. We were permitted to take photographs and our giggling Mama-san insisted on group shots — Bob, Ger, and Mama-san, Bob,

Ger, and Bruce. After we left the chapel, I asked to see the bridal booking offices; Bruce and madame were not too thrilled with my request but they agreed to show us. There, at one end of the lobby, in a huge glass pit, we watched ten couples, each with a consultant, plotting their weddings. To the right was a large counter for the travel agency that books honeymoons: Guam, Okinawa, Hawaii, and farther afield for the wealthier and more adventurous (but wherever one goes, a week is the usual length of time away). On our left, a music consultant sat at an organ keyboard as a couple, wearing headphones, selected their music.

We were told that Japanese farmers, despite the fact that they're protected by the government and have good incomes, cannot find brides. No young woman in the 1990s wants the isolation, the hard life, or the care of aging in-laws. Solution? Brides are brought from the Philippines. "Why the Philippines?" I asked someone. "They're nice and they work hard!" I'd also heard they were often abused by their husbands and in-laws and that this is becoming a social issue in Japan.

Before saying goodbye to Mama-san, I visited the ladies' washroom. Never have I seen a public space so beautifully maintained for the care and nurture of moms and babes: two lovely cots, padded changing tables, decorated nursing rooms. There were children running all through the wedding palace, evidence of the ultimate purpose of marriage.

Walking back to Bruce's apartment on the embassy grounds for tea, I exclaimed, "How wonderful it was to be allowed into the chapel! Does she do that for everyone?" (I assumed my winning ways had secured the visit.)

"No," said Bruce. "I phoned ahead." I suppose that's what a foreign service officer is supposed to do, but did I need to know?

Bruce's apartment was huge, even by Canadian standards, and beautifully appointed. I don't know that I have ever before felt domicile-envy but I did then. He showed us the guest room where we might stay, but to live that close to even the kindest of strangers is too difficult. Also, it's hard to know with government folks if you're Work, or Pleasure, or Somewhere In Between. It makes me uneasy.

I woke in the middle of the night in a foul mood, feeling out of touch with friends and family, the result perhaps of watching Japanese weddings. I was in such a state that, with a nod from Bob, I might have packed up then and there. Not having a permanent address makes planning impossible — we're always waiting for a friend or agent to call.

Monday, October 13

At least I don't have to make Thanksgiving dinner. As penance we spent the morning trying to neaten our too-small room, making lists of Japanese phone numbers, throwing out junk, sending off three bags of laundry and dry cleaning, trying to think our way through the rest of our stay, and faxing Ted in Kyoto.

Bob heard from John Harris in Toronto, a friend of the Japan Foundation, a businessman who's always on a plane, and a big promoter of this trip. He'd heard about our dilemma and made a number of suggestions, all of which we'd already tried. Bob also heard from Masako Iino, head of the Japanese Association for Canadian Studies. She's organizing a conference for March 1998, and Bob might offer some assistance.

I called the front desk because our room was unbearably hot despite the fact that the air conditioner was turned to Max. "Ah," said the sweet young thing, "it is the day when we turn off the air conditioner." Ah, annual Turn-the-Air-Conditioner-Off-Regardless-of-Temperature Day. We should have known, except it's a "limited holiday" — the corridors and other public spaces are still cooled.

At 3 p.m. Mr. Horiuchi and Ms. Iino arrived. I was on the lobby phone speaking to Ted, who thought he would not be coming to Tokyo during our stay but did invite us to pull up a futon at his house in Kyoto when we go there. I thanked him and continued to complain about our lack of accommodation after two weeks, no doubt boring him to death. I also reported that as yet there was no copy of the recently published Oxford University Press anthology of Japanese short stories he'd edited in the IH library. He said it would probably take time for the publisher to meet all the orders. Japanese reviews have been positive; one paper featured a picture of Ted, no doubt wearing his beret.

I joined Iino, Horiuchi, and Fulford scrunched over their papers: a Yellow Pages, the floor plan of a two-bedroom apartment for a mere ¥680,000 plus 5 percent taxes, and a two-storey unfurnished house that Bob and I agreed to look at to prove to Mr. Horiuchi that we were doing our part. Only later did we discover that this was the same house that the former Canadian cultural affairs officer had told us about before we left Canada, one where the owners lived next door and "would let us have some of their old furniture." We had refused then, and again when we arrived in Japan, when Mr. Aoki of the Tokyo

Housing Bureau called us on our first night in town, and again when Mr. Horiuchi handed over Bob's cheque. It was not until we were in a crowded cab heading through Tokyo traffic and the charming Mr. Aoki said, "as I mentioned in the fax I sent you," that I made the connection. Call me crazy, but I now believe that Tokyo rental agents are given one property at a time and can't have another until they dispose of it.

The house in question was located in a wonderful area, Ichigaya, about a twenty-minute walk from the nearest subway stop. We felt obliged to visit each room since we were met at the door by the poor woman who owns it and does indeed live next door. She speaks no English, which would make necessary contact difficult.

"Mr. Aoki," I said, "if we were staying for a year or more, this would be a fine place. However ... " Our objections seemed perfectly sensible to me, and I suspect to him as well.

"You couldn't really have it for a year," he explained, rather missing the point. "All this side of the street has been bought by a developer and will be torn down in January." I was sad about that. It felt like a real neighbourhood — a rice store in the middle of the block, kids playing on the streets, little traffic. In a year, it would disappear.

Just this morning I read in *A Lateral View: Essays on Culture and Style in Contemporary Japan*, Donald Richie quoting Edward Seidensticker, "The relationship between tradition and change in Japan," Seidensticker said, "has always been complicated by the fact that change itself is a tradition." This seems a wise observation from another of those post-war US experts.

We trudged towards Ichigaya station — no taxi for the return trip. Mr. Aoki, who'd begun his time with us as a loquacious, genial host, had turned petulant and depressed, transformed into a Willy Loman. He stooped, his suit looked shinier, his briefcase scruffier, his shoulders more rounded. Quietly, he offered to lower the price. We repeated our reservations and tried to engage him in distracting conversation. Because his English was flawless, we asked how much time he'd spent out of Japan.

"Only a few weeks," he said, "and mostly in Spain. My Spanish is better than my English." That was the last word he said to us. He walked in silence beside Bob to the subway. I walked ahead with Ms. Iino. She mentioned another place that's available and will fax details later. I asked her, "Where do you live?" (Is this becoming an obsession?)

"In Chiba Prefecture," she answered. She shares with a person from the office — a kitchen, bath, living/dining room, and each has her own bedroom.

I'd heard of Chiba. "Not too far away?" I asked.

"One and a half hours each way. About average."

She's a recent arrival from Fukuoka on the southern island of Kyushu, and she seems lost. She carries an air of permanent loneliness.

When we were travelling home on the crowded subway car, a young woman and her toddler got on. There were no seats so we were all standing. The Japanese who were seated kept their eyes straight ahead, or closed, in their famous sleeping mode. It occurred to me that this "blindness" served a purpose: if they didn't see the woman and child struggling to keep their balance, they didn't have to consider giving up their seat. She stood until the car emptied.

It was now 5 p.m. and Bob and I dropped into our local Wave outlet, a supercool record store in Roppongi. In recent years I'd reviewed a number of newly translated books by the Nobel-winning author Kenzaburo Oe. Almost all his recent writing, fiction and non-fiction, relates to his brain-damaged son, Hikari, who has defied overwhelming odds and become a classical composer, his work performed and recorded. I couldn't find any of his CDs in Toronto and thought I'd look here.

The clerk was surprised when I wrote out Oe's name for him, in English.

"Japanese?" he asked in a startled voice.

"Hai," I replied, "Yes."

He found Oe's work in a rack marked simply "Japanese." This segregation of local product reminded me of the years, not long ago, when Canadian recordings and Canadian books were stacked in their own retail ghettos. Here, as throughout the world, America makes everything else seem marginal.

Over another Indian meal we read letters and clippings sent by Jack Batten and Marjorie Harris, bless their hearts. We took turns reading them aloud between courses, paragraph by paragraph, savouring every word. Returned at 7:30 to IH. No faxes. No new letters. No newspapers. It was National Newspaper Day. Japan's frequent statutory holidays are one of their best-kept secrets.

TUESDAY, OCTOBER 14

Two more days and, barring a miracle, we'll be evicted. A fax from Ms. Iino was waiting for us when we went down for breakfast: an apartment belonging to an employee of the Toronto office of the Japan Foundation was available. "Dear Mr. Fulford. I'm sorry that we have not explain a difficult situation of housing in Japan before you came to Japan." (Mr. Sugihara of the Japan Foundation is indeed a force to reckon with!) "As I told you, Mr. Bunji Yokomichi, who is a member of the Japan Foundation, Toronto office, offered that he would like you to use his apartment house. He did not tell about house because he was afraid that you would think his house was located in far from centre of Tokyo." (Perhaps, but we have learned a thing or two.)

The "house" is in Kawaguchi, a bedroom community northwest of Tokyo, about an hour's commute by train. Small by North American standards, it's about sixty-two square metres. (That, too, might have made Mr. Yokomichi hesitate.) There are three rooms and a living/dining room. Also included are "electricity, water, gas, telephone, air conditioning, lighting, refrigerator, washer, TV, VCR, dining table and chair, table and chair, bookshelf, china set, oven, pot." There's a futon mattress but Ms. Iino suggests we could "rent a bed." Best of all, the apartment would be free! We're to call Ms. Iino in the afternoon.

She called us first. It seems that Mr. Horiuchi is trying to secure "a guest house" for us at Sophia University. He asked that we postpone our visit to Kawaguchi until tomorrow. One day before eviction, this is turning into a cliff-hanger. Time to enter a darkened movie and escape. Fortunately, there is a new Juzo Itami flick, *Marutai no Onna*, playing with English subtitles tonight in Ginza. Itami has provided me with many rewarding experiences during the last ten years — *Tampopo*, the noodle Western, just before leaving for Japan in 1987; *The Funeral*, while we were in Japan; and *Taxing Woman, The Taxing Woman's Return, and The Gentle Art of Japanese Extortion* in the intervening years. This last movie so angered certain yakuza that they stabbed Itami, nearly killing him and leaving his face badly scarred. I saw *Extortion* at the 1992 Toronto International Film Festival and was surprised that such a witty and notorious film was never distributed in Canada. There must have been others in the intervening years, but they never played North America either, as far as I know. Could it be that the Japanese consider him unsuitable for export? And the Western cinema elite find him too accessible?

This film, like the others, starred his wife, the great comedienne Nobuko Miyamoto. She plays an actress who accidentally witnesses the brutal murder of a prominent lawyer who was prosecuting members of a cult, The Sheep of Truth. Reluctantly, she's placed under the protective custody of two mismatched cops and forced to endure the scare tactics of the cult and their oily attorney as well as the police. The plot echoes Itami's own brush with the law as well as the recent sarin attack in the Tokyo subway by the Aum Shinrikyo cult. The film was wonderful.

As we were leaving, an impeccably dressed Japanese gentleman, about sixty years old, said to us in crisp English, "Fun, wasn't it?"

"Yes, very," we replied.

"But you don't think that that was the *real* Japan, do you?" he went on.

I replied, "I should ask you what you think?" (I'm learning.)

"Of course it isn't. It's fiction!"

I felt that this was not the time or place to discuss the power of fiction to portray ultimate truths, especially since he was walking with Bob towards the men's room.

There he apparently expanded his views, after which Bob replied, "You wouldn't say Fellini was describing all Italy in his movies, would you?"

"Are you Italian?" our Japanese movie maven asked.

"No, Canadian. And if you'd seen the movies made in my country in the last few years, well, I don't think they resemble Canadians at all!" (Nice work, Bob. Conversation ended.)

Back at IH there was a message from Marie Suzuki, the audiovisual officer of the Japan Foundation in Tokyo and a friend of James Quandt of the Cinematheque in Toronto. She called to say that she'd arranged press passes for the Tokyo International Film Festival and was prepared to let us preview some Shohei Imamura films scheduled to play North America. Bliss!

WEDNESDAY, OCTOBER 15

Very tense, first waiting in the room, then in the lobby. At 11 a.m. Bob was called to the telephone. Yes, we could have the Sophia guest house, but — as always, the but — it would not be available until Friday,

October 17, one day after our scheduled eviction. Before this, Bob had asked Mr. Ashiba, the manager, if we could extend our stay. "Unfortunately, we have been watching, but as yet, no cancellation. We will do our best but ... "

We raced to our room, changed, and took a cab to the ARK Mori building (Command Central) and Mr. Horiuchi's desk in the Japan Foundation office. "Ah," he said, "unfortunately, the offices at Sophia close for lunch between 1:00 and 2:00." Bob suggested we return to Xsitehill for lunch but I talked him into grabbing a bento and heading for the large outdoor plaza where ARK Mori workers eat on fine days such as this. There were several empty tables on an elevated platform. I pointed to a likely spot and headed in that direction.

"Right," Bob replied. In an instant I heard a loud thud behind me as he tripped onto the wooden stand. When I turned I saw him sprawled on his hands and knees.

I think I shrieked. Not again! Not here! I helped Bob up.

"I'm all right," he said, not very convincingly, but it appeared that he was. He was able to walk to the table and sit down.

There was a huge hole in the knee of his cherished checked suit pants, his left knee near the torn quadriceps, but he was able to raise his leg, a simple task he wasn't able to do after he fell down the stairs in December 1996. I felt terrible. Of course, it wasn't really my fault but how could I not feel guilty? And since this was Japan, I also felt shame. Bob insisted he was all right. (It wasn't until we returned to IH that night that he showed me his poor knee, already sliced and stitched, now with the skin rubbed off. Nothing a little antiseptic and a Band-Aid couldn't fix, I hope.)

When we returned to pick up Mr. Horiuchi, we discovered he'd been eating a snack at his desk. I'd thought about inviting him to join us for lunch, in which case we would have gone to a restaurant, and Bob wouldn't have tripped, and ... and. This is the sort of hopeless "what if?" thinking that follows any accident. While we were getting ready to leave, I looked around at the souvenirs left by grateful guests to the department of receiving: wooden mamushka dolls, pennants from Polish soccer teams, Disney ornaments, stuffed animals, all hideous. A Blue Jay cap would look right at home.

On our way to Sophia we passed the Akasaka Prince Hotel, where Bob and I had stayed during a two-week return trip when the Canadian embassy opened in 1991, and passed a row of super-swank shops devoted to Armani, Gucci, Versace et al. We were let out at the university's main gate and walked some distance through crowds of students who, on first appearance, looked much more alert than their Meiji counterparts.

"Sophia is a very good school," said Mr. Horiuchi, as if privy to my thoughts.

"Better than Meiji?" I asked.

"Meiji?" he snorted. "Much better. One of the best in the country." (Japan is the number-one place for ranking things.) "Every year," he continued, "the Japan Foundation has exams to get in. Very tough. There are always one or two from Sophia who make it."

"And where do most of your staff come from?" I asked.

"Tokyo University," he snapped. Ha! The crème de la crème. Top dogs. Numero unos.

"And where did *you* go to school?" I inquired disingenuously.

"Todai," he replied, smiling for the first time in our short acquaintance. (Todai is what the cognoscenti call Tokyo University.)

We reached the administration office, where Bob filled out an application form, merely pro forma since all the negotiating had been done. Then we were taken to see the house, which was in fact an apartment. My initial reaction was rather negative: to reach it you have to take an elevator to the sixth floor, walk along a narrow, outdoor steel corridor; then into a modern, utilitarian version of a charming Kyoto eel-house. Within about 65 square metres there were two bedrooms, one with twin beds, an office, bathroom, washer and dryer, kitchen, living/dining room and balcony.

Everything was quite new — there had been only one previous tenant — and superficially clean. But boy, was it equipped! Enough bedding for twelve bedrooms, plenty of dishes, pots and pans, cutlery, telephone, drawers, closets, a state-of-the-art vacuum cleaner, iron, and huge television. The furniture was dentist-office functional. Altogether, it was by far the best place we'd seen or were likely to see. Of course we said we'd take it, and if at all possible, could we move in a day ahead of schedule? Like tomorrow?

Not certain, we were told. Mr. Horiuchi will call us tomorrow at 9:30 a.m. It hinges on whether or not a certain caretaker is available to show us how things work. I snooped around. Like the country itself, everything looks the same but operates differently — there are three compartments to the refrigerator; four units in one stove, and two hot water heaters, one for the bath and one for the kitchen.

Back at IH, Mr. Ashiba greeted us warmly and announced that there had just been a cancellation. Bob flushed and was forced to say, "Unfortunately, we don't really know what our plans are right now. Could we let you know first thing in the morning?" Mega-embarrassment! Being "a pest," as my mother-in-law used to say, a burden to someone else, makes Bob a little crazy. Also, some concern about whether we should pack up or not.

Dinner of comfort food, Japanese-style: beer and yakitori. Oh yes, and a vodka for me. The Japanese seem to have traded in those delightful liquor-dispensing-vending machines that lined the streets in 1987 in favour of machines that sell vitamin supplement drinks, cold tea, and hot coffee. Bottle shops seem to have retreated to back lanes or disappeared all together. Cigarette machines selling packs for ¥240 are still everywhere.

THURSDAY, OCTOBER 16

We sat around until the 10 a.m. check-out time, surrounded by packed suitcases, an overnight change at the ready. Then the telephone rang in our room. It was Mr. Horiuchi. All was arranged. We could move in today. I finished the packing while Bob went to a bank machine to extract ¥500,000, about half the amount we had left. The rent was about ¥300,000 a month (a bargain at about $3,500 Canadian) — no key money, no deposit, no agent's fee, no taxes. A total of ¥450,000 (about $5,000) until the end of November.

This was something of a miracle. We can travel. We can leave our things in our own apartment. We can shop and cook, be alone to read and think and work. Everything seemed possible now.

We set out in separate cabs, accompanying our four large pieces of luggage and three small. It appeared excessive, perhaps, but there were books, a computer, printer, keyboard, and of course clothes for two seasons and two large people.

Mr. Horiuchi and Ms. Iino were standing on the curb waiting at 11 a.m. as the cabs pulled up. They both looked pleased with themselves — then alarmed by our baggage until I showed them that almost every piece moved on wheels. Mr. Akasaki, the building manager, a sweet man with no English, mimed his way through the use of all major appliances. I pretended to understand. Then I raised the issue of the six-foot pile of bedding, a looming stack of pillows, blankets, and various crocheted coverlets. All three beds already seemed perfectly equipped.

"Ah," opined Ms. Iino, "winter is coming."

"Ah," I replied, "we're Canadian!" Mr. Akasaki indicated that he would take the surplus away.

For a long while, Mr. Horiuchi sat playing with the television. "My place is not so big as this. Not so big TV either."

I felt an undercurrent of discontent bubbling to the surface of this mid-rank bureaucrat, discontent with his lot in life, a discontent that's usually held in check by political will, national purpose, inertia, fear, or *tatemae*. Perhaps poor housing and the cost of consumer goods, combined with the falling Nikkei index and rising number of government and business scandals, might bring about a much-needed redirection of Japanese fiscal and social policy. People have been expecting this for years, but it hasn't happened. Is this lack of confidence widespread? A sense that shortage and scarcity could return as it did with the "oil shocks" of the 1970s? (Japan is a country without raw materials, its citizens are quick to point out.) One day, soon perhaps, the Japanese may decide that they've made enough sacrifices and begin to demand what the rest of the industrialized world considers its birthright — easier living. What the long-term results and consequences will be, I cannot imagine, but right now, Mr. Horiuchi is jealous of me, my apartment, and my television.

Besides being our moving day, this was also the first day it's legal to use the organs of brain-dead donors for transplants. Here's an example of how slowly Japan confronts change. The debate over such subjects as "When is a patient dead?" and "What will be the result of taking his organs for someone else?" has raged for years, far longer than in other developed nations. The law that finally settled the matter passed in June 1997 and today the first transplant will take place. The length of time taken to make a collective decision is long and torturous. Once made, implementation proceeds at an unbelievably rapid pace. If the Japanese behave according to precedent, they'll soon be world leaders in transplant technology.

In our living room, besides the giant Panasonic TV, there are four tweed-covered armchairs lined up in a row, a lamp, a coffee table, a dinette suite with four chairs, and a prominent wall clock. The place has all the natural charm of a bus station. Timepieces and timers are everywhere — on clothes dryer, rice cooker, stove, and hot water heater. Time reigns. The only natural light comes in at the front and the back of the apartment, yet I'm more pleased with this place than when I first saw it.

"You must have a home ... ah, a *home*warming party," suggested Mr. Horiuchi.

"A *house*warming party?" I replied. "What's a good date for you?"

He and Ms. Iino chattered away and pulled out their electronic notebooks. Thursday, October 23 seemed to suit everyone.

"What time does one usually have parties like this in Tokyo?" I asked. "Around seven."

"Fine," I said. "Seven it is." What had I got myself into?

Later I called Bruce Barnett for advice.

"Did he say he'd bring all the food?" he asked.

"No. There was no mention of food."

Bruce told me that sometimes the guests look after this. I told Bruce that I'd just finished *The Makioka Sisters* and when they had parties they were always catered and so perhaps this was the route to go.

"I have local friends I turn to in situations like this," Bruce said. "I'll ask them."

Naturally, I invited Bruce to join us. Mr. Horiuchi also suggested inviting Mr. Honda. "He has been very worried about your accommodations as well," he said.

"Fine idea," I replied. Then I looked over at Bob, who appeared ready to flip out — his eyes wide, trying to get my attention, to stop what he clearly saw as madness. He didn't know that this party was not my idea but Mr. Horiuchi's and besides, as I told him later, "It'll be fun."

Mr. Akasaki brought us back to the task at hand with a huge grey three-ring tabbed binder, with sections for each major appliance, including the phone, the instructions in English or a version thereof. We were cautioned several times about the importance of the gas alarm, about making sure the fan in the kitchen was on whenever I cooked. Fear of fire is still strong, a holdover from the Edo days of paper and wood.

When everyone cleared out, I unpacked the clothes while Bob set up the office. There's a proper desk and lamp, a good chair, sofa, and bookcases. When the time came to plug in the Okipage 4W — new but much knocked about in a suitcase — I said a silent prayer to Caxton, the god of Printers. Eureka, it worked!

At about three, I went to forage for groceries and cleaning things. Mr. Akasaki had marked a rather inadequate map where he said? (gestured?) I could find a Green Market for necessities. These would have to include plenty of cleaning equipment (there was none) because, besides being larger and more loveable than I first thought, the apartment was also dirtier, with long black hairs dangling from the bathtub plug and sticky things on the counters and table top. I recalled my mother's golden rule for moving: set the kitchen up first, and everything else will fall into place.

I returned about two hours later, exhausted, having walked all the way to Ichigaya without finding the Green Market or anything in the supermarket family. But I did double back to a corner store and returned with plastic bags full of stuff. And guess where one buys canned tuna, oil, vinegar, and soy sauce? The sake shop! With what I bought I was able to make a great salad of lettuce, tomato, cucumber, celery, onions, and Mr. Chief's bottled dressing. For dessert, cookies and Red Rose tea, schlepped all the way from Toronto. Almost tea to China, but not quite.

It was great being a housewife in Japan. I have to admit that being domestic is a big part of my life. I love playing house, which is often the way I still feel, as if I'm playing, as if the real house is one where I'm still a child and someone else has all the responsibilities.

I'm especially glad to leave IH, as comfortable as it was in many ways. There were too many personalities; I lack the ability to ignore them. There was the middle-aged woman in the long denim skirt and short hair who breakfasted alone, reading the paper or staring into the garden. Later in the morning she'd move into her library carrel and work at her laptop until dinnertime, when she'd walk alone down the hill. What was she writing? Was she pleased to be where she was? Was this the life she'd imagined for herself? Or was she wretched and desperate to talk to someone, aware for the hundredth time that this was all she could expect, all she'd ever wanted but it wasn't enough and now it was too late?

There was the elderly lady in the kimono who entered the breakfast room each morning and said, "*Ohayo gozaimasu*" ("Good morning") to no one in particular, a noblesse oblige one had to admire. She was later joined at her table by a middle-aged woman — her daughter? — who was badly crippled and just managed, walking at a great tilt and with tremendous will, to navigate the long hallway, always smiling.

And the jolly professor (retired) from Berkeley who engaged passing strangers in animated conversation, involving them in the latest discovery or theory connected with his subject area, religion in Japan, particularly the Soga period (538–645). His wife was almost frozen with what seemed to be advanced Parkinson's. He tried overpowering her infirmity with his ebullience, his unquenchable search for data, and his confidence. He looked like a former military man of the Second World War generation. He spoke rapid-fire Japanese and often handed people he'd just met Xeroxed copies of articles he'd "discovered" in the IH library. On our last day they had breakfast with a newly arrived British couple. I heard the professor's voice rise above the others: "Oh no, she's my second wife. My first wife was born in Japan. She wasn't Japanese but she was born here. In fact, she died here." Turning to his rigid second wife, he asked, "How long ago was it we met? Ten years?" She turned her liquid blue eyes in his direction but did not speak.

They were joined by a large, bejewelled, jangling woman the professor introduced to his guests as Mrs. Richard Storry. She was the widow of the British historian who wrote *A History of Modern Japan*, often the first book on Japan read by interested outsiders of my generation.

As well, there were three American gay men, a couple and a third chap, as I saw it, artists here to work with some Japanese. They were classically built, small, compact models who toured the garden after each breakfast. I'll miss that garden but am glad to be free from scrutinizing others and having them scrutinize me. When I travel I hate to meet people I can't leave if I want to.

I can imagine myself as that solitary scholar at her corner table, but with Bob as my travel partner I'm forced to think harder and see more clearly than I possibly could on my own. Still, I do need a room of my own, even if it's the kitchen (apologies to V. Woolf). Before bed, I unrolled our newly acquired mountain scroll and hung it on the same nail that holds the clock. Damned ingenious, I say, since it is forbidden to make more holes.

FRIDAY, OCTOBER 17

I feel as though this trip is just beginning. It isn't a vacation; it's a time to live in Tokyo, exactly what I wanted. I went to sleep last night with my clothes hanging on a rack on the balcony. My clothes, my balcony. The first phone call came from Bruce, giving me a list of upcoming events connected with the Canadian embassy. (Now we can make plans.) One scheduled pianist was described as "a young André Gagnon." I asked Bruce why he thought that so many Japanese liked this style of romantic music.

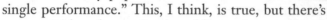

"Because it's relaxing, I suppose," he replied. Then he went on, "In a country of about 130 million, you don't have to be really popular to sell out a single performance." This, I think, is true, but there's more to it than that: crying in public can be considered a group activity — shared sentimentality. The fact that each person in a two-thousand-seat hall might be crying for a different reason matters little.

Bob worked on one of his speeches for Meiji University, and I wrote and read all morning. Around noon we headed for a restaurant lunch after a second unsuccessful attempt to find this mysterious Green Market. We did wander a subway stop away to a grocery shop called Marucho and tried to decipher the labels. That night, when I tried to cook a chicken stir fry, I found that the "oil" I bought was really cooking sherry. Bob suggested that I might take the shopping book on my next outing. It's called *Gaijin Guide: Practical Help for Everyday Life in Japan* by Janet Ashby, and gives useful translations of commonplace labels. As for the rice, I confess that the automatic rice cooker is cleverer than I am. It's an early model and looks like a Studebaker with gleaming chrome teeth and incomprehensible instructions. I placed it under the sink and will stick with the stove-top method.

Ages ago, or so it seems, when Meiji University mentioned the possibility of a place in Kamakura, I asked, "But what if the plumbing breaks down or the drains clog?" What indeed. It happened here, with the tub. When I pulled the plug, the water backed up the floor drain and covered the tile with a thick, black gunge that appeared to contain only hair, fuzz, and dirty water. I thought I'd done something wrong, but Bob had the same experience.

We used every towel in the place before we conducted our own scientific experiment: we filled the tub with a half inch of clean water, then pulled the plug. Whammy! The drain beside the tub began to gurgle and water bubbled out. It's Friday and nothing can be done until Monday. Do I still want my own place? Do I wonder how I'll cope with domestic crises? Yes and yes.

SATURDAY, OCTOBER 18

Bruce came to our apartment at about 10 a.m. and was less than impressed. I wish he'd been with us when we'd seen the three or four "mansions" before this one. He was to join us for everyone's first trip to the Edo-Tokyo Museum, which opened in 1993. Bruce had arranged a sort of VIP visit — free admission and a meeting with Ms. Yoshiko Inami, the director for public relations. Here was a woman, high enough in the hierarchy to rate her own corner office, who began by asking us, through Bruce who translated, if we knew what Edo was. Then she read from notes, repeating history basics one finds in every guidebook. Despite this, she seemed bright and involved. I would have liked to talk with her, but that was impossible. The best part of our encounter was a gift of a large and detailed book on the museum, its collection and displays.

Since both Bob and I prefer to explore a new place on our own, we managed to convince Bruce, after the mandatory tea and questions, that he should tell this fine person that we could manage on our own. We left only after assuring her that if we did have any questions, problems, etc., we would get back to her.

The museum was impressive beyond imagining, constructed so that anyone could understand it on some level: the latest whiz-bang display techniques would hold the attention of the Japanese version of the MTV generation, but the material was serious enough to make their grandparents nostalgic. This was museum as theme park, and it worked. To approach the exhibits, we walked across an almost life-size reproduction of Nihonbashi, the Edo-period bridge that was the centre of the old city, the arch immortalized in so many woodblock prints, generally shown covered in parasols and rickshaws. (Edo is Bob's favourite period.)

I was crazy about the Meiji and Taisho exhibits, especially actual objects such the "Western-inflaenicd home," as it stated in the catalogue. There were also marvellous scaled-down reconstructions of places I'd been reading about — the Ginza Bricktown and the Rokumeikan, the turn-of-the-century ballroom built to entertain Westerners. It was recessed into the floor, and every forty minutes, as the cover slid off, toy models of Japanese ladies in bustles and gents in tails stepped down from carriages and joined toy foreigners in a waltz around the room.

Another charming display was a tribute to the ukiyo-e artist Ando Hiroshige (1797-1858), whose two-hundredth birthday is this year. Born in Edo, he did a series of prints called *Hundred Views of Edo*. His more famous work, *Fifty-three Stages of the Tokaido*, depicts travellers at each of the traditional stops between Edo and Kyoto. Little is known about his personal life other than that he was the son of a fireman and lived in the Low City, the old downtown.

At one point in our tour we heard, "Bob Fulford?" (Is this becoming a pattern?) It was Liz Bradley of the Hummingbird Centre and her husband, Keith, who was on the arts faculty of York University. They're spending two weeks here, thanks to the Japan Foundation. They'd been on the run from nine in the morning until nine at night for days and looked as if they could use some down time. It was their first trip to Japan and their hosts seemed determined to show them one high-tech theatrical venue after another, including Opera City, where they'd attended the opening performance in a fifty-four-storey shrine to culture and commerce, the hope being that Liz will book something Japanese into the Hummingbird.

After lunch Bruce left, "museumed out," and Bob and I moved on to the section covering the Meiji Restoration (1868) to the Tokyo Olympics (1964). I love the speed with which a population that had been more or less isolated for 250 years came overnight to build Western buildings, trains, cinemas, and turn themselves into Western sophisticates — Gibson girls and swells. (The rallying cry of that era was *wakon yosai*, "Japanese spirit, Western technology.") There were coins melted together by fires after the Kanto earthquake of 1923. But about the Second World War, the Pacific War, there was still a reluctance to come to terms with certain facts. American bombers, it seems, appeared suddenly overhead and set Tokyo on fire. What about Pearl Harbor? Or the Philippines? Barely a mention.

Dinner at home, making do, using oil from a can of tuna and two tomatoes to make a passable pasta and salad. Vegetables here taste fresher. Japanese women consumers demand high standards. I watch them squeezing, sniffing, selecting in stores. Tomorrow I set out for another local supermarket, highly recommended.

About our drain: I decided that it was possible that our building engineer, Mr. Akasaki, might work on the weekend. Sure enough he did, clad in weekend leisure-wear that included a towel wrapped around his neck like a sign of his guild. Despite my best efforts at communication, he couldn't understand my note or my repetition of "*furo*," bathtub. (I was told later that I should have used the honorific, "*o-furo*." Honourable tub?) He did find an English-speaking office worker and within fifteen minutes the drain issue was resolved. I will end Saturday night with a long shower, and look forward to a soak in our *o-furo* without fear of flooding.

SUNDAY, OCTOBER 19

A quiet Sunday in Tokyo. Called Keith and Liz Bradley and suggested that they might want to escape to a shrine sale. I wanted to introduce two first-timers to a place that had given me so much pleasure. They seemed to like the idea. Unfortunately we stopped to have the broken frames of Bob's glasses repaired at a shop near the subway exit and arrived a little late.

"Five minutes," the nice young clerk in the glasses shop had said.

Five turned into fifteen. There were six staff and the two of us in the shop. Several clerks seemed to be running around checking figures in a large blue book. "They can't decide how much to charge you," I suggested to Bob. We spent the time playing with the in-house TV monitor which let you see how your new specs looked on camera. "Just five more minutes," the bespectacled clerk said. We decided to leave the glasses behind, marking as carefully as we could the way back, and arrived fifteen minutes late at the Hanazono shrine.

The Bradleys were already there. We wandered around for about an hour. Picked up a Japanese movie poster for Norman Jewison's *In the Heat of the Night*, the perfect gift for our friend, Jack Batten, who's researching a book on the director. Other gifts, for us or friends: a wicker basket, a lacquer bowl, a lovely decorated metal scroll carrier. This I will keep.

After lunch at Isetan department store, we bid goodbye to our fellow Canadians and headed for the food hall to stock up on essentials, or should I say, exotics? — milk and salt, pasta, pesto and olive oil — all contained within the Foreign Section. Miraculously, we retraced our steps to pick up Bob's glasses. "How much will that be?" Bob asked.

"Free," he answered. "No charge."

Bob said thank-you and we left. Was it because the repair took longer than estimated? Or were they being kind to *gaijin*? Before dinner we wandered over to our neighbour, the towering New Otani Hotel — 2,100 rooms, a world unto itself. There I found a post office and two helpful women who broke the No Mail On Sunday rule for me. Perhaps it was national Be Kind to Foreigners Day. But then that's most every day.

MONDAY, OCTOBER 20

Spent the morning making phone calls with only modest success. Left messages for Tomoko Shimizu, known as Illya, a woman in public relations at the Canadian embassy, and spoke briefly to Kanako Hayashi of the Kawakita Memorial Film Institute, another of James Quandt's contacts. She's wildly busy at the moment, viewing various submissions to the Tokyo Film Festival. Shohei Imamura, the director whose work will be featured in a Cinematheque retrospective this month, is apparently in Hiroshima shooting what he calls his last film. Bob thought he might interview him. She suggested that this could be arranged through Ms. Suzuki of the Japan Foundation. She left me with the impression that she was rather astounded that we were so much on our own, that this was unusual for the Japan Foundation. Perhaps we are something of an experiment.

Also called Mr. Horiuchi to confirm Thursday's party.

"Mr. Horiuchi," I said. (We were not yet on a first name basis.) "This is Geraldine Sherman calling. From Canada," thinking that this would be enough information to jog his memory after all we'd been through. And it had only been a few days since our last meeting.

There was a pause. "Oh, wife of Mr. Robert Fulford?" Ah, yes.

"Yes." Properly submissive.

"And how's your apartment? Is it all right?"

"It's better than all right. It's great!" No point carping over a clogged drain. Wanted to show him we were suitably grateful, not spoiled *gaijin*.

"I'm just calling to confirm our plans for the housewarming party this Thursday."

"Ah, yes. Housewarming."

"Well, I have to confess, Mr. Horiuchi, that I have no idea what I'm supposed to do."

He said that he would take care of inviting Mr. Honda, that they would "bring some pizzas and beverages. And I will ask my wife to bake a cake." I'm ashamed to confess that I did not say, "What a good idea. And please bring her as well." I felt that if Mr. Horiuchi wanted his wife to come, he would bring her.

"Sounds great," I replied. "I'll get some snacks and some drinks too." (Surely even here, beer and sake don't mix with cake?) "And could I ask one more favour? We need to fill out some forms for the Tokyo Film Festival. Ms. Suzuki has them. Would you mind getting them from her and bringing them along?" (We are without a crucial fax machine.)

"So you want to invite Ms. Suzuki?" (Had I committed some social gaff here?)

"Yes, of course. Great idea."

And so now we have Bruce, Ms. Iino, Messrs. Horiuchi and Honda, Ms. Suzuki, Bob, and me, slightly crowded in our current circumstance but better too many than too few, an entertainment rule that must apply on this side of the Pacific as well.

At 11:30 a.m. we went to Asakusa, as terrific as I remembered. It's not really old, as in centuries, but old by Tokyo standards — a few buildings that survived the fire bombs and some that went up shortly after the war. To my eyes, little had changed in ten years. There were still rows of boisterous vendors of religious paraphernalia, Miss Kitty collectibles, shoes, souvenirs, and food everywhere. Asakusa is said to be the best place to buy rice crackers, so we bought lots for the party.

There was a large display of chrysanthemums, some standing as tall as five feet, some twisted like bonsai trees, extended so far forward they seemed about to topple. Went to Matsuya department store near the Kannon, to their stationery department — every store seems to have its stationery department on the seventh floor. We were looking for computer paper to fit our printer. Everything was methodically organized by size — binders, dividers, folders, but with sizes that didn't quite fit our machine. We bought the closest match and it worked.

Bob printed out his Meiji talk for tomorrow and rehearsed in front of me. Quite impressive, although God knows who will be in the audience and what level of comprehension to expect. I left Bob and headed into our neighbourhood, pulling my small suitcase on wheels loaded with laundry and dry cleaning. The woman in the store apologized for her English, which was serviceable, and I for my non-existent Japanese, and then we exchanged cards — I wanted to be able to find my way back. Somehow I managed to prepay the bill — ¥6,620 (about $75).

"You teacher?" the woman behind the counter asked when she heard that we were staying at Sophia. I don't know why I didn't lie, to accommodate her idea of me. One of the potential joys of travelling must be to take on a new persona. Instead I tried to explain, "Sort of. Well, really my husband ... " and made a hand gesture that in the West means *comme ci, comme ça*, but in Japan might well mean, "I want to sleep with your father." The perils of cross-cultural communication.

With my empty suitcase thumping behind me, I walked to Yotsuya-sanchome subway station. Although Shinjuku-dori is an eight-lane thoroughfare I had the feeling that I was strolling through a real neighbourhood. Lots of moms on bikes, and old men with canes. Children on tricycles zipped along unsupervised. Off on the side streets smaller shops sold food, drink, and a bit of everything else. I returned home a cultural warrior with booty that included Vittel and Perrier.

TUESDAY, OCTOBER 21

Speech day, so a slower start than usual, made slower by another clog — this time the toilet. Despite tons of boiling water it refused to resuscitate itself. On my trek yesterday I spotted a hardware store and intended to stop there on our way home. This problem I plan to solve on my own!

While waiting to leave the apartment I wrote postcards and

unpacked our first full mailbox. (Our names appear on the box as "Robert Fulfordo and Geraldne Sherman," while our door reads "ROBERT FULFORD" with "and Geradine Sherman" in small type underneath.) Among the letters was one from Jack Batten and one from Anna Porter, as well as two invitations to embassy events: one from Joseph and Mrs. Caron inviting us to a buffet supper, Monday, October 27 from 1900 to 2130 at their home in Roppongi. This was expected. What was not was the list of honoured guests: "Canadian authors Ms. Joy Kogawa, and Ms. Geraldine Sherman, and Mr. Robert Fulford." Journalist, okay. Writer, perhaps. But author? I thought that I should take advantage of distance from home to upgrade my station a little, but here someone had done it for me. Forget about the mailbox and the front door. For one glorious night I shall be "an author." (Should I use the occasion to complain about exhausting book tours?)

The second invitation was also amusing: "a fairwell [sic] soiree" for eight German-language broadcasters who were guests of the Japan Foundation and were now heading home. The party is being held across the street in the New Otani. There will no doubt be food and drink aplenty, but conversation? Forget about it! We RSVP'ed, with regrets.

We set out for Meiji with plenty of time — Bob was a tad nervous. Stopped at a subway vendor and picked up two sandwiches to eat at the university. We chose from a typical selection — strawberry sandwiches with whipped cream, cold noodles on rolls, and cold wieners with bands of orange (mustard?). Bob selected ham and egg on pillow bread (crusts removed); for me, basic fried cutlet with mayo.

Bob was to meet Professor Bowers, who teaches something called Speech Communication, so they could try to access our e-mail and transmit Bob's column, his first from Japan. We arrived at noon, two hours before the lecture, but Bowers was late. We huddled in Professor Arai's office, choking down lunch.

Arai and Bowers appeared, contrite. Arai immediately put on his beret and left the building. Since he doesn't speak English and seems most interested in his foreign trophy collection, this was okay. Bob and Bowers disappeared into another room and I read a novel by Haruki Murakami, *A Wild Sheep Chase*, more magic realism than I normally can tolerate; but I'm coming to think that the "authentic" Japan of the late 1990s might actually resemble the bizarre fictional worlds of Murakami and Banana Yoshimoto.

About an hour and forty-five minutes later, minutes before the lecture was to begin, I took some photographs of the Meiji offices, and of Bob and Bowers sweating over antique computers. When that was done, or done as much as it was possible to do, Mr. Egawa appeared to escort us to Bob's lecture. Bowers apologized that he had two meetings and regretted that he was "not able to watch" Bob's presentation.

We went next door, past the most animated students I'd seen at Meiji, all gathered in the lobby looking through travel brochures at tables set up by various agencies. They were planning Christmas holiday trips to Hawaii. Up an elevator to a grey classroom where about fifteen students were waiting — all Japanese except for a York University student who was remarkable in that he was the only one who took notes. About five more students eventually joined the lecture in progress, anywhere from thirty minutes to an hour after it had begun.

Professor Egawa gave a feeble, poorly prepared introduction to Bob and then left the room. *He left the room!* I couldn't believe it. There was no one from the faculty present. Not one. But what a show they missed! Bob abandoned his chair behind the desk, held his notes in one hand, and gave a highly animated performance. While comparing Canadian and Japanese newspapers, using lots of topical examples, he moved across the floor, emphasizing his points with his unencumbered hand. It was the closest thing to a song and dance act I've seen a teacher give, although he looked more like Mohammed Ali than Fred Astaire as he swooped and dodged to amuse the onlookers.

I wish Bob's greatest fans had been there to enjoy it with me — Julian Porter, John Fraser, Jack Batten, and John Macfarlane. Or that someone had videotaped it. I'll always remember Bob in front of this audience, most of whom looked as if they'd been coerced. Several slept. Since the subject was a comparison between Canadian and Japanese journalism, you'd think they might have been alert: I had understood that they were, after all, journalism students. I'm not an uncritical observer of my husband's performances, but this was truly spectacular.

Bob asked for questions after the speech. First question: Have you ever been censored? The answer was funny and included the time Bob, the young sports writer, wrote that athletes who didn't smoke would perform better: his editor asked the advertising department if this might create a problem! Second question: What did you think of the coverage of Princess Diana's death? A savvy answer here too.

When it was almost over I stood at the back of the room and took a few photos. I had to turn away, misty-eyed — I had that Chief Dan George feeling. "My heart soars like an eagle."

Then, as if he'd heard a whistle blow, Mr. Egawa reappeared in the company of a middle-aged woman. He thanked Bob for what he was sure was an informative talk, introduced us to Masako Iino, a professor at Tsuda Women's College and head of the Japanese Association for Canadian Studies, and escorted us back to his office. She was charming and talked a bit about the upcoming conference where there would be professors specializing in Canadian studies from China, Thailand, Indonesia, India, and of course, Japan. A call for papers went out on the Internet and there were about forty replies; fifteen were selected. As usual, funding from some of the poorer countries is a problem.

I wasn't quite sure what she was doing there or why she hadn't attended the lecture, but her presence somewhat made up for the social ineptitude of the people from Meiji. (What else would you call no lunch, no dinner, no invitation of any kind?) She'd recently spent a year in North America, including some time in Canada where she'd met Jack Granatstein and Ramsay Cook, among others. She's the author of a recent book on Canada and Japan that's, sadly, available only in Japanese. She'd come all the way from Kamakura to meet us.

Mrs. Iino did her graduate work in American history in the United States and was away for a year at that time also, travelling and studying. She took her young daughter with her but left her husband behind. North American friends told her they envied the stability of the social codes of Japan; they felt that they were making it up as they went along and longed for structure, especially in the face of increased multiculturalism and a shaky value system. She might have agreed with them until she came home and received a heavy dose of social codes. As Japanese normally do, she visited her neighbours on her return, bringing each of them a small gift. She said that she was shocked by the comments of one female neighbour after another: they all told her how hard her absence had been on her husband, having no one to look after him for so long. "Not a single person said that it might have been hard on me, working and travelling, with my daughter to look after. That's 'the code' all right."

Japanese women are demanding greater control over their lives, she said, and this has affected her exclusively female college in a negative way: the brightest girls now want to go to a co-ed university and have a chance at challenging work. She said that commuting time from her home to the college was two and a half hours. This she does three times a week, and some weekends. (And of course two and a half hours for the return trip.) Her husband also travels a great distance.

"If I get on the train by 6 a.m.," she explained, "I can usually get a seat."

"That gives you time to read?" Bob asked innocently.

"Well," she confessed, "I mostly sleep." And no wonder. She gets home at 9 or 10 p.m. The next time I hear someone complain about a twenty-minute bus ride to work, or even forty minutes, I hope I'll remember Mrs. Iino — not complaining, merely explaining. Part of the reason for her tolerance must be that her house is ten seconds from the beach. And who, closer to Tokyo, could afford a house at all? She offered to take us for tea, and when we declined, she invited us to come to Kamakura to see her.

Returning from Meiji on the subway, I watched my groggy fellow passengers, imprisoned in the Land of the Sleep Deprived. Men and women who would never dream of saying, "Hello, nice day," doze side by side, the head of one banging against another's shoulder with complete indifference. Beside me a young man nodded, his head on his chest. In his lap he carried a towel that read, "Let Me Sleep." How can decisions be made and people be productive when so many are sleepwalking? Could this condition account for the necessity for group activity and consensus? What if no one is sufficiently awake to take full responsibility? For women, the idea of avoiding an intolerable commute and staying home in a little apartment with one or two babies must seem comparatively attractive. My perspective appears to be shifting. Situation ethics, I think it's called.

I find Japanese women fascinating to observe on subways, in stores, and on the street. More of the older ones are abandoning the heavy dyed-black helmets they wore ten years ago, and are either turning grey — or going orange. Among the young, I've observed one fashion innovation: perfectly hideous ankle socks worn by schoolgirls.

They are long enough to cover the knee but so loose that they fall down the leg and bunch up at the ankle. Advantage? Girls with fat ankles look like everyone else. Pregnant women dress mostly like school girls, minus the gross ankle socks. They wear one-piece navy tunics, white blouses, flat shoes, something like Western expectant mothers of the 1950s. Like schoolgirls they are in transition and in training and we are to see them that way. No subway journey is ever a waste.

We remembered to stop for a toilet plunger. To do this, I'd brought a Japanese-English dictionary. When we found the hardware store I prayed that we would spot a plunger, point to it, and deal done. But no, none could be found, high or low. I looked up the correct word and pointed it out to a clerk in a smock, who said, in a voice loud for one her size, "For toilet?"

"Yes," I whispered. "For toilet."

Then she beetled out the back door, down a laneway to what must be an adjacent storage area, and returned with a standard black plunger, no turquoise or pink, but industrial strength and just fine.

To celebrate Bob's speech and our new purchase, we had one of the best meals so far this trip. It was in a Korean barbecue not far from the hardware store. The place was filled with men, two or three at a table, with only two other women — one in the company of a man, the other a sad Edward Hopper type, drinking and eating alone in a corner. To me, the men all looked like central-casting yakuza; Bob thought they were accountants. Perhaps these distinctions have blurred and now there are only corrupt businessmen everywhere. Two chaps finished off a half bottle of J&B and several beers; three other guys in my line of vision polished off a large 26-ounce bottle of Scotch. One by one, as the evening progressed, off came the coats and on went bibs so they wouldn't get dirty as they ate round after round of meat, vegetables, and seafood, grilling it at their tables and filling each other's plates as if this were a church picnic.

I had two beers myself as we barbecued a vegetable platter that included squash, okra, mushrooms, onions, sweet potato, and green pepper. The beef was Kobe, heavily marbleized and delicious. There was also a tinfoil container filled with garlic buds and butter that sat cooking on its own. The staff clearly thought we didn't know what to do. Each waiter who passed by turned the flame under the charcoal either up or down. Finally, one English-speaking server came over and started to cook for us until we assured her we wouldn't set the place on fire.

At the end of the meal, a shy girl asked if we would like some ice cream. "Oh no," I answered. "We couldn't possibly." Then the English-speaker on staff walked by and added, "It comes with."

"Ah," we said, in unison. "In that case ... " I ordered wimpy vanilla but Bob had green tea. He professed to love it.

While we ate dinner I asked Bob how he'd been able to give so much of himself in that afternoon's lecture, staring out at a sparsely filled room. "I was speaking to you," he answered, and I teared up again.

On the way home on the Sophia campus, on an outdoor bulletin board we pass each day, a poster showed seven smiling middle-aged guys, naked from the waist up, their torsos and arms covered in writhing tattoos. Underneath, in English, it said, "Seven Ex-Yakuzas Tell My Boss Is Jesus — English translation. Thursday, October 23 at 5:30 p.m. Room 507." (This was one of the fringe benefits of living on the Japanese campus of a Catholic university founded in memory of the Portuguese Jesuit missionary of the sixteenth century, St. Francis Xavier — yakuza and salvation.)

Lying in bed before falling asleep I thought about Masako Iino and "codes." We have them too, of course. They may not be universally followed, since we are such a large receiving country for immigrants from all over the world, but many codes are shared by a majority of people. One I've never seen broken demands that the host attend the lecture of a guest he's invited to speak. I can't imagine a Canadian professor introducing a visiting lecturer and then leaving the room.

The plunger, an under-appreciated tool, worked like a charm.

WEDNESDAY, OCTOBER 22

Spent the morning making calls because we have not figured out how to make the answering machine work. First, Illya Shimizu at the Canadian embassy, someone Katherine Ashenburg said we must look up. She invited me to lunch on Friday, and both of us to come to her home in Yokohama, with a visit thrown in to Yokohama's Chinatown, a tourist attraction that guidebooks say "rivals Disneyland." This would be followed by a tea ceremony with her mother who "teaches tea," as they say, and end with "a typical home-cooked Japanese dinner."

She asked rather nervously, "Do you like Japanese food?" (I don't remember ever having been asked this before.)

"Of course," I replied. "We love it." (Most of it anyway.)

She said that she'd also invited Stephane Jobin from the embassy so that he could drive us. Apparently tea is taught by Illya's mother on Wednesdays and Fridays only. "Would Wednesday, November 5, be all right with you?" she asked. "That's the first day Stephane is available." We would leave at three in the afternoon and arrive in Yokohama about forty minutes later. By train it's an hour and forty minutes. The conversation automatically turned to commuting.

"It's not so much the distance or the time," Illya explained. "It's that I can never get a seat and sometimes it's so crowded I can't breathe."

We agreed to go with Stephane on the fifth.

I spoke with Bruce, who said that he was mailing us a list of the guests who were coming to the party being held for us at the Carons. He reported that he's thinking of cooperating with Sophia to set up a journalist-in-residence program. (I guess he didn't think our accommodation was that bad after all.) To that end he has added Professor Kimitada Miwa of Sophia to the guest list. As well, he promised to bring a bottle of whisky to our housewarming. That will most certainly appeal to Japanese guests. Or I think it will.

Then, Joseph Caron called to apologize to Bob for not having been in touch sooner but with no ambassador in place, so busy, etc., etc. He also wanted to warn Bob that he would be asked to say a few words at the reception for us — a few words on his behalf and mine. (Ms. Kogawa would speak for herself.)

"Have you got your e-mail up and running?" he asked. Bob gave him the condensed version of our troubles, ending with the hope that when Professor Bowers comes here on Friday we would be connected. "Amazingly," Bob remarked, "Japan is light years behind North America where this sort of technology is concerned."

"Absolutely right," Caron agreed. He knew several large cultural and philanthropic organizations that use no e-mail at all. He said, "It's not in the Japanese nature to use e-mail." I'm not sure what he meant by that: Is it too instantaneous? Too demanding of the individual? Faxes arrive at a central location in an office whereas e-mail appears on the screen of a single person. Is this the explanation?

Then, once again, after ten years, we were on the hunt for ukiyo-e woodblock prints, only now we know that they are pronounced "ukiyo-ay," as in "way." We were partially rewarded this time. On the sixth floor of the Ginza Tokai bank building, a jewel of a gallery was celebrating Hiroshige's two-hundredth birthday. The bank owns many editions of his prints, including his famous *Hundred Views of Edo*, a faintly satirical, urban version of various Views of Mount Fuji, including Hokusai's *Thirty-Six*. To celebrate the bicentennial, the bank commissioned a talented photographer, Narumi Yasuda, to revisit the same sites as Hiroshige, and photograph them from similar vantage points, in the same season, and at the same time of day. They hung the originals and the recent versions together, with text in Japanese and English, explaining what it was that Hiroshige had depicted and Yasuda had photographed. In many ways it's a lament for the past. It's also a tribute to both artists, and to the bank for such an imaginative celebration.

There are some particularly poignant examples of change. One Hiroshige print shows logs, covered in snow; now, probably for environmental reasons, it never snows in that part of Tokyo. Yasuda had to settle for a dusting on a few spindly branches. The entire show, about thirty prints and photos, was displayed in a small, circular room, its surfaces expanded by a Plexiglas circle in the middle. To keep us from coming too close to the prints, a thick white rope was laid on the floor about eighteen inches from the wall, the space between rope and wall covered in small white stones like a Zen garden. Ultimate tact.

A kind supernumerary set up a ten-minute English-language video for us in a glassed-in viewing room. It recounted the few known facts about Hiroshige's life, his art, and printmaking in general. (I learned that one set of prints can be so different from another that entire images can disappear — one impression will include a mountain, another won't.) On our way out we were given little Hiroshige hand towels as *presentos*. A totally satisfying museum experience.

Stopped for lunch next to a cooking school, Toyo Recipe, housed in a gleaming white multi-storey building with potted herbs and giant video screens playing loops of greenery of unknown origin in their outdoor public foyer. Walked on and stopped for tea and cake, which arrived in a tinfoil wrapper covered in waxed paper. Two coffees, two pieces of cake, ¥2,400. A silly waste of money, but we ate in a lovely room overlooking a florist's window filled with this month's favourite plant, the potted orchid.

Picked up our search for the second gallery on our list, the Riccar, mentioned in all my books as home to a large, permanent ukiyo-e collection. It was said to be near a railway track, very close to Ginza, a snap. Rule no. 1: when looking at a map do not say, "It's got to be right around here." This is the sort of touristic hubris that leads to disappointment. We stopped first at a police box and asked a bilingual policewoman who nodded sagely at the bilingual reference in my handy-dandy *Tokyo Atlas* and replied, "Up this road, two lights, opposite the school on your right."

It's true we did get slightly side-tracked by a Sakura Bank machine whose code Bob eventually cracked, but then we picked up the trail. We strolled through a lovely area of small, private galleries and stumbled on a George Segal exhibit. Surprising new pieces — soft body parts rather than the larger, more familiar plaster dioramas; a gentle hand resting on a stomach, a face in a door. It was timed to coincide with Segal's arrival in town to pick up an international art prize.

Before leaving this gallery, I took out my trusty atlas once again, pointed to the Riccar Gallery on the map, and asked the assistant where it was. She pointed up the road and indicated a left turn. We did as she suggested. No gallery. Then we asked a well-dressed woman on the street, who asked a local shopkeeper watering her outdoor plants; she informed us that the gallery was in the next building, just around the corner. She happened to be going that way and invited us to join her. We did. She stopped and pointed. "Here," she said. "Arigato," we said, and went inside.

It was dark. An ancient person manned the reception desk. I pointed again to the map. "Here?"

"Ah," he said, and reached into a drawer. He pulled out an envelope, handed it to us, and grinned. The Riccar Art Museum, renamed Hiraki Ukiyo-e Museum, had moved to Yokohama, in March 1993, four-and-a-half years ago. Should we retrace our steps, stopping to deliver the news to everyone we'd met? We didn't. Instead, we had a lovely time strolling around this area, new to us, proving once again that in Tokyo one is never lost but always on a magical mystery tour. Also tried to find the entrance to the Yamanote line for a circle trip around Tokyo. No luck. Next time I'll swallow my pride and call Teletourist (English) for instructions.

THURSDAY, OCTOBER 23

Every morning, starting at about six, a high-pitched hooting noise like the sound of a castrated crow comes into our bedroom from the parking lot of the New Otani hotel. Dozens of gigantic tour buses pull in to pick up passengers. Out of each empty bus jumps a young woman, costumed in pleated skirt and cute bonnet. She runs behind the bus, guiding it into an empty parking slot using incessant, high-pitched shrieks that grow sharper as the bus manoeuvres into place. Since the huge parking lot is entirely vacant except for other waiting buses, the only clear and present danger is that the hostess will fall under the bus.

In the evening there's another intriguing show, this time on television. We don't have cable and therefore receive only the basic eight channels, none in English. Watching is a rewarding experience even if it leaves an incomplete and perhaps inaccurate impression of Japanese broadcasting. Nevertheless, as a careful student of TV images, I have drawn the following conclusions:

1. There must be many illiterate Japanese, or many foreigners learning Japanese as a second language, because there's one channel that devotes much of its prime time to Japanese language lessons. This could also mean that Japanese is so hard one spends a lifetime learning it.

2. Many Japanese are deaf or otherwise physically impaired. One channel spends many hours a night teaching sign language. It also features the latest equipment for the disabled. Since Japan has often been criticized for insensitive treatment of non-perfect people, this strikes me as extremely odd.

3. Japan is a nation of foodies to an extent we in the West cannot imagine (and I include the French in this generalization). During prime time, when women must be home alone while their salarymen husbands are drinking with cronies, three channels broadcast cooking shows — with a difference. They regularly begin with a group of friends sitting around eating, making contented noises — including slurping, which is de rigeur, especially in the case of soups, tea, etc. Because raw seafood and fresh vegetables dominate gourmet meals, chefs are judged as much by the quality of their ingredients as their cooking skills. Cooking shows become shopping, travelling, and myth-building shows. Guided by an elderly country person, we search for the perfect rice flour, the silkiest tofu, the freshest seabream, the purest sake.

4. Only on news and serious panel shows do performers look directly into the camera. Everyone else speaks to an unseen, unheard interviewer off-screen. Where emotions, not facts, are involved, eye contact with the viewer barely exists.

5. Documentaries are more highly produced than on North American television. While someone is being interviewed, we're given visual guides to what's being discussed — if it's about an old-style comic, we see a circus clown; if it's about the Pacific War, we see planes bombing Tokyo.

6. While there are more single news readers than there were ten years ago, the stuffier shows have retained two people — a man who reads and a woman who sits beside him, nods, and says, "Hai!" or "Ah so?" each time he makes a point. This reflects a conversational convention — it's okay, even mandatory to interrupt, because it indicates that the listener understands.

7. Crazy antics shows continue to prove a single point: people will do anything on television. No costume is too silly, no action too outrageous (short of copulation). One quiz-variety show I watched so humiliated a young female guest that she burst into tears while the host continued to badger her.

8. Respect for expertise is intense and far-reaching. On one channel, viewers are treated nightly to a graph, a diagram, or a set of equations, as well as a pointer and an off-screen voice explaining something. On another, a woman "cooked" something that looked like a porcupine but turned out to be a plant that produces a natural dye. I also watched a man build an apartment building out of a deck of cards while his daughters watched, madly clapping their hands, then pressing them to their foreheads in prayer as he reached for the top.

9. There's tireless coverage of endless holidays, all involving travel to the countryside, regional food and drink, and ceremonies of dubious provenance — all in answer to the city dweller's desire for roots, nostalgically referred to as a longing for one's *furusato* (literally "old village"). Since most Japanese live in large urban areas, *furusato* is largely a romantic construct promoted by governments and the tourist industry. According to Carol Gluck's study of the late Meiji period (early 1900s), it was born out of a need to reconstruct or reinvent missing traditions.

10. In the Human Interest category there are shows that feature docudramas on particular forms of abuse — bullying in the schoolyard,

domestic beating. Shocking re-enactments are shown to the home audience and a studio panel. When that ends, doors open and the real victim slides forward on a moving chair. The panellists, still recovering from the squalid video, wipe their eyes and proceed to question the subject. Fascinating.

Yesterday, while on our ukiyo-e hunt, we picked up a new English-language magazine, *The Aliens*, intended for the *gaijin* in Tokyo. The cover featured a large mandarin orange called a *mikan*. Inspired by the Big Apple, Tokyo calls itself the Big Mikan, which also means Big Bureaucrat. Inside was a cartoon series on a group unknown to me until this trip — *sokaiya*. They're a type of yakuza who specialize in blackmailing corporate executives — unearthing various scandals or misdemeanours that a company wouldn't want their shareholders, or the government, to know. For large sums of money, company shares, or other benefits, *sokaiya* promise not to disrupt the company's next annual general meeting.

A recent case involved an executive with the Matsuzakaya department store chain, which has been run by the same family since the seventeenth century. Its current president and a former president are facing extortion charges because it's as much a crime to pay bribes as to receive them. (They had been giving "gift vouchers" worth millions of yen to blackmailers, apparently without their board's approval.) This sort of crime is reported daily. Frequently we see, in newpapers and on TV, distinguished looking elderly gentlemen bowing to company members, to government officials, and to the press as they apologize and resign. Has this been going on forever? Is it only now being exposed? Is it purely formal, or will the offenders really pay a price?

The Aliens cartoon asked, "Are you a Sucker or a Sokaiya? Take this quiz and find out: At the bank, does the bank clerk remember your face because she gave you a packet of tissues last year ... or does the bank director deny knowing you because he gave you ¥200 million in cash last year?" Or, "Before Shareholders' Meetings, do you receive notice of decisions that will be made on your behalf ... or do you receive a parcel of money thanking you for not attending?"

At the same newsstand I read that the defunct *Tokyo Journal*, so satisfying to read when we were here last, will be returning in November. Good news. With only slight trepidation, I look forward to tonight's housewarming. Guests to arrive any minute.

FRIDAY, OCTOBER 24

It's hard to imagine a worse party than the one we had last night in our apartment. It was largely, but not entirely, my fault. I wish now that I hadn't made a commitment to keep a journal and could spend the day forgetting, but that's not the deal. I feel awful and deserve to. Long ago, in my teens and early twenties I was a terrible hostess — nervous, insecure, and bossy. I would bully my guests: "Why don't you all start dancing?" or, "Doesn't anyone want to eat?" I thought that was behind me, that I could be the mistress of the soiree, that if I planned well, the atmosphere would be relaxed and people would enjoy themselves.

Without knowing it, for most of my adult life I'd been a follower of the Zen axiom *ichigo ichie*, which states that a host must treat all guests as if their visit would be their last and make the occasion perfect. Was I not once included in *Toronto Life*'s list of great partygivers? Last night I broke all my own rules about being a good hostess and a guest in someone else's country.

In fairness to myself, I was not the only one at fault. Nor do I think that others will necessarily be as hard on me as I am on myself; some, of course, might be more critical than even I can imagine. I must remind myself that I am in the land of *Rashomon*, of shifting narratives that all purport to be true.

Simple things first: although I did give some thought to what I should wear, I came to the wrong conclusion. Experience had taught me that being too dressed up is threatening, too casual is disdainful, and that, as with the Tao, the middle way was best. Whatever, then, made me think that old black stretch pants and a black top would be appropriate? My appearance spoke of a lack of concern, announcing that this occasion was of little importance to me.

Bruce called early and asked if there was anything we needed. He was bringing a bottle of wine and Canadian Club.

"How about dessert?" he asked.

"Seems to be taken care of. Mr. Horiuchi's wife is making a cake."

Another mistake. I should definitely have asked Mrs. Horiuchi to come, even if she'd refused. It would have been a gesture in keeping with my own inclinations, but I'd assumed that I understood the rules of this culture and abided by them. Wrong and wrong.

When Mr. Horiuchi arrived with Ms. Suzuki and Ms. Iino twenty minutes later, there was no pizza and no cake. They brought a basket of small pink and white carnations, a huge bottle of sake and one of German white. I should have had an alternative plan. Why had I not anticipated this? (The mandarins and rice crackers I had laid out looked pitiful.)

Ms. Iino promptly got on the phone and called a pizza delivery from a Xeroxed copy of some Yellow pages. (Why hadn't I at least made a big salad?) Mr. Honda, I was told, would be about an hour late. It seemed that it was budget preparation time and his whole office would be working through the night. Ms. Suzuki was truly wonderful — wry, gentle, and savvy. She'd spent a year at Amherst College in New England and immediately felt like a friend. The other guests, forgive me, I did not find as congenial.

Bruce insisted on talking business with Mr. Horiuchi. An occupational hazard, I suppose — not being able to separate social occasions from work. The topic? Bruce's latest scheme to install a Sophia journalist-in-residence. Mr. Horiuchi, to his credit, would not play. He did his iguana imitation, sat back and appeared not to understand a word. For all I know he was sleeping, drafting a memo, or costing Bruce's suggestion.

There were certain topics Bob and I agreed in advance not to discuss. One was the apartment, as I was afraid it would either appear embarrassingly small to some of our guests, or grotesquely large to others. I'd also decided not to "interview," so to speak, our guests about subjects that interest me at the moment — Japanese corporate crime, for example. However, all evening, whatever subject came up had a slightly offensive or condescending tone to it: the ladies who escort the buses at the New Otani (me), the way postcards are still hand-cancelled in some places (Bob), the *sokaiya* phenomenon (me).

Much of the talking took place as I was refilling everyone's glasses, especially mine. Bob and Ms. Suzuki drank Coke or mineral water; Mr. Horiuchi had a little wine; Bruce drank several glasses; Ms. Iino nursed a beer; and I drank some of everyone's gift, afraid to offend while being offensive. I'd read about evening excesses and how straight-laced office workers would break into song, and how *gaijin* were often asked to sing a solo. I was prepared with my version of "I'm Just a Girl Who Can't Say No," complete with hand gestures. But there was no singing. I must have been reading an outdated guidebook.

Then the phone rang. The pizza man, calling from his cell phone to say he couldn't find our apartment building. Small wonder — it has a recessed door and no lights. Ms. Iino and Ms. Suzuki ran downstairs to meet him. When they returned with three pizza boxes (I'd neglected to offer to pay!) we opened them and laid them on the counter. I couldn't stick them in the oven because I hadn't yet figured out how to make it work. (Before she left, Ms. Suzuki instructed me in the operation of both the conventional oven and the microwave which share the same space. And how to use the answering machine.)

As for the pizzas, the toppings remain something of a mystery. I can say for certain that there were hot dogs, eggs, cheese, ham, and possibly okra. A cross-cultural culinary disaster, similar to the conversation that alternated between "The Japanese do the darndest things!" and "Aren't *gaijin* a hoot?" with more of the first than the second. Everyone was speaking English for our benefit and that should have provided us with the intellectual edge. It didn't.

Bruce asked Mr. Horiuchi how many guests he "received" each year for the Japan Foundation. "About seven hundred," he replied.

"That's a lot of parties," I interjected, Lord knows why, perhaps trying to loosen up Mr. H., who only smiled in that "If-you-only-knew" way of his that implied this would be the last barbarian affair he'd attend.

Bob spoke about how much Margaret Atwood and Graeme Gibson had enjoyed their two weeks as guests of the Foundation.

Atwood, he remarked, had wanted to go to a pachinko parlour. (We did in 1987.) "She was told that it would be on her tour but it somehow never happened. Then it was time to go home." Apparently her hosts didn't think pachinko parlours were proper places to take guests. We realized too late that this comment could be interpreted as criticism of the Foundation.

There followed more talk about noisy, smoky pachinko parlours where Japanese spend hours in front of vertical pinball games, dropping silver ball bearings into a slot, trying to win cartons of cigarettes or toasters. (Yakuza run pachinko, one of Japan's most profitable businesses.) Then on to the Japanese interest in adult comics; then, the conversational highlight of the evening, a comparison of the Canadian raccoon and the Japanese badger. We trotted out the usual stories about how large our raccoons are, how bold, how they turn over garbage and have become daytime as well as nocturnal animals. The Japanese badger, not surprisingly, is more interesting. At the entrances to temples and inns, you see statues of the little critter, dressed in a lotus-leaf hat that looks like a Stetson. He's called a *tanuki* and is found in folk tales and songs and is actually not a badger but a raccoon without rings on its tail. In Japan he's thought to have magical powers and be able to transform himself into a human, often a Buddhist monk. A crafty person in Japan is said to be a *tanuki*. Thankfully, no mention was made of their lusty reputation and their huge testicles, which account for all the giggles whenever a *tanuki* is mentioned.

From there right into cultural theory. This would have been all right had I allowed our Japanese guests to speak for themselves. Instead, Bruce and I became authorities on the subject. On re-entry problems of Japanese who've been abroad, Bruce said, "The Japanese have so much trouble integrating back into their own society because the Japanese language changes so quickly they find it hard to communicate." I went on about Japan as a uniculture that excludes immigrants, that doesn't even allow long-term residents the opportunity of citizenship, and accepts almost no political refugees even though it's a signatory of various UN resolutions in support of the principle. I believe I heard myself saying, "Japan may have let in ideas from the West, and technical innovation, but they haven't the porous exterior that allows people to enter their monoculture."

Fortunately, I became my most bellicose after Mr. Horiuchi had opened his eyes and excused himself. Bob said that he kept trying to interrupt my rants, but I was in full throttle and couldn't be stopped. Bob simply stood up and started to clear away the debris. Ms. Suzuki, Ms. Iino, and Mr. Honda appeared only too happy to assist. Then, after a scramble for the door, the party ended.

In the kitchen, Bob, quite rightly, highlighted my outrageous behaviour and I felt as if I'd irretrievably screwed up our entire trip, that Ms. Iino would describe for Mr. Horiuchi the evening's downward spiral, and nice Ms. Suzuki, who had invited us to visit her in Kamakura where she lives with her parents, would withdraw her invitation. She'd also been kind enough to bring our accreditation documents for the film festival and information on all the Imamura films in the Foundation's archive that she'd be willing to screen for us. How would she act when I called on Monday to set up an appointment? Would she tell James Quandt at Toronto's Cinematheque, whom she described as "the nicest guy I work with," about my performance after all the kind things he did for us before we left, including arranging the meeting with Ms. Suzuki?

Bob finished the dishes and I fell asleep with the blankets over my head. In the middle of the night, when I guess we were both reviewing our performances, Bob apologized for making such a fuss. I would not be consoled, even after Bob told me that as our guests were leaving, no doubt overcompensating, he bent down and kissed Ms. Suzuki on both cheeks, then Ms. Iino, who seemed truly astonished. (Social kissing is a no-no here.)

Had the day ended before the party, it would have been perfect. In the morning, after three telephone calls to the free English-language tourist service, we tracked down the Yamanote line and managed to buy a ¥150 ticket that allowed us to circle old Tokyo.

On the way, we committed the Eating on Public Transport offence because I absolutely had to have coffee and a waffle dripping with maple syrup. It was my national duty! We were still eating when the train pulled in. Once seated, Bob spilled syrup all over the map he was following, and I had a giggling fit. Here we were, fulfilling our dream of travelling the Yamanote line, but the car was so crowded that unless we sat backwards in our seats all we could see were the torsos of other passengers. Groins, actually. And out the window? Grey buildings, pachinko parlours, bicycles, and one neighbourhood looking much like the next. Is it the Chinese who say, "May your wishes never come true?" That worked for both the hour-long subway ride and the endless party.

And so it came to pass that I spent much of the day reliving, atoning, and recovering, not a physical hangover so much as a deep lethargy bred of self-loathing. Bob was sweet but I was pretty unreachable. Intended to have lunch today with Illya Shimizu, but she called in the middle of last night's debacle to apologize and cancel because she was coming down with a cold. I crawled out of bed and tidied the apartment; Professor Bowers was due to arrive at 10 a.m. to try to connect our e-mail. We rearranged the living room so the table was closer to the telephone jack. I was glad that I could alter *something* from last night, even if only the décor.

Bruce called at 12:30 and told Bob that it was a lovely party, that he hoped they hadn't kept us up too late (10:30?), and that he found Mr. Horiuchi quite unapproachable. "No small talk," he said. I decided I would have to write up my journal for yesterday and be damned. But first I did a few errands: some grocery shopping at Marucho and a pickup at the dry cleaner's.

I returned with an arm-numbing load. Bowers was still at work, his shoes off to one side in the front hall. Odd, in a Western-style apartment with Westerners, but habits die hard. At noon he gave up, saying something about the phone system in this area and that he would need to bring his own computer when he came again. Then he called Mr. Ko at Meiji and asked him to take Bob to the audiovisual department to get him set up on the Internet and e-mail. Why is this so complicated?

When he'd gone, I booked myself in for a foreign ladies' ikebana class at the Sogetsu School, next to the embassy. Katherine Ashenburg had taken the course and written a charming piece about it for *The New York Times*. She had insisted that I register while I was here. Bob went off to lunch at the Akasaka Prince with Mr. Ogawa, former ambassador to Canada, an enthusiast of both French- and English-Canadian literature, recipient of an honorary degree from Queen's University, and friend of Mary and Cy Taylor. I took to my bed with my Murakami novel and *Individualism and the Japanese: An Alternative Approach to Cultural Comparison* by Masakazu Yamazaki. I met him a year ago when he spoke at the Japan Foundation in Toronto. An elegant, grey-haired man with a quick wit and broad learning, he's one of the most appealing Japanese men I've met.

In the evening, after a cold soba supper, we heard a lecture by Donald Levine, a University of Chicago sociology professor, an expert on Ethiopia, and a keen observer of Japan. He spoke in a rather dilapidated building, the International Education Center, about three blocks from our apartment. He was in Tokyo lecturing at one of his university's branches. There were about 150 in the audience, mostly Japanese in their thirties, with more than a sprinkling of Africans and East Indians. Bob and I were the only whites. The two hours Levine spoke were over too quickly for me.

He began where my afternoon reading left off — Yamazaki writing about the "specialness" of the Japanese, an attribute they like to ascribe to themselves. It allows them to say, "We are unique, so special we cannot be compared with any other people."

"Well," Professor Levine said, "in many 'primitive' societies, the word for being human is often the same as the word for being a member of that society. They are unique and superior. When applied to Americans, it's called exceptionalism. Jews are the chosen people. France is the cradle of civilization. So the Japanese are not alone in their specialness."

Then he began an astounding cross-cultural comparison between Ethiopians and Japanese, two groups one would think shared nothing except the planet. "Ethiopians see themselves as the authentic bearers of a divine mission inherited from the Jews and the Christians. The Ethiopian says, 'You can't possibly understand us!'" As he spoke, I found my respect for sociology being restored. (I graduated from McGill in 1964 with a degree in sociology and anthropology, but my appreciation for those disciplines had diminished over the years.)

He described the value of having a "trained outsider" offer a disinterested look at Japanese society. Their sense of uniqueness can make it hard for them to relate to outsiders, and hard to find realistic solutions to national problems. "Increasingly we must all relate effectively with others and this might be particularly hard for the Japanese."

In Japan, Levine said, there's been a conflation of the public and political realms, revealed in the term *kokutai*, meaning "body politic" or "national essence." It's a pre-war concept used to define the uniqueness of the Japanese state. According to the Kodansha *Encyclopedia of Japan*, the term was first used in the seventeenth century to argue that Japanese government and ethics were not adapted from China but arose in conjunction with Shinto, the indigenous Japanese religion. In the modern period it was used to promote unquestioning obedience to one's superiors, first to one's lord or immediate superior, then, after 1868, to the emperor. This obedience made the Meiji Restoration possible and heightened nationalistic feeling during the military buildup in the 1930s. "Although officially denounced by the Occupation and in the constitution of 1947, it is *kokutai* that inspires corporate and bureaucratic loyalty and halts debate and public dissension." Levine referred to Japan as "a pseudo-democracy, without public discourse." This habit of "falling in step with one another is hard to break."

How *can* this pattern be broken? Levine asked. By challenging, through disciplined study, the deep-rooted Japanese belief in their uniqueness. He argued for a verifiable comparative analysis. First, examine countries that appear the same but are in fact different; then start with the notion that Japan is unique and compare it with other countries, and find similarities; finally, use these comparisons to move past the idea of uniqueness.

If this is done, it will be easier to examine Japanese solutions to universal problems, like economic growth. Traditional Western sociologists, such as Max Weber, argued that one had to have Christianity, then Protestant Calvinism, before there could be capitalism. Levine sees in the Edo period the origins of the Japanese post-war economic miracle, and the causes are not so different from those found in early industrial Europe. Japan's growth during the Edo period led to the establishment of a hierarchy based on profession — warriors, then artisans (who provided tools and beautiful objects for the warrior class), then farmers (who provided food and wealth for the warriors), and merchants (who exchanged surplus goods). In Ethiopia, by comparison, these professional classes never developed.

The Pure Land sect of Buddhism became increasingly popular during the Edo period, with its belief that the key to salvation was faith in Amida Buddha. One could experience a state of grace in this world by "showing diligence in production and economy in expenditures," which Levine compared with Calvinism. This form of Buddhism remained popular even after the Meiji Restoration and the enforced introduction of state Shintoism. In addition, samurai values flowed into the merchant class, "valorizing commerce." This unique Japanese history, while different from the West's, produced similar results.

He then focused on the issue of conflict resolution, a historically interesting cross-cultural comparison that seemed to bring us to today's front page. Most Asian cultures prefer to resolve conflicts privately. In ancient Greece, it was agreed that the airing of conflicts was good, witness the dialogues of Socrates. In East Africa, litigation is relished and any bystander can be called upon to participate, while in China, court is avoided in all but extreme cases.

In Japan, conflict has traditionally been viewed as "unnatural and an embarrassment," so one minimizes any differences in ideas and positions. In the West, the technique for consensus is bargaining; in Japan, it's persuasion. There is a "lack of transparency in Japanese decision making" and principles are often subordinate to loyalty. If there's no public debate on issues, no encouragement to express different views, there's less emphasis on absolutes and more loopholes left unclosed. Japan says that it desires administrative reform but these are "not necessarily benign" changes and some people will inevitably be hurt.

I found the lecture terribly exciting, the sort of mind-stretching exercise that I had wanted from last night's guests but that it was grossly unfair to expect. I certainly didn't anticipate feeling this exhilarated again so quickly.

SATURDAY, OCTOBER 25

I can't think why I didn't want to go back to kabuki, except that I was perhaps afraid that I wouldn't like it as much as I did in 1987. Oddly I never resent the price of a kabuki ticket — it was about $100 ten years ago and double that today at the private Kabuki-za, off Ginza. As early as 1830, audiences were complaining about the expense of kabuki when a single reserved seat cost a worker about four months' wages. It is true that I found the first drama more interesting than moving. It was designed to fill in the background of the famous incident of the forty-seven *ronin*, which occurred at the beginning of the eighteenth century, in the middle of the Tokugawa shogunate. Their master, ruler of the Ako region of Japan, was humiliated and forced to kill himself. His property was confiscated and his retainers, forty-seven now masterless samurai, known as *ronin*, waited two years but finally avenged the death.

They decapitated his killer and took his head to the grave of their former lord. Although they acted according to Bushido, the samurai code, they were violating new laws. Forced to commit *seppuku*, they were buried beside their lord at the Buddhist temple, Sengaku-ji. (The plot, the perfect illustration of *kokutai*, is a favourite with Japanese audiences.) These *ronin* are still regarded as heroes. Many plays were written about them, including one by Monzaemon Chikamatsu, who was alive at the time of the incident.

The version we saw today begins before the death of the Ako daimyo but recounts examples of loyalty and betrayal in the case of one retainer and dozens of people around him, all of whom are affected but know only part of the truth. The program notes told us this "dark, sardonic play" by Tsuruya Namboku is rarely staged. I thought there were two outstanding performances, but one by an aging *onnagata* fell far short of excellent. (I realize that for me to comment on kabuki requires great chutzpah.)

This play, with its approval of the warrior code, illustrates why General MacArthur had doubts about allowing kabuki to continue after the war and briefly banned it. As before, I found the ambience as fascinating as the on-stage action. Some in the audience nibbled snacks wrapped in noisy Cellophane; some shouted *kakegoe* (appreciation, often the actor's stage name); everyone grew silent at key moments, such as the death of a child, or the suicide of a wife.

The second piece was a mesmerizing dance, performed by an exquisite *onnagata*, Tamasaburo, with "her" partner, Shinnosuke, described as "the popular young actor." The musicians, all fourteen of them, were on stage. The set, costumes, and choreography were heart-wrenching. It was called *Yoshiwara Suzume* (*The Sparrows of Yoshiwara*), "the story of a husband and wife who come to the Yoshiwara pleasure quarter to sell caged sparrows for the Hojo-e, a ceremony to gain Buddhist merit by releasing things." The program went on to say that caged sparrows were also images of the courtesans of the pleasure quarters, and the dance depicted a romantic meeting between a courtesan and her lover. It seems impossible that this short dance within a dance, between two men, could be so tender, so erotic, but it was.

A young Japanese woman on my left during the performance told me that she used to go to kabuki as a student, even though it was very expensive. Then she married and had children who kept her busy. "Now, I start to come back."

"Does your husband also like kabuki?" I asked her.

"Yes. But today he is with the children."

We agreed that this was a good idea for everyone.

SUNDAY, OCTOBER 26

A day like Sundays anywhere — laundry, letter writing in the morning, and then some business filling in the accreditation forms for the Tokyo International Film Festival (TIFF). The directions were classic

Japanese — type in capital letters only (we printed); family name and professional position (ignored); circulation figures of the publication you work for (Bob guessed 400,000 for *The Globe and Mail*; I adopted *Toronto Life* and guessed 120,000. Who's to know? The numbers are so small by Japanese standards it's embarrassing); a business card (we obliged); a three-centimetre-square photograph (no ruler but we had stopped at a photo booth in the local subway for a cheap series of three each in which we both look like mummified anarchists). Anyway, it's done.

By noon we were on our way to a shrine sale at Togo in Harajuku. It made the Hanazono market look like a Unitarian rummage sale, lane after lane of stuff, junk to treasures. Unfortunately we didn't get there until about one o'clock in the afternoon; their hours are from 4 a.m. to 2 p.m. Some folks were already packing up.

Before arriving we wandered through Harajuku, along the infamous Takeshita-dori, where the hip and the wannabes hang out. Pleased to see that crepes have not been replaced entirely by waffles in the Snack Food Battle. An article I read in Wednesday's *Daily Yomiuri* (one of four English-language dailies available in Tokyo) reported on the number of African merchants who have set up businesses in Free Park Harajuku since April 1996; they pay a small fortune each month to rent a ten-square-metre spot. The Japanese consider their imported things "cool."

Meiji-dori, another big shopping street, was partially closed for the most organized and boring Hallowe'en event imaginable, parents and kids in costume, carrying black and orange balloons, marching around

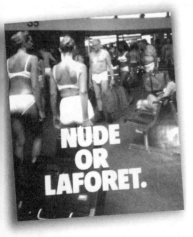

a huge oval about the size of a football field. One man had spiked hair and a leather outfit with studs; his son, no more than four, wore precisely the same get-up.

By this time we were ravenous, having resisted the crepes, and ventured onto the fifth floor of Laforet, whose logo is "Naked or Laforet." Their billboards feature unappealing *gaijin*, a middle-aged man in the foreground, walking the streets in their underwear. The store is a zoo, with different "cages" for different merchants, an indoor bazaar specializing in the fashion du jour — thick-soled footwear, including running shoes; Naomi Tami dresses in embroidered stretch material, size 1, at exorbitant prices; and woollen duffel coats, a cashmere blend, mostly in beige, all the rage at about $600. But The Look for women is prepubescent — Mary Jane shoes, frilly dresses, pale makeup, and hair like two doggy ears.

The restaurant, Pista, featured Italian food, currently Japan's favourite Western cuisine. I had spaghetti with eggplant and tomato sauce and Bob, a pizza with five kinds of mushrooms. Both were delicious. I couldn't resist taking photos in the store: these young people, most living at home and some still at school, suffer from too much discretionary money and too little sleep. I took a picture of two of them — a girl sitting upright against the wall and a young man sprawled out on her lap on a bench in front of a bank of elevators, both sound asleep.

Loaded with groceries on the way home, I stupidly tried to use my plastic telephone card in the subway turnstile. Bob, ahead of me, was already on the train. It pulled out, Bob waving, as I continued to search for my subway pass. We met five minutes later on the Yotsuya platform, both laughing uncontrollably. The Japanese fellow travellers must have thought we were genuine nutters.

MONDAY, OCTOBER 27

A koan is a Zen Buddhist riddle intended to lead to enlightenment. My personal koan goes as follows: What can one foreigner learn in one day at an ikebana course? Like the tea ceremony, ikebana started centuries ago as the exclusive preserve of priests and samurai. It was intended to remind them of the brevity of life and the continuity of time, that sort of thing. Eventually it became part of Buddhist ceremonies and Shinto rituals, war camps and weddings. Always, it requires flowers of the season, so in winter one makes selections not on loveliness but on "withered desolation." Today, various schools of ikebana emphasize different materials and permit their practitioners more or less independence.

What can I hope to learn, or unlearn, in a single day? First, I have been a close friend to two wonderful gardeners: Marjorie Harris, known throughout Canada as a writer and editor on gardens, and Barbara Frum, a gifted amateur. These two women have tried, in different ways, to induct me into the legion of passionate planters. Marjorie simply brings her clippers on frequent summer visits and wades in, telling me my lawn is hopeless and I need more of this, less of that. As a birthday gift one year, she insisted I remove some pebbles I was fond of and gave me three climbing plants, with detailed planting instructions (two died). Barbara was more tactful. About a certain rock or corner poplar she would say, "Why don't you work with that?" and offer several suggestions. Or, "Here's a book about Japanese fences. Have a look." I would look but a gate in my imagination would remain closed. One could consider that I had already mastered the Zen thing since, as I understood it, the ultimate goal of flower arranging is to arrive at an inner realm where no worldly passions can enter.

But here I am, trying to overcome my hortophobia in a baby-step course given in English for about $50. Perhaps, I thought, I was intended to garden in an elongated dish — or jar. If I felt my ego was being destroyed during the class, I could always return home early. But it was a glorious autumn day and I was up for the challenge.

At the entrance to the building there was a magnificent rock and water sculpture by Isamu Noguchi, completed this year to mark the seventieth anniversary of the Sogetsu school of ikebana. The founder, Sofu Teshigahara, was the father of the current head, Hideo Teshigahara, best known in the West as the director of a 1964 film classic, *The Woman in the Dunes.*

Although the word ikebana comes from *ikeru* ("to keep alive") and *hana* ("flower"), it generally means "natural" but in fact appears anything but natural to Western eyes. My impression of ikebana is that it follows interventionist principles: if a plant grows up, you should hang it by the roots, beautifully. The Japanese, on the other hand, argue that they are being faithful to nature, seeking a natural balance rather than an artificial symmetry. I remained sceptical.

In the elevator to the fourth floor I was joined by an elegant blonde woman. "Is this your first time?" I asked, seeking moral support.

"Oh no," she replied. "I'm working on my fourth certificate." Hortophobia rising.

I arrived at about 10:01 a.m., paid my fee, and pulled up a stool beside a long Arborite table, joining three young Dutch women and an older couple who turned out to be their parents. There was a booklet with diagrams and a pair of formidable clippers at each place. A junior sensei (teacher) was already at the board, explaining some of the origins of ikebana and telling us that we could buy our own booklet at the end of the lesson if we wished.

Then a tiny, perfectly coiffed, middle-aged Japanese woman took over the blackboard and began our serious instruction. All around me, at three long tables, eleven other women from advanced classes were busy picking their containers, selecting their flowers and twigs, holding them to the light, and choosing a *kenzan*, a metal holder the teacher referred to as a "needlepoint," into which one "sticks" flowers and branches. (I believe Westerners call them "frogs.")

We would be using three main branches. "We don't use two branches, or four branches," Major Sensei told us, "because we Japanese like things to be asymmetical [sic]. Any kind of material can be used, and ... " here she paused for emphasis, "they can be used by any nationality."

We were then told a brief history of the school's founder ending with him receiving the Legion of Honour from the French government for his "international work." (In artistic matters, French recognition remains the highest accolade in Japan.) She told us that his son, the current leader and former film director, encourages the use of unconventional materials. In one photograph in the brochure the caption states that "Hideo Teshigahara attempts to resuscitate a war-torn church in Milan by means of his massive bamboo installation in 1995." (I was surprised that there were any war-torn churches in Milan fifty years after peace was declared.)

"We work on a basic upright pattern called *moribana*," she told us. We should place the "needlepoint" always in the left-hand corner of the container. The three elements we work with are called the *shin* (the longest), the *soe* (the middle), and the *hikae* (the shortest). The first two can be anything; the third has to be a flower. We calculate the size of the container by using a stem — multiplying the diameter by the height. (The math was making me edgy!)

The *shin* has to measure twice the size of the container and be placed at a ten- to fifteen-degree angle towards the left shoulder. The *soe* has to be three-quarters the length of the *shin* and be placed at a forty-five-degree angle, also towards the left shoulder. (I considered a bailout right here.) The *hikae*, half the length of the *soe*, is to go at a seventy-five-degree angle towards the right shoulder. It must also be cut three times, always under water. (Numbers were swimming in my head. I drew a diagram. I sweated. I looked towards the door. Could I leave now?)

No. We were ready to select our material. There was a polite stampede, everyone trying, without much luck, to control competitive instincts and get into contemplative mode. I'd inferred from sensei's demonstration a new axiom that I thought would serve me well: ugly is good; hideous even better. I chose several branches that were badly misshapen, asymmetrical as all get out, and some deep-blue cornflowers with lots of branches since she had told us, "The needlepoint not so attractive. Good to cover it up." I planned to do just that.

I also chose the ugliest container I could find — oval, dark brown, and chipped. Imperfect should be right up there with asymmetrical. I grabbed a clear plastic bowl of water so I could cut my *hikae* properly. We were told to place the needlepoint in the container and cover it with water. (In for a sen, in for a yen, as we say in the East.) I grew fond of my gnarled, bald branches, especially one with a bulge resembling a brown bird of paradise or a tumour. I measured the sides, about two inches, and the length, about twelve inches. This meant that I needed a *shin* about twenty-eight inches high. I began to measure.

"Excuse," said the roving Minor Sensei, "but you must measure from the top, not the bottom."

Of course. (Obvious if I had thought about it for a minute.) Process repeated. Branch successfully cut. Angle ten to fifteen degrees. Miraculously I got the base of the sucker to stick in the needlepoint and stay there while I bent it to the required angle, or so I thought.

Next, the *soe*. I chose a piece somewhat thinner than my *shin* and placed it at forty-five degrees towards my left shoulder.

"With oval pot," said Minor Sensei, "we do not put needlepoint in the left corner. We must move it a little to the middle." (What was this? The exception that proves the rule?)

The tiny teaching assistant moved me aside and rearranged my needlepoint, causing both branches to collapse. I began again. Edo wasn't built in a day.

Damage repaired. Began to cut my flower, underwater, half the length of the *soe*. When that was done, the needlepoint failed me. There was no way I could make my flower tilt seventy-five degrees without resting on the lip of the container or falling out. Minor Sensei removed the bloom and examined the base. "Must be straight." I'd apparently cut the flower on the bias. She cut the flower again, and jammed it on the needlepoint and twisted it to lie at seventy-five degrees, more or less. (No one had told me that this was a brutal art.)

I don't want to give the impression that I was the only one in for special attention. Harsher criticism was directed at the middle-aged mom on my right. While she had managed to grab the best branches, when it came to flowers she was stuck with roses and then forgot to remove the thorns, for which she was severely reprimanded. Major Sensei was off coaching her more advanced pupils: we were told that she would examine our work when we were finished.

The last part was fun — using bits of leftover cornflowers to cover the *kenzan*. (I felt that I was now qualified to call it by its proper Japanese name.) Minor Sensei still stalked. "Too much space behind."

(Had they never heard of positive reinforcement?) She moved in and plunked a branch at the "back" and the overall effect was improved dramatically. "Thank you, Sensei," I said, hoping to earn Brownie points. "Much better."

Then I asked what must be the dumbest possible question at this stage: "So, this part I'm looking at — is it the front?"

"Very good question. The front is here and you walk one side to the other. Not at the back." This information was passed down the line.

Throughout the room, cameras flashed. The Dutch dad, who'd come along strictly as photographer, was snapping like crazy. I did the same to my own magnificent work, as did the other women in the room, even the most experienced, all of whom came with cameras. Shamelessly, I asked "Dad" if he would take a picture of me. Ikebana, I decided, was pure photo op.

Time for inspection. I was first in line. "Who did this?" Major Sensei asked. I stepped forward.

"Very good depth," she said.

Very good depth? I had very good depth! I wanted to give her a big hug! However, I knew it was that final branch, placed by Minor Sensei, that made the difference. (I'm ashamed to say that I kept quiet. I even blushed a little.) Major Sensei moved a few things around, clippers clacking at her side, and then moved on. She worked her way down the line, snipping a twig here, a leaf there, removing an excess flower. After each correction she asked, "Better, *ne*?" (Who would dare to disagree?) She particularly admired the work of the last student in our line.

"How old are you?" she wanted to know.

"Thirteen."

(That's it. I'd begun too late.)

It was demonstration time again. Major Sensei in front of the entire class, pros and tyros. "This time, I choose very interesting container," she began.

With the help of an assistant, she hoisted in the air what looked like the remains of a wrought-iron calèche that had been in a serious collision. "This is a very good time for fruit-bearing branches." She reached for what looked like a small tree with red berries and held it upside-down, removing almost all the leaves — the "almost" is the artistic part.

"If you have too many leaves you cannot appreciate the fruit-bearing part." (On the other hand, I reasoned, too much fruit means you can't appreciate the leaves. I did not share my insight.)

Then, with the branches still upside-down, she plunked it in the middle of the calèche, then reached for her second element, a spindly, bare red branch. "This is family of maple. Such a dynamic branch!"

Several of the advanced students were madly drawing her work-in-progress, trying to keep up. I felt they were working against time since the entire construction looked ready to topple. She and Minor Sensei grabbed it. I averted my eyes, expecting the worst.

"Please, let me wire on spot here."

With reconstructive surgery completed, Major Sensei bounced back and added a white, leafy plant to the top of her upside-down wired-together thing. "Like a bird, don't you think?" (Dutiful applause.)

I was not sure what to do next. (Should I destroy my near-perfect specimen, or run out and let someone else deconstruct it?) I watched to see what my fellow students were doing and followed as they picked up some newspapers and plastic cord, laid the unused branches on the newspaper, then the *hikae, soe,* and *shin,* also the little branches and flowers, and bundled up the whole messy package, tying it with the plastic cord. I picked up my purse and camera, about to leave.

"Don't you want your flowers? You paid lots of money." Not wishing to appear profligate, I pretended that I had forgotten them and snatched up the soggy pile.

On my way out I wandered through the gift shop: containers of all shapes and sizes lined the shelves — vases and bowls in glass, clay, straw, and lacquer; "needlepoints" in all sizes, brass and silver; shirts, hankies, books, all with the Sogetsu logo. A staff of four was doing a brisk catalogue and telephone business. I left with only my flowers and memories of ikebana.

I walked next door to the Canadian embassy and handed my "bouquet" to the receptionist, explaining that I had to meet someone for lunch and didn't think that I could take the "flowers" with me, and perhaps, if she had a vase? She looked befuddled but tactfully accepted my gift — part of the job, I imagine. I'm sure that without a single lesson she could do something wonderful with them.

I heard later in the evening, at the party given for us by Mr. and Mrs. Joseph Caron, that Sogetsu is a bit like pyramid-selling: a sensei at Grade 1 level can rise to Grade 2 when she signs up enough pupils. Ikebana gossip says that Hideo Teshigahara has been spending too much time and money on large-scale projects — filling too many churches with bamboo, I dare say — and his daughter is being groomed to take over.

I suppose there were political issues as well at the party tonight, but since so few guests spoke even passable English and I kept nattering on, asking inane questions, I'd be the last to know. I did hear one classic Nobel Prize story involving Robertson Davies from Professor Akira Asai, a Canadian literature specialist. For three years in a row, one of the Japanese newspapers had asked him to stand by because they'd heard that Davies had a good chance of winning the Nobel Prize and they would need a background piece. They called a year ago and asked Arai to get ready once again. This time he had to break the sad news to them — Davies had died the year before.

I was happy to meet Dr. and Mrs. Kimitada Miwa, a retired professor of international history who taught for a time at Princeton and is a long-time associate of Sophia University.

"I enjoyed *Obasan* so much," Mrs. Miwa said, "I thought you and

Ms. Kogawa would enjoy this as well." She presented me with a book which told the story of the Catholic community in Nagasaki. I did thank her for her kind gift, and told Professor Miwa how happy we were to be living at his university.

Among other interesting guests was a pony-tailed chap visiting from the Toronto office of the Japan Foundation, Toshiaki Aoyagi, a rebel with a passion for kabuki that was as large as his personality. He'd seen both Kabuki-za productions the day after arriving for a short visit to Tokyo and confirmed that the afternoon production was better. Drats, and the run is over.

He always returns to the third balcony with ¥4,000 tickets and poor sight lines. "That's where I spent my youth," he said. Since I'd heard he was a kabuki expert, I asked him one of my typically inane questions, "And where did you study kabuki?"

"There," he answered. "In the balcony at the Kabuki-za!"

We discussed the appeal of kabuki, various *onnagata* he'd seen, and the general performance standard of today's actors.

"For a while," he replied, "a few years ago, I would have said it was very bad. Now I think it is much improved. There are many 'new generation' performers."

When I asked which he liked better, the Kabuki-za or the National, he said that he preferred being in the Kabuki-za but that both were too big. They both use the same actors. He recommended that we see kabuki in Kyoto: "The theatre there is wonderful!" Then he pulled out pictures he had bought of actors in recent shows he'd seen, drooling over them, laughing with great delight. He's been in Canada for fifteen years, the last four at the Foundation. Before that, he worked for the Canadian Opera Company. "Opera's the best place to learn things," he said. "Everything in the culture comes together there." He's a landed immigrant and although he admitted he'd never return to live in Japan, he said he'd also "never change the chrysanthemum on my passport for a maple leaf."

"Why did you come to Canada in the first place?" I asked, suspecting I was in dangerous water.

"Oh, no," he feigned surprise. "It's much too soon. I would have to know you a long time to tell you." Perhaps after we spend November 3 at the National Theatre, which we plan to do. Perhaps not.

Joseph Caron spoke in Japanese about Bob and Joy — if he mentioned my name I didn't hear it. Bob responded briefly and

Kogawa, passionately, exhorting Japan to be more open in its attitude to strangers since as a Japanese-Canadian she'd experienced the misery of being treated as a second-class citizen. It hurt her, as a Japanese with a deep connection to the country, to see the Japanese mistreat other nationalities within its borders.

Mrs. Caron, a Turkish-born daughter of a diplomat and herself once a diplomat, now works as a translator of technical documents from Japanese to English. Tiny as a terrier and just as tough, I should think. She was rather icy at first, which might just be diplomatic self-preservation, but she thawed a bit afterward.

Their apartment, large and elegant, within walking distance of the embassy, was beautifully furnished and decorated with Japanese ceramics and scrolls, with not a single piece of Canadian art in sight. They've lived in Japan for fifteen years and seem to have adopted a Japanese aesthetic. Who could blame them? The food and drink were good and plentiful and everyone behaved, including me.

TUESDAY, OCTOBER 28

A most wonderful afternoon in the Japan Foundation's screening room, watching our first two Imamura films. The Cinematheque has organized an Imamura retrospective to start in Toronto while we are still here. Bob will write something, if he's inspired. Today we saw *The Pornographers: Introduction to Anthropology* (1966) and *The Profound Desire of the Gods: Tales from a Southern Island* (1968), two remarkable films from a director not so much obsessed by aesthetics — although his camera angles in the first film, and his colour in the second, are spectacular — but with what it means to be Japanese. We have two films scheduled for tomorrow, two the day after.

Before going upstairs to the twentieth floor we couldn't ignore the Starbucks outlet in the lobby. The smell hit me the minute I entered the building. Their coffee's cheap by Japanese standards (a medium Guatemalan was only ¥290, about $3.50). Upstairs, the audiovisual department was chaotic, like most offices I've seen here. Despite the glories of their public spaces, Japanese offices are open fields filled with desks — overcrowded, cluttered, and badly lit. None of this mattered once we sat down in our own private screening room (never mind that it doubled as a storeroom) and watched Imamura while we sipped

Starbucks coffee and munched sticky buns.

We'd arrived at the ARK Mori building by taxi since it appeared to us in the past to be fairly inaccessible by subway. But as we pulled up to the front door I noticed what seemed like a subway entrance a couple of buildings away. When we re-emerged at 6:45 p.m. we headed past the Hotel Ana and sure enough, there it was, a subway line so new that it didn't appear on any of our maps — the Namboku line, and it goes directly to our home station, Yotsuya. For urban explorers, this discovery was equal to Jacques Cartier navigating the St. Lawrence. We were home in record time.

John Fraser had called early in the morning, full of home-grown gloom — teachers are on strike across the province and the stock market took its worst single drop in history. If I recall correctly, the same thing happened when we were in Japan in 1987. Teachers out and the market down. As it happened, both of these stories were in the Japanese papers — the teachers' strike because it was the largest ever recorded, and the financial disaster because it hit the Japanese market as well. I've been trying not to look at the headlines.

Without this apartment I would never know how delicious Japanese food is — the eggs, bean sprouts, lettuce, cherry tomatoes, green onions. I'm not enchanted, however, with the packaging. I opened a box of ordinary crackers; there was an outside layer of Cellophane, then six squares of foil with six individually wrapped crackers in each. Admittedly, they were super-fresh, but I ask, Is this necessary? Then there are the disposable bamboo chopsticks. In private homes, each family member has a set that are washed and re-used. But in restaurants one is given a set of *hashi* in a paper sleeve. Each year, 540 million pairs are used and thrown away in Japan alone.

There's much press coverage of the international global environment conference currently underway in Kyoto and much criticism of American reluctance to lower carbon-dioxide levels. The delegates, no doubt, are all using disposable chopsticks.

WEDNESDAY, OCTOBER 29

The campus seemed in a bit of a tizzy this morning: black limos by the metre, campus security by the dozen, over-equipped police by the gross, and red carpet by the mile. There was even a rope laid the length of the drive to the library, one-third of the space for pedestrians, two-thirds for cars. I felt obliged, for freedom's sake, to walk on the section allocated for autos. The cars were full of executive types. There's no telling whether this was an event of real importance or a pseudo-happening, such as a class reunion or a president's retirement. As Ted Goossen told us ten years ago, the Japanese love pomp and circumstance.

Down to the Japan Foundation for another 1:30 screening and two utterly engrossing Imamura films, *The Insect Woman* (1963) and a documentary, *A History of Postwar Japan as Told by a Bar Hostess* (1970). They're both about rough women who are treated roughly. They play like Russian epic novels — an unsteady domestic peace against a backdrop of war. Incest was routine, as we saw in yesterday's films as well, along with other kinds of adolescent sex and prostitution. In *The Insect Woman*, a daughter who recently gave birth is working beside her father in the field. She stops and asks him to ease her pain by sucking her engorged breast. He does, and calls her Mama. Towards the end of the movie, the middle-aged daughter returns to visit her dying father. He's lying on a futon surrounded by old crones, including her mother. He gestures to his daughter to lean in and whispers in her ear. His last word, "milk." She responds by unbuttoning her blouse and inserting her nipple into his mouth. He dies peacefully.

There's a terrible realism in all of Imamura films, a sort of cynicism that doesn't remove you from the subject but rather convinces you of its truth. They're humanist documents, and I'll hate for them to end.

THURSDAY, OCTOBER 30

Woke up realizing that Bob and I had completely forgotten the Jacques Israelievitch concert last night at the embassy! I'd been in need of people and music and would have enjoyed going. On holiday, even a working holiday, dates somehow don't seem important until they're missed.

Bob went off this morning with a Sophia University graduate student, a young woman named Jun recommended to him by Professor Miwa after Bob grew desperate and asked if he knew someone who could help him access his e-mail. Jun seems the ideal person; she's getting a master's degree in 1950s US-Japanese relations. She improved her English by studying for two years at Earl Haig Collegiate in Toronto.

"It was full of Chinese students," she said. "Students from everywhere."

When Bob returned he reported that there'd been about three hundred new e-mails, but only one was personal and that barely so. Tel-net, the means by which we access our University of Toronto account, is painfully slow: "Punch a key and wait." They worked in the university's computer sciences centre, so the delay wasn't caused by equipment or personnel. The world is not yet as wired as one might like, or as it will be in a few years.

The only news that seems to matter in both Asia and America is "the collapse" of everything — the market, real estate, political leadership, and confidence. I hope this is journalistic hyperbole and only a blip in the great heave upward from world poverty. Right now it appears that the stock market is experiencing the domino effect: markets are falling in a row, starting with Thailand. (Who besides traders, the Thai, and those who do crosswords had ever heard of the baht before all this?) I'm giving up on the news until it improves.

As if all this wasn't designed to put me in a foul mood, I had an upsetting lunch at the Akasaka Prince Hotel with Patricia Bader-Johnson of the Canadian embassy. The restaurant, called the Potomac to set the Yanks at ease, serves ersatz American cuisine. We all opted for the clubhouse sandwich and it was godawful. Theory: whenever the Japanese want to make an American dish, they add a fried egg. It rarely works.

Perhaps I was the only one who felt uncomfortable, I don't know. I also felt somehow responsible. I'd asked her if she could help us plan two trips out of Tokyo, and she'd taken her task seriously. A large woman with bottle-red hair, she exudes boundless energy, enthusiasm, and confidence.

"I've just come back from skiing in Aomori Prefecture," she announced. "Now I've been to every prefecture at least once." A Saskatchewan girl, she came to teach English thirteen years ago, learned Japanese, and has worked at the embassy for six years in charge of their academic programs. "Anything to do with schools — teachers, exchange programs — that's me!"

Her most recent accomplishment has been to help establish the only postgraduate program given entirely in Japan by a North American university — an MBA from McGill. After passing "those ghastly math exams," she herself was admitted to the first year. She has a Canadian-born husband and a couple of kids. Once, she might have engaged me. Now, she seemed to drain all the oxygen from the air, leaving me feeling old, incompetent, and a mite breathless.

The trips, described as her "personal favourites," focus on western and central Honshu. One part involves an hour ride up the side of a mountain in a gondola and an hour-long walk back down, surrounded by deer. "Whatever you do, don't take food. They'll stand with their front legs on your shoulders and sniff through your pockets." Lovely!

I felt drowned in possibilities, smothered by information. Because of his limp, I'm nervous about Bob falling just going up and down stairs. But a mountain? I realized for the first time at that lunch that Bob had a permanent injury and there will be things we cannot attempt. I need to adjust.

In the taxi to ARK Mori, I asked Bob if he was willing to help me plan our trips "away," because I didn't think I could handle them alone as I sometimes did. He said that he would be happy to, but suspected that my question contained poorly veiled criticism. I told him it was true that I was nervous. If things didn't go well, I didn't want to shoulder all the blame. I was well aware that I enjoyed being in charge but I don't always like the consequences.

Thank God for Imamura. *A Man Vanishes* (1967) was totally engrossing. A documentary made over the span of years, it explores the story of Oshima, who had disappeared without a trace; as Imamura said, he'd "dropped through a hole in the earth." Imamura declared in the film that he'd developed a dislike for the man's fiancée, Yoshie, and had burrowed deep into her family, exploring her hostile relations with a sister she accused of having had an affair with Oshima. He encourages Yoshie to fall for the actor-interviewer and secretly films their intimate moments. In the end, Imamura justifies his questionable behaviour. "It's all a film."

This is both true and not true, since he made events happen that would not have otherwise. In the final scene, when the two sisters are forced to confront one another, Imamura himself enters the room just as the walls are being removed, exposing the stage set, shattering reality. It's a delicious postmodern deconstruction of a documentary.

The candour and introspection in Imamura's films will stay with me a long time. I think I was fooled into thinking that all Japanese energy is directed towards motion, activity, simply getting from A to B, navigating this intensely complex society. Now I marvel at the depth and complexity of the interior monologues of Japanese characters in film or literature, and at their perceptive responses to personal questions.

The second movie was one we'd seen at the 1987 Tokyo Film Festival, an early Imamura and the least successful of the six, *Intentions of Murder* (1964). Already evident were the signature low camera shots; the freeze-frames where the soundtrack continues; the concentration on abused and tough women; and some of the roughest, least pleasant sex ever filmed. I've had no sexual experiences with Japanese men but if what the movies show is even close to the truth, they must be among the most inept lovers in the universe — self-absorbed, fast, and sadistic. Even one of these characteristics is bad enough. Women are always having their breasts squeezed, pulled, and bitten: it makes me sore to watch. After reading the material prepared to accompany the Imamura retrospective, I think that Canadian audiences may be shocked by the rawness of the material.

We raced to the Canadian embassy for the last three-quarters of Joy Kogawa's talk. Stephane Jobin let us in a back door so we could take our seats as quietly as possible in the last row. The auditorium was almost full. I think that if I had been there from the beginning I might have behaved in a way that would have shamed me, my family, and my nation. Kogawa rattled on about love and connections, about being kind to one another and to animals, about being a Christian and Japanese, about not feeling entirely at home in Canada or in Japan. Her trip was sponsored by the Canada-Japan Friendship Society, and I suspect she gave them exactly what they wanted.

One audience member asked her what she thought of contemporary Japanese fiction: "Well," she replied, "I can't really answer that. When I write I can't read for fear I'll be influenced." In fact, she has written so little she should have plenty of time to read. I confess I've never been able to plow past the opening sentences in *Obasan*.

Wine and cheese after. I spoke with a Japanese man who is one of thirteen employees at the Quebec government office in Tokyo. "I've never heard of Mrs. Kogawa before," he said. "How is she regarded in Canada?" Oh Lord. I began by mentioning the Order of Canada, perhaps more for her work in securing war reparations for Japanese-Canadians than for her fiction.

"She says," he interrupted, "that she's Japanese and Christian. To me she is mostly Christian. So much love!" Indeed.

FRIDAY, OCTOBER 31

Revisited Kanda, the book district, today. Last time we were there we were astounded to be handed a map showing 135 new and used bookshops, some cramped and rickety and jammed with treasures, others large and commercial combining stationery and CDs. Many were multilingual. One shop, Ohya Shobo, claimed to have the world's largest collection of old Japanese illustrated books, maps, and woodblock prints. I bought a lovely reproduction for about $20, a water scene with a boat circling a submerged torii. It could be Miyajima.

Ten years ago we were told that the area would likely disappear under development pressures. I'm happy to note that there are more bookstores than ever, trailing up and down side streets. I went crazy buying books about Japan; I can't get enough. Being here is a a full study program for me — experiencing, reading, discussing.

I had a hunger for sushi and we found a wonderful place in the basement of a new pencil building — tall but with a ground coverage not much larger than the tiniest bookstore. There, for ¥1,000 each (¥600 for my beer) we had a great sushi platter that would easily have served three or four in Canada.

Bob lugged the books back to the apartment while I did more grocery shopping. After a pasta supper, we spread out a large Tourist Office map of Japan, opened our new Fodor's (one of the day's purchases) and Patricia's notes for Trip No. 1 to Western Honshu. Slowly it all seemed possible. Bob and I worked together, calmly. I still have a few phone calls to make, hotels and things, but it is, as they say, do-able. Might leave on Trip No. 1 during the first week of November and miss some of the film festival. This is not as disappointing as it might be. I don't care about *Titanic* or *Air Force One*, and unfortunately for me, many of the Japanese films will be screened without subtitles.

SATURDAY, NOVEMBER 1

Two film festivals in one year — Toronto and Tokyo. My cup runneth over. To think there are people who spend their lives going to film festivals and being paid for it. I feel a twinge of envy. The Bunkamura Gallery, where we saw the French photography show last month, has been transformed into a press centre filled with the usual scraggly filmgoers, hair too long, skin too pale. Daily bulletins in Japanese and English litter the area, and bilingual signs list extra screenings and cancellations.

This year, China has pulled its two official offerings to protest the screening of *Seven Years in Tibet*, a lament on the death of an independent Tibet. Marie Suzuki, whom we met at our second screening of the day, said that Japanese-Chinese cultural relations might improve once Beijing recalls the hard-liner who is now their cultural officer.

It's to Marie that we owe our smooth registration. They didn't bat an eye at our entirely unworthy photographs. In no time we found ourselves in a stark and smoky press lounge: tables, hardback chairs, coffee, water, harsh yellow light — rather like a hospital waiting room. Fortunately my festival-going muscles are still well-toned. Bob and I tackled the printed schedule, comparing our previous commitments with the movies we really wanted to see. We came up with about a dozen that are scheduled between now and Friday, November 7, when we will make our first foray outside Tokyo.

We concentrated on old Japanese movies, four of them shown here for the first time in sixty-five years. They're among the many films thought to have been lost in various natural and man-made disasters but that turned up in Russia, in the Gosfilmofond, their film archive, and were brought back for viewing by a new generation of filmgoers. We began bravely with *Oichi no Kata*, one of the "recovered" films running eighty-eight minutes at the Shibuya Joy cinema, located after weaving through the crowds that make Shibuya such a treat. I said "bravely" because there were no English subtitles. By 2:50, the supposed starting time of the movie, the medium-sized theatre was reasonably filled but far from full. A long trilingual announcement was broadcast on the public address system — Japanese, German, and English — informing us of copyright laws, prohibitions against taking photographs, and the risk of having our equipment "restrained" should we disobey.

Then there were speeches by Sadao Yamane, a film critic and program coordinator for the festival, and Shigehiko Hasumi, president of Tokyo University and chair of the Committee for the Centenary of

Film in 1995. The first chap was short, completely bald, with dark glasses and soft shoes. He could have been a monk. The second was taller, a more commanding figure, clearly passionate and informed about movies, who ended his brief description of several movies in this Nippon Classics series with a tribute to Samuel Fuller, that quintessentially American moviemaker whose films drew on his early years as a crime reporter. Fuller had died yesterday.

"I met him once," Hasumi said. "It was five in the morning and he talked for many hours. I have a happy memory of our time together." It's hard to imagine Mr. Fuller and Hasumi-san in the same universe, let alone the same room.

The movie revealed itself like a scroll across the screen. It was set in the sixteenth century and was based on *Momoku Monogatari*, a novel I had never heard of by Junichiro Tanizaki. The program notes said that it was regarded as "a pro-imperialist film." Without subtitles it was hard to understand how this could be, except that the daimyo who demanded complete obedience from his mother, his wife, and his vassals, was betrayed by some, and eventually gave his wife to his rival before committing *seppuku*. Nothing unusual there.

The battle scenes were restrained and the black-and-white cinematography under the direction of Akira Nobuchi had a Hollywood gloss. Our hero had the jutting jaw of Dick Tracy, the black-lined eyes of Errol Flynn. His wife, our heroine, had two expressions: wisely sad and sadly wise, seen through a lens loaded with Vaseline. She did have a remarkable collection of kimono and wigs.

While waiting for the movies to start, an older Japanese man sat down beside me. He was rather shabbily dressed with worn-down shoes. I'd been imagining how much he must have loved film to have left his single room two hours' train ride away to come to this arcane example of classic cinema. He turned and asked me where I was from. "Canada," I replied. "Toronto."

"Oh, I've been there three times," he said. "On holiday." He'd apparently worked in Canada for a while, which explained his flawless English. His love of cinema, if indeed that was his motivation for attending, was insufficiently strong to keep him from sleeping through much of the film.

As with the Toronto film festival, there's a cafeteria of choices and we decided to expand our selections with a sampling from a series called Cinema Prism, largely movies about movies or moviemakers.

There's a long interview with Ingmar Bergman and a documentary about Luis Buñuel later in the week. *Titanic* is the coup of the festival; James Cameron was clever to launch his epic in this sentimental, spectacle-loving country. The sustained, hysterical screaming later in the day signalled the arrival of Leonardo DiCaprio at the Bunkamura. Hundreds of frenzied girls in school uniforms lined the gallery steps overlooking Bunkamura's French Café.

For dinner we went across the street to Poco a Poco, which has mastered the fine art of the thin pizza crust. Then back again to join a long lineup inside the building for Theatre Cocoon. We followed the line as it coiled down the stairs like a snake, flight after flight until Bob and I arrived at the very bottom. Soon "the snake" started to make its way back up the stairs on the far wall. We were fortunate to be standing on a small flat surface because we had to wait there for about twenty minutes, ten minutes after the scheduled starting time of 6:30. There was so little air in the stairwell, I thought I might faint. No one spoke. Everyone concentrated on breathing. We couldn't leave if we had wanted to. And we couldn't move until we were allowed to. Finally, slowly, we made our way up the stairs. In the lobby we met Marie Suzuki and my sleeping partner from the afternoon, who waved at me from a distance.

In the end I'm so glad we hadn't been able to escape. *Nani ga Kanojo wo Sosasetaka* was a silent film, a masterwork by the director Shigeyoshi Suzuki and one of the treasures rescued by Russian and Japanese film scholars. Made in 1929, according to the catalogue notes, "it followed the trend towards mass production of leftist-tendency films." It also followed the Perils of the Innocents films of the Mary Pickford type common in North America. This movie was so popular when it was released in 1930 that a sequel soon followed starring the same ingenue.

Before the screening we were subjected to a forty-minute introduction. First there was the program coordinator again. Then two full-bodied Russians, a bureaucrat in a beige suit and big shoes, and an artistic type in ill-matched jacket and pants who went on and on thanking his six hundred colleagues at Gosfilmofond and their counterparts in Tokyo. He was having his fifteen minutes of fame on the backs of the poor audience, not to mention his remarkable translator. Working without a note, her hands clasped behind her back, she spewed forth great lumps of Japanese, intelligible to most in the audience. (A poorer Japanese-to-English translator had the impossible task of following her.) Also remarkable was the ability of the audience to sit in silence while being bored to death. Many slept; some quietly left their seats; most accepted this self-indulgence with the passive attentiveness of schoolchildren. I can't imagine similar behaviour from Westerners.

Finally came the longest and most painful speech, this by Teruo Yamakawa, the fiftysomething grandson of the founder of the production house responsible for this film, Teikoku Kinema. In excruciating detail, he recounted how the film was believed lost until he heard from a friend that a print had been shown in the Soviet Union in the 1930s. He asked that friend to check for him and indeed he found it — preserved, but in fragments. In 1987 it was transferred to non-flammable stock, but with the collapse of the Soviet Union — and on and on.

Suddenly and without warning, Mr. Yamakawa shifted into confessional mode. "This film was particularly important to me personally," he said. "My grandfather died before I was born and my father was killed in the war when I was only four years old. I was missing the father-feeling, so I decided to stay in the same business, the movie business. I manage a cinema in Osaka and have produced one film."

Finally, almost an hour past schedule, Günther Buchwald entered the orchestra pit. He's the German conductor and composer in his mid-forties, here to lead the Tokyo Metropolitan Orchestra in a score he wrote for the film. Herr Buchwald is an anomaly — a contemporary composer dedicated to writing silent movie scores. He founded the Silent Movie Music Company in 1986 and "restores old film music, composes for films and improvisation."

We were warned when the evening started that the beginning and the end of several reels were missing. Since there were no English titles, much of the time Bob and I were left, literally and figuratively, in the dark. Even so, it was a marvellous experience, heightened by the score — flute, drums, violins, cellos, double bass, and trumpet. The movie tells the tale of a plucky heroine who's living with a lecherous old man with rotten teeth when the reel begins — not the original beginning, which was lost. The leitmotif is quickly established: these are poor characters, probably played by poor actors, and they all have poor teeth. They are shown eating rice ferociously. I was certain he was going to ravage her before our eyes; instead, he steals some of her money before taking her to a family with too many children in need of a servant. Charles Dickens could not have conjured up a viler brood of seven or eight maniacal children, a drunk and useless wife, and a lecherous husband.

Again I was certain we were in for a deflowering, but no, again she's robbed and this time sold to an alcoholic with rotten teeth and a scarred face, which we soon discover resulted from occupational injuries: he's a knife thrower with a travelling circus. Our maid becomes his newest target until she's gallantly defended by a fellow worker, and together they run from the circus — only to be separated against their will. She becomes a maid for a rich matron, her cruel daughter, and groping husband, who makes a pass at our young heroine. She flees into the arms of the young man from whom she'd been separated.

Alas, he's still penniless so they decide to walk into the sea together. The end? Not at all. They're rescued separately, each not knowing the fate of the other. Convinced that her young man is dead, our heroine joins a convent and there follows some kaffuffle about a letter she attempts to smuggle out once she hears he's alive, followed by many screens of kanji that recap the missing finale.

Earlier, the maids in the rich people's home put on a phonograph record and began to dance, the live orchestra played "Ain't She Sweet." It was utterly charming. Later, Buchwald added a musical nod to Kurt Weill's "Mac the Knife," also very clever. The audience ended the evening with the briefest applause and raced for the doors.

SUNDAY, NOVEMBER 2

A later start than usual. Managed for the first time to sleep in, the result no doubt of actually staying awake past nine o'clock. Carrying our official Film Festival bags with our pink press passes on chains around our necks, we headed for Shibuya, changing subway lines part of the way there. On the 180-metre walk — all distances from one line to another are marked on pillars along the route — Bob was reading me something from yesterday's *Japan Times*, when I caught the eye of a small, twitchy Japanese man with unruly teeth. He came towards us, stopped in his tracks, moved back, slipped forward, then struck a pose that would have been excessive even in kabuki. Could we have been the first foreigners he'd ever seen? Impossible. Had we met before? I thought not. Was I a dead ringer for someone he once knew? Perhaps.

"Hello," I said. (That seemed neutral enough.)

"Excuse me," he replied, "but are you going to the Tokyo International Film Festival?"

"Why yes," I replied, thinking we were closer to solving the mystery. Even Bob was intrigued.

"I am going too," said our new best friend. Oops, I thought. We were going in the wrong direction and he was going to set us straight. Not so.

"Are you going now?" Bob asked, working around various possibilities.

"No. First I must go somewhere else."

"It's been nice meeting you," Bob and I said in unison, totally baffled. He continued to walk backwards, staring at us as we moved further and further away. What had really happened? No idea.

Sometimes, even in Tokyo, you can't find lunch where and when you need it. This seems impossible in a city that eats all day long but there we were, minutes to go until our first screening of the day, and nothing to eat. Well, there was a McDonald's. So we did the Tokyo thing, chickenburgers, fries, and Diet Cokes, leaning against a pole on the street opposite the theatre. Was it really delicious, or was I just starving?

This culinary delight was followed by a genuine cinematic treat — *Zangiku Monogatari* (*The Story of the Last Chrysanthemums*), a 1939 talkie with English subtitles directed by Kenji Mizoguchi when he was forty-one. It's based on a novel by Shofu Muramatsu that was originally serialized in the Sunday *Mainichi*. It tells the story of a kabuki actor and his lover Otoku in which his career became her reason for living and the cause of her death, a plot of innocence betrayed, family loyalty tested, and the ultimate sacrifice — as always made by a woman in love.

It was wonderful to see kabuki on screen. It gave me some confidence that I know when it works and when it doesn't. There's a revealing scene towards the beginning of the 143-minute movie. Our hero has just given a terrible performance, and although everyone in the company is talking about it behind his back, no one will tell him what they really think, except Otoku. She's the family nursemaid, and this is the first of his shows she's seen. Admitting that she is "impertinent," she tells him that he has talent but needs to work hard to earn his adoption into one of Tokyo's great acting families. Only at the end, when the male lead plays an *onnagata*, does Otoku's faith in him seem justified. His success, however, means her death.

The stage scenes appear to have been performed in real kabuki theatres, so much smaller and more intimate than those I've seen. It made me yearn to see kabuki that way, each raised eyebrow, every curl of the lip. At the end of the film there was a burst of applause, a first for me with a Japanese movie audience. (At the Toronto International Film Festival it's quite common.)

Afterward, in the cinema lounge, I saw two men crying — one discreetly blowing his nose, the other, in his late twenties, early thirties, giving full vent to his emotions. Walked back to Bunkamura slowly because the weather was divine and the crowd impenetrable. The lineup to get into the parking lot outside Seibu department store was several blocks long and had house police, in regulation outfits with white gloves stationed every few cars. In one car, a man was reading; in another, a father clenched the wheel while his wife and baby slept.

We watched a crepe-maker at work in a little truck in an alley, operating two hotplates. I'm sure the crowd derived as much pleasure from watching him create the crepes as from eating them. It's a labour-intensive, highly skilled performance involving a huge wooden spatula and cans of every topping under the sun. He was still there at 9:30 p.m. surrounded by batter, whipped cream, Hershey chocolate sauce, all possible fruit mixtures, bananas, nuts, and sprinkles, and admiring customers.

As we move into fall, the sweet potato seller has appeared, as old as Edo, as up-to-date as tomorrow. He drives slowly through residential neighbourhoods, his plaintive, centuries-old cry now on a tape loop, issuing from a loudspeaker on the roof of his vehicle. A perfect example of a cultural skiamorph, the retention of an old form in a new function. Bob introduced me to this term, which he'd found in a *Globe and Mail* article. The word is from Greek — *skia* meaning shadow and *morph*, shape or form. It refers to a holdover from older technology. Glancing at the icons on my Windows tool bar, I spy a paste pot, another skiamorph.

Back in the press lounge for an hour or two, trying to relax, then off to the Shibuya Joy. We'd scouted a fish restaurant on the seventh floor of the theatre building and decided to eat there. Our eager waiter found us a window table even though the place was jammed at 6 p.m. The Japanese eat early, or perhaps they eat one of their dinners early. Hard to say. In a private dining room with a wraparound aquarium, young people were whooping it up, having a whale of a time. "A university theatre trip," said our waiter — part explanation, part apology.

The other diners were young men and women who sat surrounded by shopping bags. They were enthusiastic eaters, trying new things, one dish after another, sampling from one another's plates, nibbling slowly and carefully, discussing what they were tasting. There were also tables of guys in work clothes and hard hats doing much the same thing. Bob and I played it pretty safe and ordered two different "sets." Still, I had only the faintest idea what I was eating, but I loved it.

Then back to the theatre for two more silent films: one was a puzzle, the other a bore that proved even Shimizu could make a dud. It was called *Minato no Nihonmusume* (*Japanese Girls at the Harbour*). The first film, a curiosity, was introduced by Mr. Yamane, the critic and program director, and a French colleague, a charming film expert forced to speak English. "*La Trahison de Daimyo* was a fifteen-minute film shot by Pathé in 1912," she told us. "It was filmed either in Paris, or perhaps in Toronto, one of the places Pathé had studios at the time." This print was tinted like an old postcard, pinks, blues, and greens; the clothes of the main characters — a drunken daimyo, an honourable samurai, and a geisha with a heart of gold — were each a different hue.

"We just discovered," the French scholar said, "that one of the actresses is not Japanese. We do not know who she is so we will be staying to watch the movie on a large screen, looking for clues." A Japanese viewer, she said, had noted that the maid wore her kimono in an odd way and seemed "un-Japanese." When I saw the disputed scene, there was no doubt the actress was a *gaijin*: her kimono was loosely tied, like a bathrobe; she stumbled onto the set as though drunk; and, most important, she carried the tray with one hand, something a Japanese person never does. The audience burst out laughing.

It also occurred to me how radically the Japanese body has changed in two or three generations. The film was made when a low-protein, low-calcium diet produced short legs and large heads, making the actors look like dwarfs. Today, young Japanese closely approximate Western proportions. Like many changes in appearance in Japan, it came about quickly.

By the time we left the theatre, usually noisy Shibuya was quiet and empty, as if an evacuation alert had cleared the district.

MONDAY, NOVEMBER 3

A long weekend for the long-toiling Japanese. It's called Culture Day, or, according to some, Constitution Day, celebrating the signing of the 1868 Constitution; or, as in a new book I am reading about the three last emperors, Meiji's birthday. But there's no rest for the high-energy kids at Sophia University who are in the third day of a marathon school-spirit weekend that could only be called cultural in the broadest sense.

We noticed changes about a week ago with the mysterious appearance of two banks of sinks set up along the walkways and attached to an outdoor water system. We speculated this was a health measure for a highly toxic lab experiment, but that seemed unlikely. (The campus is dedicated to arts types, with music often pouring out of classrooms.)

Then folded stalls appeared, followed by the delivery of dozens of boxes of bottles, paper products, and food of every sort. The students took up the remaining space to lay out reams of brown paper and the sign painting began. Every sports, arts, and language group had its own stall. Extension cords hooked up various heating elements — hot plates, waffle irons, and electric frying pans. The enthusiastic selling began yesterday, fading only slightly today. Boiled hot dogs on sticks are popular. Also waffles, noodles, sausages with cabbage, and sausages with onions. The air was filled with the rich smell of soy sauce and oil.

Some booths sold plants, or key chains, or stuffed animals, the latter in aid of a Club Freiheit (founded in 1977), another was for the Windsurfing Club. Liquor was available day or night — Campari, Scotch, crème de menthe (with hot dogs?) along with the ever popular beer and sake. Strangers seemed to wander in as well as supportive relatives, staff, and the odd local newsperson. Nothing in evidence was directly "educational."

Our day was far more cultural, in the narrow sense: we saw kabuki at the National Theatre as guests of Osamu Honda and Toshi Aoyagi, Japan Foundation chaps from Tokyo and Toronto. They met us accompanied by a third man, the very model of a salaryman — slicked-back hair going grey, steel-rimmed glasses, blue suit with print tie.

Toshi said, "This is Mr. Kojiro Kataoka, the kabuki actor. You'll see him in today's performance."

It was true. Mr. Kataoka handed us his card along with an official photograph which showed him as an attractive *onnagata* in a stunning costume we later saw displayed in the National Theatre's museum.

He apologized for his suit. "I'm dressed this way because it's opening day." His English was rapid, enthusiastic, and beyond my understanding. We took two cabs to the theatre: Toshi and the actor in one; Mr. Honda, Bob, and I in the second. This actor, he told us, had performed a one-act show at the Japan Foundation in Toronto in September and would appear on CBC TV before the Winter Olympics in February in Nagoya. While he was in Canada, he travelled to several cities putting on makeup and costumes for audiences while he explained the art of the *onnagata*. Later we learned from Toshi that he's not from a kabuki family and took a degree in Western philosophy at the University of Kyoto. There he became involved in theatre. Only after graduation did he decide to make kabuki his life. "Today, unfortunately, he has only a small part." (I didn't recognize him when he appeared as one of several village women in the day's second production.)

The first show was a disappointment, a drama that both relied on and subverted historical facts: *Gion Sairei Shinko Ki* (*The Tale of the Believers at the Gion Festival*). It did star three national treasures in major roles, however. Nakamura Jakuemon IV, an *onnagata* over seventy years old whom we'd seen earlier at the Kabuki-za, appeared as Princess Yukihime, "one of the most famous roles of the *onnagata* female role specialist repertoire." There was Nakamura Tomijuro V as a wildly costumed villain, a shogun who has killed the heroine's father, captured her husband and mother-in-law, and now wants her as his mistress. Because she's the granddaughter of Sesshu, the great artist, he also wants her to draw a dragon on the ceiling of his pavilion in Kyoto. Then there was the hero, Tokichi, played by Nakamura Ganjiro III, who rescues all the prisoners.

There's a brilliant piece of stage business when the shogun decides to test the intelligence of Tokichi, who claims he wants to lead the troops although his true loyalty rests elsewhere. The shogun throws a lacquer bowl into a deep well and asks the would-be strategist to retrieve it without wetting his hands. Tokichi succeeds by holding a piece of bamboo, one end in a waterfall and the other in the well, until the water in the well rises and lifts the bowl into his hands. At another point, when challenged to a game of Go with the shogun, he describes his intention thus: "The best strategy is not to win, but to appear not to lose."

I was looking forward to one of the play's most famous scenes where the princess, roped to a tree surrounded by fallen cherry blossoms, uses her toe to draw a rat, or in this performance, two white mice, who gnaw through the rope and set her free. But I remained unmoved, perhaps because of the brightly lit stage and the lack of mystery.

I resolved before we joined our two hosts, who sat separately, that I wouldn't say what I thought of the first show. But as soon as we sat down for lunch, Toshi declared that he thought the production a bust.

We agreed that the three national treasures delivered unfocused performances, disconnected and mechanical. Perhaps three treasures are too much for one stage, although Tokichi (Ganjiro) and Daizen (Tomijuro V) were individually strong. The audience seemed as disengaged as the actors. Toshi suggested, "First night, you know," but I doubt that was it.

The second drama was a scene from one of the most famous Kansai plays, *Shinju Ten no Amijima* (*The Love Suicides at Amijima*) by Monzaemon Chikamatsu. Born in 1653, thirty-seven years after the death of Shakespeare (with whom he's been compared), he's the author of a hundred plays, written originally for puppets and later adapted for actors. His domestic plays, like this one, involve four main characters: a middle-class merchant, his faithful wife, his honourable courtesan-mistress, and a villainous rival. Critics say that his strength lies not in plots or characters but in his ability to build to a single, high-tension moment when love is weighed against honour, passion against duty. In Japan, there is little contest.

The acting was more accomplished, and it contained something I didn't know existed in kabuki, improvisation on a theme — but of course within certain rules. Ganjiro was utterly convincing as Jihei, a married paper seller in love with a courtesan, who loves him equally. After receiving a pleading letter from his wife, she decides to break off their relationship. She arranges to entertain a samurai, played by Tomijuro, when she knows the paper seller will overhear them. She asks the samurai to rescue her from her lover's "unwanted attentions."

Although neither man knows, they are brothers. The two share a moment of verbal recitative that is pure magic (afterwards Toshi told us this was entirely improvised). In the end, during a fairly comic turn of mistaken identity, there are murders and suicides, and the stage is littered with corpses.

It's been my experience when I'm taken somewhere as the guest of a Japanese person that the outing usually involves a surprise which reveals itself slowly as time passes. Today was no exception. I couldn't understand why Mr. Honda seemed less than thrilled when I described going backstage ten years before to meet a master bunraku puppeteer. It turned out that he and Toshi had a similar plan to take us backstage to meet Ganjiro III. On the way, Toshi, a true kabuki groupie, met several young men he'd worked with about ten years ago when the Japan Foundation arranged a Canadian tour for Ganjiro's company and Toshi worked as a backstage interpreter. Many theatrical hugs and kisses.

We entered Ganjiro's private dressing room, removed our shoes, and knelt on tatami mats before the great man and his wife. Happily we were able to tell him honestly, through Toshi, how much we'd enjoyed his performances, both that day and as Sanjiro, the boatman, earlier at the Kabuki-za. This National Treasure wiped his brow and apologized, saying how nervous he'd been on "opening night."

He and his wife (regal in glittering kimono wrapped with a diamond-studded obi sash) spoke with us through translators; she speaks excellent English, but he doesn't. We talked about Mizoguchi's *Story of the Last Chrysanthemums*, the movie we'd seen. She told us they had once starred together in a theatrical production of the story — she as the maid, Okuro, and he, the struggling kabuki actor. Her acting career behind her, she's now a member of the Japanese parliament, in the ruling party.

She signalled to a young lady-in-waiting, who ran for four hand towels, individually wrapped and decorated with the Nakamura family crest. This seemed a perfect gift since it's been a tradition in kabuki to save the towel an actor first presses against his face after a performance, something like a brass rubbing. Authentic old face pressings have become valuable collectibles; hand towels seem to be the current *presento* of choice.

Unfortunately I'd neglected to bring my camera, not realizing that there was to be an Act 3 to the afternoon performance. Since Mr. Honda knew, he'd come prepared. Bob and I posed for several shots with this attractive couple before saying goodbye to them.

While the four of us walked together to a café, Toshi answered many of Bob's questions about kabuki for a piece he's writing. It was good to hear my suspicions confirmed that the *kakegoe*, the skilfully timed calls of appreciation made by fans in the audience, do come largely from hired retainers in the third balcony at the Kabuki-za or at the back of the National, where they can barely see the actor on the *hanamichi* runway.

Throughout our conversation over coffee, Toshi found it difficult not to voice his poor opinion of women. He giggled and apologized in advance before saying that he found it "upsetting" when women in the audience called out. As we began the walk home, Mr. Honda excused himself; he looked exhausted. I couldn't help wondering if he and his family might not have preferred to have him home on Culture Day.

After he'd gone, we continued to walk along Shinjuku-dori. Toshi explained how easy it is for a stranger to assume that Tokyo is a disorganized city. In fact, he said, it was "highly structured into specialized commercial zones," not through any overarching plan, but for convenience, convention, and good business sense. He mentioned a few of these zones, such as the Akihabara district for electronics or the area around the temple in Asakusa for household shrines.

"There are also special areas for the sale of toys, and believe it or not, an area for cakes and all kinds of sweets." Pointing to a nearby shop, he declared, "In fact, we're in it." I'd noticed that our neighbourhood had more bakeries than I'd seen elsewhere but had assumed I only noticed them because I was a housewife.

"Why are they together?" I asked Toshi.

"It's fashionable," he sneered. "The young ladies just love their sweets!" He invited us to go with him to Shinjuku, where we could buy good-luck rakes, "special for this time of year." We declined. How much culture can one consume in a single day?

TUESDAY, NOVEMBER 4

Woke up worried about our trip to Kyoto, which will start in two days. Felt somewhat better when I actually sat down with guidebooks and rehashed the itinerary with Bob. Then, while he wrote a column for the *Globe* on Imamura, I did errands. A call had come while I was out, with a request for Bob to address the Canada-Japan Friendship Society; he'd accepted. Length of speech? One hour (standard). Location? Probably the Akasaka Prince (also standard). Title for use in the newsletter? Bob had suggested "A Canadian Journalist in Japan," remarking to Michiko Asami, secretary-general of the association, "then I can speak on just about anything. Ha, ha." Ms. Asami was not amused. Humour is the last imported commodity.

Decided to skip the afternoon at the film festival — there was no Japanese movie we particularly wanted to see — and headed for the Japan Rail (JR) office at Shibuya station to "activate" our rail passes, that great boon to foreign travellers. Without the pass, internal travel would be too expensive for most foreigners, as it is for many Japanese. Now that we know when we'll start travelling, we have to find a View Plaza in a major train station and activate our first pair of one-week passes.

Finding the place was not easy. The word "plaza" can mean many things in Japan: it could be an underground tunnel, for instance. One thing it does not mean is a strip mall, as it does in North America. View Plaza was in fact a grimy hole-in-the-wall closer to a bus terminal than a train station. Once inside, we were asked to take a number and wait. It was by then 4:45 p.m. We'd assumed there would be time to book our train seats and hotels, have dinner, and be watching a movie at Bunkamura at 6:30.

The woman whose sole responsibility was travel passes spoke English "a little," and was terribly sweet. She did her best, but it occurred to me afterward that we were probably asking her to perform tasks outside her job description. Our intention had been to go straight through to Miyajima and stay there for two nights, then two in Kurashiki, one in Okayama, and one in Osaka. Well, Miyajima was completely booked. We'd forgotten it was the designated weekend for viewing autumn leaves.

All the ryokans and hotels we'd carefully selected were full; others she suggested were out of the way or expensive. All thought of Bunkamura at 6:30 dissolved. I felt the trip dissolving as well.

She booked alternate accommodations and told us we'd have to pay the full amount of ¥158,000 or about $1,800, in cash. All the guidebooks said that inns and hotels take credit cards.

When Bob objected, she disappeared, reappeared, and said that we could pay the full amount by American Express at the View Plaza in Shinjuku station. She would fax them our itinerary so we wouldn't have to put in another hour making the old arrangements anew. We said we'd do that and wandered out into Shibuya. This was an area we loved, but today the whole district looked about as appealing as the wrong side of Yonge Street. We had an appropriately dismal dinner in an Italian place where we sat next to a disagreeable young man who managed to talk, smoke, eat, drink, and cough, all at the same time. I doubt that the man, or the restaurant, has long to live.

On the way home, it occurred to me that we'd gone about booking our hotels in the wrong way. I got on the telephone and began calling every place we'd wanted to stay. Everyone was gracious and most had rooms, perhaps for only one night instead of two, but it was a start. We're now booked for all but the last two nights. Every hotel said they took credit cards but didn't ask anything of me in advance except my name and Tokyo telephone number. Tomorrow I'll play Naughty Tourist and not go to the Shinjuku station. All they have are our names, passport numbers, and JR reservations.

WEDNESDAY, NOVEMBER 5

It's no longer a scandal a day in Japanese newspapers; it's an entire front page of scandals. Yesterday, for the first time since the Second World War a securities company declared bankruptcy — a shock even though the government has guaranteed investors they'll get their money back.

At about 3:30 we headed for the Canadian Embassy to meet Stephane Jobin and his wife, Annick Goulet. We piled into their little white car and headed for Yokohama to visit Illya Shimizu and her family — her mother, Oneko Hiyoshi, the tea ceremony lady; her husband, Yasunori Shimizu, a salaryman; and their two sons, Shota, nine, and Takumi, three. Illya has worked for about eight years as the media relations officer at the embassy. We'd never had our scheduled lunch because her bronchitis kept her at home for about a week, so this was our first meeting.

Stephane certainly knew his Tokyo side streets. Despite the rush-hour traffic, we were soon zipping across the elegant, newly opened bridge spanning Yokohama Bay. "This bridge has really shortened the travelling time into Tokyo," said Stephane. True, except it still takes Illya an hour and a half each way: a seven-minute walk to the bus stop; twenty minutes on the bus to the JR station; thirty minutes on the train; another twenty on a Tokyo subway; and finally a ten-minute walk to the embassy.

We chattered happily during the half-hour drive. Annick is a fellow McGill graduate, class of 1992, exactly thirty years after me. She studied Spanish at CJEP, Russian and Japanese at university, worked in Paris for Radio Canada, then moved to Asia — rather a lot crammed into such a young life; I don't think she's thirty. Stephane told us that the night before there had been an embassy reception after the opening performance of the Famous People Players. (We'd declined the invitation to attend.) Celebrants were in short supply, so the staff literally stopped passers-by on the street and invited them to come to the party in the embassy.

"It was wonderful," Stephane said. "They had a chance to visit the embassy, which they'd never done before, and there was plenty on the buffet for everyone." I thought this a rather expensive way to save face, but I suppose the food would have been wasted otherwise.

Annick and Stephane had made this trip to Illya's many times before, once with Katherine Ashenburg, but they insisted that they didn't mind going again. "Each time it's a little different," Annick said. "I learn something new."

"Last time we went," Stephane added, "we arrived a little too early. This time I was told to take you to Chinatown and the shrine before coming to their house." We parked on one of the impossibly narrow streets and started walking through what looked like the set for *The World of Suzie Wong*, garish, seedy, frozen in time, a Chinatown of the late 1950s with carved dragons, fiery vermilion storefronts, and restaurant after restaurant, gift store after gift store.

It was quiet. There were few pedestrians, and they were Japanese not Chinese. "It wasn't like this when we were here last with my parents," Annick said. "We didn't know about Double Ten day — Sunday, the tenth of October. The streets were jammed, worse than Shibuya."

As we walked along, we nibbled steamed rice buns, gawked at the gaudy temple, and decided that six o'clock was about the correct time to arrive at Illya's. More narrow streets, residential, single-family houses, small and close together. We stopped and entered with our *presentos*: bottles of wine and sake, and an inscribed copy of Bob's *Accidental City: The Transformation of Toronto.*

We were greeted at the front door by the entire family except for Mr. Shimizu, who was not yet home. We removed our street shoes and put on slippers.

The tea ceremony was to take place first, conducted in a special tea room. Bob was the first across the threshold — with his slippers on! Loud admonishments from our hosts about leaving our slippers at the door and nervous giggles from the rest of us, grateful that we hadn't committed this footwear gaffe. Mama-san was tiny, dressed in a brown kimono with an autumn-leaf pattern, naturally. Around two sides of this eight-mat tatami room was a red carpet, one of the many special touches introduced because the following day was "the day of new tea."

Mama-san was desperate to pass on as much information as she could in the half-hour she'd been allotted. Illya is not too keen on the tea ceremony: she and her mother seem to have established operational spheres of influence. Illya, dressed in blue jeans, stayed in the kitchen until the thirty minutes had passed.

Poor Stephane had a hard time keeping up his translation. We did manage to grasp that fresh tea arrived twice a year in a large ceramic caddie elaborately tied with orange silk rope. To mark the occasion, sensei would invite her disciples, about a dozen local women, for the occasion.

"There's a special autumn flower with some red leaves in the vase in the tokonoma," she told us, "and also the scroll contains a seasonal message." The calligraphy on the scroll had been executed by our tea mistress but the wording was never clearly explained, although we understood it referred to autumn. "The tea ceremony is the most complex of Japanese rituals," she told us, "because it includes calligraphy, ikebana, and even ceramics."

Near one corner was a small pit of burning charcoal with an iron cauldron on the boil, a bamboo ladle at the ready, powdered green tea in a small bamboo container with a long-handled spoon beside it, a bamboo whisk, and four bowls for tea, each with a different autumn design. We were told that even the pieces of charcoal had been placed in the pit in a pattern that formed a kanji particular to the season. We were given seasonal cakes to start, made with rice flour, tinted pink, green, and yellow and stuffed with red beanpaste, presented on small lacquer plates with lacquer spoons. We were served in the order in which we had arranged ourselves, entirely correctly by age and rank: Bob, me, Stephane, and Annick. I wore pants, knowing this would be a kneeling experience, although after about ten minutes I gave up and lapsed into crossed legs. This was fine, Mama-san said. She'd encountered *gaijin* before.

"She wants to know if you have ever been to a tea ceremony?" Over to you, Bob, I thought.

"Not really." A positively Japanese reply. I was proud. We both silently recalled our first tea experience in prosaic Don Mills, Ontario, in the home of a woman who taught tea in a room quite similar to this. Ken Richard had been our guide. We were instructed to bow to the woman serving tea while placing the bowl on the palm of our left palm, supporting the bowl on the side with the right hand. After a single sip, we were to stop and praise the taste of the tea before downing the rest in two noisy slurps, without ever resting the bowl on the tatami. Before returning it to the tea master, we were to turn the bowl slowly, admiring its beauty before handing it back, presentation side facing the tea master.

Mama-san's eyes twinkled behind her gold-rimmed glasses, her face framed by her heavily sprayed black hair. She invited Bob to make tea first. All instructions and criticism were being relayed through Stephane, who was beginning to sweat though the room was chilly. Initially Bob's whisking needed improvement, but this was remedied

once Mama-san was told that he was left-handed and made the necessary adjustments.

"The husband must now give the tea to the wife," he was commanded.

So there was Bob, bowl in both hands, crawling on his knees towards me, afraid of spilling the tea on the tatami. I was deeply touched, the only person besides Bob who knew what a triumph this represented after all those months of injury and recovery.

My sympathy did nothing to quell my competitive spirit, however, when my turn came. Despite my desire to impress, I made many errors, more than Bob I think, until I was redeemed by my whisking. Even an occasional baker knows about whisking, but when Mama-san commented, "very good," in unaccented English, I nearly dropped my bowl. Stephane, knowing the way to my heart said later, "I've never heard her say a word in English before. Usually she thinks that if she speaks loud enough and fast enough in Japanese you'll eventually get it." Since I am guilty of the same sin, mutual respect and affection grew between Mama-san and me.

With the tea ceremony concluded, more or less on time, Shota, the older boy, offered his own form of cultural expression. He appeared dressed in his karate outfit and with great dignity went through the ten or twelve moves he'd recently performed when he traded in his beginner's white belt. He was so serious and so adorable. As he walked out beside me I wanted to give him a big hug but limited myself to saying, "That was really great!" He replied, his only English for the night, "Thank you very much," and blushed. I think there was a little love on both sides.

When we were all standing, Mama-san asked if we would like to see the garden where she grew the flowers on display in the tokonoma. As we gazed into the tiny garden through the open shoji doors, I saw that just outside the tea room there rested a piece of bamboo used to carry rainwater from a downspout into a stone basin to provide the water used for tea.

"Would you like to see the rest of the house?" Illya asked. We agreed, despite the perils of loose slippers on polished wooden floors. On the upper floor Illya and Yasunori share a large bedroom with a king-size bed. Their usual sleeping partner is Takumi, the younger boy, who also has a bunk in the room he shares with Shota. Tucked behind the big bedroom was the grandmother's storeroom — beautiful wooden and paper boxes covered in calligraphy and filled with extra tea ceremony equipment gathered over a lifetime. The room smelled sweet, like a Kanda bookshop.

The boys' bedroom was chock-a-block with stuff, almost everything designed with education in mind. Illya was on a rant about the pressures schools put on parents and kids. "And he only goes to the little local school, not even a private one!"

She pulled out his daunting hard-leather school backpack, opened it up, and showed us all the notebooks containing assignments. "Look at the kanji he has to learn." There were sheets for Grades 1, 2, and 3, where he is now. "Here are the fractions they're learning in math." The workbooks are all multiple choice, or fill in the blanks, no essay writing. "And this is the homework for parents." Each night one parent has to fill in how much time Shota spent reading, writing in his diary, doing math, science, and physical exercise. On another chart, Mom or Dad has to report how many times he brushed his teeth.

"Even during the summer," she said, "he has homework and we must report on the physical exercise he's done." Each child is under pressure to do two or three extracurricular activities as well: Shota has karate and swimming. I commiserated with her about the time it must take, especially for parents who have to drop off and pick up their kids at school.

"It isn't allowed," was her response.

"Not allowed?"

"They must come on their own." (If this is true in Tokyo as well it would explain the huge number of unaccompanied minors in school uniforms I see on subways.) "He's so tense," she added, "he has a stiff neck. That's why, when he comes home from school he watches *Mr. Stiff Shoulder*."

"*Mr. Stiff Shoulder*?" I repeated, dumbfounded.

"A cartoon they watch. It shows kids how to do exercises to relax." We're talking about a nine-year-old here.

Illya has resisted sending her son to cram school. "But next year? I don't know. It costs so much, but he must do it. There's too much pressure, though, and I worry he'll be a dropout." The worst fate a Japanese parent can envisage for a child.

"Right away they want him to be part of the group. He mustn't think for himself." I wanted to suggest that, given his mother, it seemed unlikely he would not express himself, but I didn't want to trivialize a real problem in Shota's life and the lives of all Japanese schoolchildren.

Illya's mother had been an unusual woman for her time; she wanted her daughter, her only child, to go to university and to travel. When she was nineteen, Illya signed up for an international friendship exchange, passed the exam, and lived with a blue-collar family on Merrick Island, off the coast of Florida, where she went to school for six months in the early 1970s. Both adults in that family worked at the Kennedy Space Center and had a daughter away at university.

"When I went there I was in shock. I'd never seen a dishwasher before." There were several Chinese students at the school she attended, but at the beginning she was too shy to speak. The experience no doubt improved her English and helped her get into Sophia University when she came back. (It wasn't until we were on our way home that we learned that despite the tea ceremony and its Buddhist roots, Illya and her mother are practising Catholics.)

We continued the house tour with a visit to the downstairs washroom, home of the *o-furo*. Illya rolled back the *o-furo* cover that kept the water warm for successive occupants. It turned out that the tub also doubled as a learning centre. "Look at these books," Illya pointed to piles of books inside and around the tub. "We spend so much time in the tub, this is for my little boy to study." She fished out several plastic books. "They ask questions like 2 + 3 = and when you hold the page in the hot water, the answer appears here," and she pointed to a black rectangle. "Crazy, isn't it?"

Annick and Stephane had stayed downstairs on one of two long leather sofas in the living room. They were reading Japanese children's books and laughing. "Ah," I thought. "They're pregnant." We moved to the round dining table with a big boiling pot on a gas burner in the middle for *nabe*. Soon a mountain of food, including chicken, mushrooms, cabbage, and other root vegetables, was taken apart, piece by piece, and cooked in the pot. You could pick whatever you wanted from the pot, try out various dipping sauces, and eat at your own pace.

The boys stayed briefly; when the little one started to fuss, he disappeared with his grandmother. We joked about how easy it was having children, how simple it was to stay married. Ha! Bob, Illya, and I did most of the talking. It turned out that Stephane and Annick had been married for less than a month, on October 14, which explained why her parents were in Japan. "We'll do it again when we get home," Stephane said. Their first ceremony was a civil one in Tokyo where the marriage certificate came out of a fax machine.

Then Mama-san reappeared, looking diminished in Western clothes and carrying a beige kimono neatly folded. She jabbered away while Illya translated. "My mother wants to show you how to fold a kimono. We don't use hangers, you see." Mama-san grabbed me by the sleeve and pulled me over to the sofa. She opened the kimono as if it was a lover's gift and put it on. It fanned in a circle around her feet.

"This one too long," she said as she began pulling and tugging, showing me how it should fit, the way the cord went around the waist (she didn't use an obi) and how to blouse the top. Then she took it off, still instructing me in Japanese, and held it out at arm's length.

"She wants you to put it on," Illya informed me. I'd had only one bottle of Drafty beer but was feeling slightly giddy. Next thing I knew the kimono was on, Mama-san was darting all around, pulling, tugging, scolding, until there I was, a 150-pound, grey-haired, fifty-six-year-old Jewish woman all dolled up, posing for a picture in a beige kimono.

Then she whipped it off me and summoned me back to the sofa to witness the painstaking refolding, her hands flying; me nattering on, gesturing to make a point. "I do have a couple of kimono, back home. In Toronto. Usually I hang them up, but I see this is better. Much better. So compact! No wonder they can fit into tiny drawers." Many years ago, two of my great-aunts, my grandfather's sisters from New York, visited Chatham, Ontario. They wanted to teach me, as they had taught all the other children and grandchildren, the train stops between their hometown in Russia and the next village where they had family — from Mogilov to Kovna Gaberna. Knowing the secret of folding a kimono would, no doubt, prove equally valuable. For her enthusiasm and generosity, I felt a deep affection for this woman.

Once we got back to eating, it became an even livelier party, as if we'd been friends for ages.

"Did you see *Shall We Dance?*" I asked. Everyone had. Bob described how he'd been deeply touched, had even found tears in his eyes. "When the movie began, though, I thought, 'This is going on too long. Nothing's happening!'" he said.

"You think *that* was long," Illya laughed. "They cut it down for American distribution!"

She wanted to know why Bob was so moved.

"It was the man's frustration, his limitations. When he realizes that. And in the end, how kind he is to his wife. And she to him as well." We all agreed that realistic movies about marriage were all too rare.

"But that is so Japanese," Illya added. "They never say anything, these men. I've been married for fourteen years, and my husband still has not said he loves me. Or that I am beautiful." There was a stunned silence around the table while that sank in. I think I leapt into the breach with some inane remark: "Well, you know, it's an easy thing to say. North American men say 'I love you' all the time. It doesn't mean much."

Soon Yasunori, her husband, arrived and dashed into the kitchen. Illya is a lively, intelligent, funny, and accomplished woman but she is not beautiful. Her husband is. Their marriage, like all marriages, was a complex enterprise. "He's very handsome," I said as I leaned across the table. I'd switched to sake.

"Yeah, he is," Illya smiled. "I had to ask him to marry me." I admitted to having done much the same thing. Bob, ever gallant, denied it.

We returned to Illya's life in America, and she recounted a memorable incident. "I was learning how to swim in Florida and this kid, a boy, came up to me and said, 'How come you don't shave your legs?' Don't Japanese girls shave their legs? I had no idea what to say."

"Women's body hair," I commented, "still a big subject for girls, even for women my age." I told stories about my own problems deciding when and where to shave. I reported on the ever-shifting attitudes towards body hair held by my daughters at various times in their lives. Annick said how surprised she was to discover that, contrary to popular myth, French women do shave under their arms. This was the sort of comfort level we had reached.

We then moved on to a more subcutaneous subject: the importance the Japanese attach to blood types. Illya said, "Yes, I'm AB negative. What are you?" She asked everyone at the table. I was the only one who knew (I'm O positive). Illya was flabbergasted. She explained to Stephane and Annick, for whom this was brand new, that blood type can determine hiring selection, among other things. "I got the job before this one because I was so unusual. They didn't have an AB."

We moved on to other "superstitions" that have survived the post-industrial world of the knock-on-wood and fear-of-black-cats variety. "You should see what happens here when you have a baby!" Illya exclaimed. There's superstition about naming a baby, based on the number of lines in the characters of the chosen name, combined with the characters in the surname. "We had books and books. One said one thing; the other, something else. We couldn't find a name we liked that would be all right." The first time they were desperate and consulted a fortune-teller.

"Did you pay for this?" I asked.

"Yeah, sure. You pay for everything," Illya said.

Illya's salary at the embassy was about $50,000 Canadian, comparable to someone doing similar work in the private sector in Japan or Canada. Her husband, while not an aggressive salaryman, had a responsible job working for a Tokyo company set up by a fisherman's union to monitor ocean pollution; her mother worked teaching tea, which allowed her time to help with the house and the children. She owned the home they shared. Financial concerns weighed heavily on Illya. Taking the family to the movies cost about $200 and was out of the question. "Maybe for birthdays," Illya added.

Yasunori had quietly joined us at the table after getting his own supper, breaking another stereotype. "He doesn't speak much English," Illya informed us. I think he understood more than she credited. "Every year," she told us, "we take the children and drive to see my husband's family in Shimane Prefecture, on the northern coast of Honshu. We have to pay $200 just for the fees and the toll roads."

"It cost us $700 to drive to Hokkaido for our honeymoon," said Stephane. When one sees the crowded trains and highways, it becomes clear why high fees are set as a disincentive to travel; the infrastructure couldn't support more Japanese on the move. Travelling abroad is usually cheaper, especially when the yen is strong.

"We've been to Hawaii maybe three times, yes?" Illya turned to her husband and he nodded.

"And to Okinawa too?" someone asked.

"No. It's too expensive." Of course. Okinawa is now part of Japan.

On the return trip to Tokyo, Stephane commented that Illya would be worried about the inheritance tax she'll have to pay when her mother dies and leaves her the house. "That would come to about a million dollars," said Stephane. "That's why so many Japanese families are forced to sell off part of even a small property." I could see where this would be a constant worry. It also explained the intrusion of "pencil buildings" into every sort of area, commercial and residential.

Around the dinner table, we talked about why the Japanese seemed willing to put up with high taxes, long working hours, etc. They'd elected the same party, the Liberal Democratic Party, more or less consistently since it was formed in 1955, except for a few years when it was overwhelmed by scandal. Since the war, and probably long before that, the country has relied on bureaucrats to act in the nation's best interest. In the past they've been able to huddle together in a crisis, reach some sort of consensus, and bring about necessary changes. Stephane suggested that this might not be the case today.

"Those with personal experience of the war or the terrible poverty after the war aren't running things anymore." There was a sense that "this time, they might not be able to pull it off," the "it" being the next crisis that already seems to be brewing.

"I think I should have learned Chinese," Annick mused.

Stephane was mildly annoyed. "Don't say that. There are at least a billion people to bring up to the level of the Japanese. Can you imagine how long that will take?" We continued to wage the battle over who would control Asia in a most amiable way over a delicious dinner.

I, for one, was reluctant to end the evening and Bob felt the same. How wonderful to exchange ideas and confidences with a Japanese family in Yokohama. I like Illya so much. All her family. How can we thank her? Our *presentos* seem woefully inadequate.

THURSDAY, NOVEMBER 6

A day getting ready to travel with two wildly different movies thrown in: *Cure* by Kiyoshi Kurosawa (no relation to Akira Kurosawa) and a long, close-up screen interview with Ingmar Bergman. *Cure* starred Koji Yakusho, the lead actor in *Shall We Dance?* and Imamura's last feature, *The Eel*. He has a tightly chiselled face, all planes and angles, that reminded Bob of the young Jack Palance. The story, alas, went nowhere, a fact acknowledged by the director in an interview we were handed at the screening: "I didn't really know what I wanted to do." Because K. Kurosawa was assistant director on *The Funeral*, I'd expected more.

The film did have a promising beginning — serial killings by different murderers who freely admit to their crimes but can't explain them: a husband kills a wife, a policeman his colleague. Our hero is a strung-out cop with a loopy wife. Then things fall apart. We encounter a wandering amnesiac under the influence of a Mesmer-like dead person, hypnosis that goes wrong, and the eternal Freemason conspiracy. The movie literally and figuratively moves into the dark — perhaps in homage to *X-Files*?

Then there was Bergman, not at all a likeable fellow but divinely inspired when he talks about movies, making his and watching those of other directors he admires in his own little cinematheque on the island of Faro. He admired men (and they were all men) who were possessed with the idea of seeing the world through a small beam of light. He described the filmmaking process as "a kind of insanity." He was both inspired and meticulous in the answers he gave to off-camera questions by an interviewer who sounded terrified. Bergman seemed to have been given his questions in advance. He is, without doubt, a master of control.

Stopped on the way home to buy shampoo and was assisted by an over-eager clerk, anxious to practise her English. When I had settled on the cheaper of two bottles, she reached over and pulled a third off the shelf. "Conditioner?" she looked up at me and asked.

"I have some," I snapped, teeth clenched. "At home."

"You have damaged hair?" she asked, grinning.

Of course, I have damaged hair, I wanted to tell her. And crow's feet, varicose veins, enlarged pores, benign moles, fallen arches, ground teeth, yellowing toenails, and a bruised ego. I've earned every defect and abrasion, damn it. Instead, I grinned back and said, "Yes, I have damaged hair," then paid my money and left.

FRIDAY, NOVEMBER 7

Not much sleep. Bob up at 3 a.m. calling *The Globe and Mail* to see if they'd received three columns he'd e-mailed. They had. Then bustled around to leave the apartment by 8:30 a.m. for a train that left Tokyo Station at 10:07. Slight problem with our reserved seating — Car 13, Row 1, Seats A and B, except that seat A beside the window was occupied by an elderly Japanese woman. We took B and C, preferable anyway, and hoped for the best. In Yokohama, a man entered with a ticket clearly marked Car 13, Row 1, Seat C. We showed him our tickets and let him negotiate from there. Imagined translation: "Excuse me, Respected Older Person. There seems to have been a mistake. It's probably these stupid *gaijin*. Should never have allowed them into the country. Nevertheless, to get them off my back, could I please see your ticket?" It turned out the woman was in the right row and seat but wrong car. International incident avoided.

End of contact with Mr. Yokohama, who did an imitation of a sleeping bat whose sonar informed him when either Bob or I stood to go to the toilet or to get something to eat. There he'd be, hands folded, eyes shut. I'd just reach for my purse and whammy! he was on his feet and in the aisle. The same remarkable response when we returned, on tiptoes.

Foolishly, when they announced over a loudspeaker at the station that there was no cafeteria on this particular train, we'd stocked up at one of a half-dozen food outlets on the platform — sandwiches, milk, water, and beer. What they had meant of course was "no cafeteria," not "no food." There was in fact a tsunami of food, wave after wave passing through the compartment, the vendor bowing as he or she entered and exited — whether or not there was anyone awake in the car. By 10:30, twenty-seven minutes into the five-hour trip, the sounds of plastic bags crinkling and bottle caps popping were everywhere.

I walked the entire length of the train, all sixteen cars, twice, and everyone was either eating or sleeping with the single exception of a nursing mother — who was feeding *and* sleeping. I counted eight *gaijin* in all. Not surprisingly, we pulled into Hiroshima at 3 p.m., exactly on schedule.

I'm not quite sure why I booked the city's most expensive hotel, the Rhiga Royal, for our one-night stay but I'm glad I did. Our large and luxurious room has a panoramic view of the reconstructed castle and shrine. On first encounter, Hiroshima seems a liveable city of slightly more than one million people, rimmed by mountains, much like Vancouver. I realized that I'd been leading a fairly modest existence when I thrilled at the appearance of a bath mat, more than one towel at a time, a magnifying mirror, a scale (won't use that!), and terrycloth slippers ("Please feel free to keep these"). Our daughter Sarah once asked me, as we were completing a long and particularly harrowing family trip, "Mom, what are the two best words in the world?"

"Love Mom?" I guessed.

"No," she informed me. "Room service." And that's what we did then and what Bob and I did tonight.

What I liked less was the Peace Museum around the corner. I'd spent the last few days reading the newly published book by Stephen S. Large, *Emperors of the Rising Sun: Three Biographies*, about the Meiji emperor (Mutsuhito), the Taisho emperor (Yoshihito), and the Showa emperor (Hirohito). My anger at the last emperor and his advisors, the Japanese elite in both civil and military service, had mushroomed despite the author's academic even-handedness.

The museum was grand, similar in scale, tone, and texture on the outside to Yad Vashem in Jerusalem, and with a similar mandate. But the truth is still not being told. Most contemporary Japanese refuse to accept, or even share, responsibility for the war and the devastation that resulted. Even if wartime decisions were made by a cabal of the few, the majority now has the opportunity to place blame retroactively. They refuse to do that, even in school textbooks, which shape the opinions of the young. That the ashes of executed Hideki Tojo, the German-trained general and wartime prime minister who commanded troops in Manchuria, expanded the war against China, and ordered the bombing of Pearl Harbor, now rest at Yasukuni, the shrine for fallen soldiers, is a travesty equal to the Germans erecting a monument to Adolph Hitler.

The entrance to the Hiroshima museum was architecturally impressive. Inside, small bilingual signs made it clear, for the first time to me, why Hiroshima was bombed. Its port facilities were crucial to the war effort and it had served as a military headquarters on and off since the Meiji era. More important, in the last days of the Second World War, the military had divided their command into eastern and western sectors: Hiroshima was the western hub. There, on the wall in black and white, the military and the government stated their objective in 1945: "Let there be ten million honourable deaths." If they said this (and I assume they did) and if they meant it (I believe in taking people at their word), then by dropping one bomb on Hiroshima, as horrible as that was, the Americans saved millions of Japanese lives.

The few Japanese visitors who were in the museum raced past this section; they seemed far more interested in the subsequent set of wall texts. One said, Why was the bomb dropped? I have to paraphrase because I didn't write it down, but here are the three reasons given: the Americans wanted to limit their casualties; the Communists were about to invade Japan, and the Americans wanted to prevent that; and the Americans wanted to test the effectiveness of their new weapon.

Yes, there were the terrible photographs, films of the dead and dying, and mannequins with plastic flesh peeling. All death is awful. Premature death, terrible. Humanly inflicted death, almost unforgivable. Atomic bombs, gas chambers, land mines, bullets, spears — all awful. But what was the message of the Peace Museum? Over and over we were told "No more Hiroshimas," and "This evil must stop." What about no more territorial aggression? No more leaders willing to sacrifice their own people for glory? No more people unwilling to accept their responsibility for the atrocities in China and Southeast Asia? No more false history that could lead to its repetition? Unfortunately, these messages were not to be found in the Hiroshima Peace Museum.

I did find on the streets of Hiroshima — the bustle, the construction, the twinkling lights outside our window — a tribute to the human spirit. I remembered that about fifteen years ago, in our series *Canada and Japan: Images and Realities*, Ted and Ken had prepared an entire hour comparing automobile manufacture in North America and Japan, concentrating on the Hiroshima-based company, Toyo Kogyo, that produced the Mazda. After the war, when bomb survivors suffered not only poor health but a stigma that made it hard for them to marry or find work, this company was established in Hiroshima and hired only local workers. Every time a car rolled off the assembly line, the driver would sound its horn. The idea of getting on with it, rising above it, touched me then and still touches me. (Since 1982 I've driven only Mazdas.) But, I wonder, would these optimistic citizens who rebuilt their city oppose a leader who asked them to fight a distant enemy? That, I'm afraid, remains to be seen.

SATURDAY, NOVEMBER 8

"I'd really like a room with a view of the torii," I said to Bob, as we were approaching Miyajima.

"You'll certainly have a view of something interesting. But the torii?" Bob had his doubts.

But we were lucky. Room 506 at Ryokan Iwaso has an unimpeded view of one of the most familiar Japanese images, the vermilion arches rising out of the Inland Sea at Itsukushima, "one of the three most sacred scenic attractions" according to the guidebooks. Torii are gateways that purify Shinto worshippers as they pass into the Shinto shrine precinct. Two crossbeams are held aloft by two upright columns — a simple but elegant design. Because the word torii is written with Chinese characters that represent "bird" and "dwelling," some people believe they were originally used as perches for chickens about to be sacrificed. I've seen them made from various materials — wood, concrete, and stone. The Miyajima torii, the largest in Japan, was built of camphor wood in 1875.

From our window we could also see the Five Storey Pagoda, a 1407 confection that "skilfully combines Japanese and Chinese architectural styles." That means ornate, and it certainly is.

We arrived with minimum effort, sticking to the JR train and ferry so we could ride "free," or rather "prepaid." I saw the torii, small at first, then growing larger as we approached by water, the columns buried in the high tide. Although the entire island is considered sacred, Itsukushima shrine dates back to 592, when several female deities were said to have appeared on the site. Until the Meiji era, ordinary people couldn't set foot on the shore and used to travel by boat under the gates to view the temple. Women weren't permitted until after 1945.

Behind the temple we could see the blazing maples that seem to cover the island. It would be hard to imagine a more splendid show for the tourists. (Apparently the spring cherry blossoms are as beloved as the autumn maples.) Local deer met us (along with several hundred other visitors, Japanese and a few *gaijin*) at the dock. They were small and seemed harmless if you left them alone, which we did. There are only two taxis on the small island, thirty kilometres in diameter. We were fortunate to grab an Iwaso van as it parked to drop off three departing guests — two *gaijin* and their Japanese host.

"We've had a wonderful time. It's a great place," the woman said to us. "Don't miss the walk to Mount Misen." Their host seemed pleased. We boarded the van and approached the front desk to register. Because I'd booked late at night, spoken to someone hesitant about her English, and hadn't been asked for our credit card number, I was afraid there would be a mix-up.

"Fulford, Robert?" the concierge asked, and we gladly answered in unison, "*Hai.*"

Staying at this inn is something of a miracle, as well as the result of perseverance and cash. According to Fodor's, Ryokan Iwaso has been "host to pilgrims and vacationers for 130 years," since the Meiji restoration of 1868. One can even imagine Meiji, on his many tours of the islands, staying in the older wing that looks onto Momijidani Park.

Check-in time was 3:30 p.m., check-out at 10 a.m. Since it was not yet noon, we deposited our bags at the front desk and headed for the "Rope Way," a two-stage ride, first in a cable car that held six to eight people, then transferring to a gondola that held about thirty. The day was clear and sunny, the view magnificent. At the top the hillside was covered with monkeys, yipping and scrambling over the sandy slopes designed for them, although they were free to ramble if they wished. We headed in what we thought was the direction of Mount Misen's peak but quickly lost our way. The going was a bit rough so we decided to settle for the second best view, back where we'd disembarked from the gondola.

On the way up the mountain Bob leaned over and said, "It's a real privilege to be here. I hope I never stop feeling that way." I assured him that he never would, for I believe that to be the case. If he felt any regret or injustice at not being able to make it to the top of Mount Misen he certainly didn't show it. "Almost there" was more than good enough for both of us.

We had lunch at the lookout, walked around a bit, came back down, and roamed the town — and what a town. At every corner we turned there was a surprise, and someone taking a picture of it, as delighted to be there as we were. We visited half a dozen temples, each one different and wonderful in its own way. I waded, shoes in hand, into the Inland Sea, fulfilling a long-standing dream. I approached the Itsukushima shrine as it was meant to be approached, by water.

Everywhere we walked in the town we could smell cooking sugar, the principal ingredient of the world-famous (well, in Japan anyway) *momiji manju* — seasonal cookies in the shape of a maple leaf, filled with the ubiquitous red beanpaste. I've grown quite fond of red beanpaste and consumed about half a dozen of the local delicacy. There were seasonal clams for sale, cooked on open fires that lined the main shopping street leading from the dock. I wanted to buy everything: handmade trays, saucers for Japanese teacups, all expensive and not useful in my life but beautiful to look at. I stuck to postcards and Bob ended his search for a calligraphic mug to put pencils in. We bought an extra one as a gift.

By 5:30, weary, we headed back to Iwaso. Our night's accommodation, besides the view, is a dream — a ten-mat tatami room with a small "smoking area" that consists of chairs and a mini-bar. At the other end, a toilet and private Japanese-style bath. We seem to have been assigned a wizened Japanese woman as our permanent caregiver. She popped up everywhere. Thank God, Bob and I remembered to remove our shoes before we entered our room or she might have bitten our legs. She was fierce, like a god of fury — four feet seven inches, brassy dyed-red hair to match her personality and orange lipstick, smeared at a forty-five-degree angle across her mouth. Her English was minimal. She might have been particularly enraged since we forgot to tip the manager when we arrived and to say, as they do in novels I've been reading, "Thank you for taking such good care of us," or something like that. (I suspect that few *gaijin* know this, having had it impressed upon them that in Japan there's no tipping. This, after all, is a bribe.)

As in all ryokans, our meal was served on a low table in our room. The food received an A for presentation but was not top-of-the-line gastronomically. The raw stuff was excellent: sea bream sashimi among other delicacies and a *nabe* that we cooked ourselves. Thanks to Illya, I was able to exclaim, "Ah, *nabe*!" when the brazier and clay pot were introduced, thus earning effusive praise from The Terrier. We were grateful when she returned with pickles and rice, signalling the end of the meal, a version of *kaiseki ryori*.

It's considered even by the Japanese to be a light meal, and originated with the tea ceremony around the turn of the sixteenth century. *Kaiseki* means "stones in the pocket," and referred to the habit of Zen Buddhist monks to place small, heated stones on their stomachs to keep from getting hungry while meditating or fasting. The meal is primarily an aesthetic and social experience. It involves two kinds of soup (miso and clear) and three dishes of fish and vegetables, followed

by rice and pickles. Sashimi, *sunomono* (sliced vegetables and seafood with a vinegar dressing), and *aemono* (seafood and vegetables dressed with sesame seeds, miso, and other seasonings) may also be served. This is followed by cooked foods and broiled fish or seafood. The meal contains a balance from land and sea, and plenty of sake. The freshness of the food and the artistry of the presentation are paramount.

Aware that lighting plays a part in dining pleasure, I decided halfway through the meal that the atmosphere would be markedly improved by turning off the overhead fluorescent. I did, and everything looked much softer. Immediately, the pint-size Tojo charged into the room with another course, glared at us in the romantic glow, and said, "Light no good?" Before I even tried to answer, she hit the switch and departed. I may be nervy on my own turf, but in this ten-mat tatami room, I was her slave.

A sumptuous dinner given as a farewell gift to Bob and me by Nancy Lockhart and Murray Frum featured osso buco and a parade of vegetables. One of the guests, *Globe and Mail* editor William Thorsell, who'd spent an unhappy summer working at Canada's pavilion at the 1970 Osaka Expo said, "You're sure to miss this in Japan after all that seaweed and squid!" Mostly he was wrong, but today? Not in his wildest anti-Japanese moments could he have imagined Ilse of Iwaso. Nor could I.

She seemed to find us equally amusing, and made a great fuss finding a yukata large enough for Bob. I must say that dressed in our matching blue-and-white robes complete with tabi — short white socks that separate the big toe from the rest (like mittens for the feet) — we looked ridiculous. With the meal over and the two of us ready for bed, Her Loveliness ushered in a young man and woman who swiftly and silently moved our dining table to one side, spread the futons and quilts on the floor, and disappeared. "Whew!" I said. "That's the last we've seen of her."

"Not necessarily," Bob replied. "She could be here in the morning."

"No way. It's already 9:30. She couldn't!"

SUNDAY, NOVEMBER 9

Bob, damn him, was right. There she was, first thing in the morning, wearing a plain white dress, exhorting us to go to the first floor for breakfast, instructions we'd received when we checked in. She kept repeating, "Mama-san, mama-san. Number one. Number one!" I had no idea what she meant. "Hai," I said. Why not?

I had ordered the Japanese breakfast and Bob, the Western. When we sat at our table, various elements were missing — spoons, milk — that sort of thing. Out of the corners of their eyes, an older Japanese couple at a nearby table watched us trying to cope and called a waitress to our aid. I had smoked mackerel, pickles, three small salads, rice, nabe ('tis the season), green tea, miso soup, and a mikan (tangerine). Bob used the toaster installed at our table with slots large enough for two slices of pillow bread. He also ate the salad and coffee on his tray. It seemed that something was missing, like a main course. When he'd finished, the waitress returned and said, "Scrambled?" to which Bob nodded. A few minutes later his eggs arrived, like dessert. Since we'd both slept well on the holy island, we bore our trials with good grace.

Several people in the huge dining room were dressed as traditional Japanese travellers should be, in yukata and slippers. Through the window, we even saw a group getting a jump on the leaf viewing, walking through the park in their breakfast attire. You have to get up pretty early in the morning to beat the first ferry full of tourists, who land at 6 a.m.

Our travel arrangements for the day were flexible. Japan is geared to train travel and the JR posts information in English that permits us to make errors but rarely irreparable mistakes. And so we went first by Shinkansen, the bullet train, to Okayama, an hour-long trip, then transferred to the Sanyo line for Kurashiki. The original town was built by wealthy merchants who grew cotton and rice on reclaimed land and shipped it inland to Osaka on a series of canals. Today, in the old part of the city where we're staying for two days, there are about a dozen museums and galleries, as well as remnants of the canals. Each year four million tourists, almost all Japanese, come to stroll and admire. A good number are here today.

We knew in advance that many of the museums would be closed tomorrow, Monday, so, after dropping our bags at Ryokan Kurashiki, where we would spend the first night, we raced to the museums we most wanted to see — the Ohara Museum of Art, and the Kurashiki Folkcraft Museum, both remarkably good. The Ohara collection is housed in several buildings, the largest a neoclassical structure reminiscent of the Roman Pantheon, a strange sight on the old canal.

Magosaburo Ohara (1880–1943) was the second-generation president of the Kurashiki Spinning Corporation. Under the guidance of his friend, the Western-style painter Torajiro Kojima, Mr. Ohara collected largely French painters — Corot, Gauguin, Toulouse-Lautrec, and the all-time Japanese favourite, Rodin. In response, I suspect, to injured national pride, Mr. Ohara's son added a wing in 1961 dedicated to modern Japanese art.

The Folkcraft Museum was particularly memorable, especially the pottery and the textiles. We weren't the only ones impressed by the simplicity of the designs, the elegance of the execution, and the relationship between beauty and utility. On the wall of one room hung a framed letter dated December 1954, written in English and translated into Japanese. It said that this museum "did more than preserve the past," that it provided "an example of the beauty in ordinary things," and suggested that study of these objects could "serve as a guide to new methods of production." It was signed Walter Gropius.

We returned to our ryokan at 4:00 p.m., an hour after check-in time, and were shown to a terrace tea room cluttered with art deco pieces from Vienna. Seated at a refectory table, we were served green tea in proper seasonal bowls and ate our first red bean cakes of the day while Western chamber music played in the background. As we were sipping and nibbling, we were given the fire safety instructions to read and forms to fill out stating the time we'd like to have dinner, our beverage preferences, what sort of breakfast — Japanese or Western — we'd like, and when. As we were being escorted to our room, we smiled at the owner who was sitting surrounded by ceremonial tea-making equipment and his camera collection.

Our room was charming, furnished in dark mahogany and paulownia. There was a late-thirties radio cabinet in the tokonoma, right in front of the calligraphy scroll and stately ikebana arrangement. Jump thirty years ahead to a low table against the same wall and there was a 1960s television set beside a mother-of-pearl dressing table about six inches off the ground with a small makeup mirror on top. On the next wall was a formal sideboard holding a gilded clock that had stopped at 8:14, as well as a wooden writing box containing traditional stationery (with vertical lines), envelopes, pencils, as well as a small lamp with a Tiffany-style shade made of paper. A long extension cord indicated that it was to be dragged across the room and used as a reading lamp once we were snugly in our futons. On the third wall, bringing us into the 1980s, was an electric radiator with a remote control. In the "smoking room," separated by a shoji sliding door, there were two large chinoiserie carved chairs, a small marble-topped table between them. There was no mini-bar and not a single lock on any door. Everything was clean but slightly seedy, crammed with hybrid objects — East meets West.

Outside the window of the smoking room was a beautifully laid out miniature garden — a bamboo gate tied open, stepping stones. *Ishidoro* stone lanterns, designed for candles but now electrically wired, lined the path leading to the larger garden outside the tea room we'd just left. I wanted to explore the garden tomorrow but needed my shoes back. They were left at the front door in exchange for plastic slippers.

Our luggage was waiting inside when we arrived, as well as more tea and a pink-and-blue "sleeping setto." The Western hospitality industry should come to Japan for graduate courses. Perhaps as a legacy from Edo times, when travellers rode from inn to inn with only a single outfit, and were provided with indoor footwear, a sleeping outfit, towels and cleaning equipment to use in the public bath, and given meals in their private dining room — the opposite of the West, where we eat in public and bathe in private. We could check into Ryokan Kurashiki with no luggage and have a wonderful time. One disadvantage is there's no place for a nap, but since the Japanese can sleep on all sorts of moving conveyances, probably even horses, this wouldn't have been a problem.

Napping in our room would have been impossible in any case, as a boisterous wedding party was breaking up right above us. The incessant *Arigato gozaimashita!* sounded more like a Buddhist chant than communication. Maids were running upstairs and returning with huge trays weighed down with hundreds of dishes. These same women, four in all, brought us our ten-course dinner. I was all ready for them — showered and wearing my yukata and slightly soiled tabis I was sure the Ryokan Iwaso wanted me to keep. When the first server arrived, she pointed at my feet and said, "Tabi, *ne*?" started giggling, and called a friend over to peek.

The second server thought Bob was a sketch because he was only drinking Coke and I was having beer and sake. When she saw that he didn't like wasabi, the powerful green horseradish, in his soy sauce, she became almost hysterical with laughter. (Like real geisha, they laugh at men who are, according to them, just little boys craving their mama-san's breasts. "Rude" would perhaps be too strong a term for their behaviour, but certainly their style was not up to the otherwise high hospitality standards set by the inn.)

The meal was spectacular. Almost every course involved seafood — raw, barbecued, boiled, breaded and fried, baked in broth, or on its own. The sashimi, red tuna and white mackerel, was cut into cubes and reconstructed into patterned squares. Other parts of the meal looked liked cross-sections of a tree, or geological layers of the earth. The number of women hours put into this meal was alarming. Bob wasn't nuts about his fish, so we did a quick swap of our plates in a brief moment when we were alone. Eating took about an hour, a mostly glorious hour.

For bedtime reading matter, we'd each allowed ourselves only one book on this trip, intending to trade. Since Bob had finished his, by mutual agreement we traded. I received one we'd recently bought in Kanda: *Fragments of a Past: A Memoir,* by the historical novelist Eiji Yoshikawa, and Bob started *The Buddha Tree* by Fumio Niwa, a novel set in the home of a Buddhist priest, drawing on the author's own childhood. Growing up, in both books, is a horrific experience. Reading about Japan in Japan is like our dinner — layers upon layers, illusion and reality, old and new.

While Bob was undressing and I was tucked into my quilts, I mentioned that there were no locks on the door and what a wonderful symbol of trust that was. "Interesting," he said and slipped off his underwear. At that exact moment, when Bob was entirely naked, the door to the hall flew open. Three ladies rushed in, babbling, trying to explain something to us that we couldn't understand, apparently not noticing that Bob was hopping about shouting, "I'm naked! I'm naked!" He grabbed his pyjamas and headed for the W.C., underpants abandoned in the middle of the floor.

Meanwhile, the ladies were gathering up our belongings — emptying the closet and the drawers — carting everything off somewhere. They were moving us somewhere. "So sorry. Noisy, *ne?*" They made stamping motions with their feet and smiled. Apparently the party above was continuing, or a new one starting, and they thought we would be disturbed. "Okay?"

"No, it is *not* okay." Bob had reappeared, almost dressed. "Moving people in the middle of the night is not okay."

I stopped laughing long enough to suggest to Bob that he continue dressing and just go where they were taking us. Other than wrestle our belongings out of their hands, I could see no alternative. "And it *is* awfully noisy here," I added, following that unwritten traveller's rule that when one person loses his sense of humour, it's up to the other to restore balance. I suppose it was thoughtless of me to laugh quite so hard, but I couldn't help it.

By the time I collected myself, the three overworked hotel women had their job completed. The new room down the hall was much like the old one — more exuberant flowers, a smaller smoking area. It doesn't feel like "my room," as the other did. Bob drifted off to sleep first. I couldn't stop laughing, silently, a schoolgirl's trick that still comes in handy.

MONDAY, NOVEMBER 10

Last night, lying on my futon and looking up at the brown-and-white squares on the ceiling, on the shoji, on the lamp, and the tatami, I felt almost as if we were living inside a Mondrian. How different the world looks from the floor. I began to understand something of the shoe obsession in Japan: here the floor serves as the place you store your clothes, write, cook, eat, sleep, make love, and, of course, walk. I could hear Bob tossing, still miffed at being relocated, I suspected. No doubt these overworked ryokan ladies, powerless in many ways, take pleasure in bullying grown men, perhaps especially *gaijin*. Life in a ryokan is a play. As actors, Bob and I know little of the drama we've entered and even less of the language in which it's performed.

This became clear again at 7 a.m. when a man's voice boomed out over the inn's loudspeaker. He said good morning, all that I could understand, and he sounded calm. But then sirens went off, as if we were in the middle of a fire or, this being Japan, an earthquake. (Where were those escape instructions, and why couldn't I remember what they said?)

This time, Bob was dressed. He headed out the door, where he met one of the maids who'd moved us in the night. She indicated in a stream of Japanese that everything was all right. Apparently feeling a little residual anger, Bob bellowed, "An announcement on a loudspeaker at seven in the morning, and then an alarm! If that's all right, what *isn't* all right?" Of course she understood not one word but the tone was unmistakable. Bob disappeared in the general direction of the front desk and returned reassured that the building was not burning or falling down, although we still didn't know what had happened.

Breakfast soothed our ruffled feathers. Bob's Western breakfast was a many-splendored thing. First, a battered red toaster arrived, followed by two slices of pillow bread, two fried eggs, salad, and chopsticks - a tricky business, eating eggs with chopsticks, but he was managing quite well. Still, I suggested to our server that a "forku" would be nice. (I'd been told that adding vowels at the end of English words was one way to communicate.) She returned just as Bob's toast was turning nicely beige but she began to dance around the toaster as if Bob was intending to burn the place down. He took charge: the etiquette of slippers he might not understand, but toasters? He flicked her away with his hand and waited, Buddha-like, until his toast was acceptably brown.

We left our bags at the ryokan so that we could plot the distance to our next hotel, the Kurashiki Kokusai, and see if we needed a cab. Ambling along beside the canal in the nippy air, I decided I needed a hat, generally a traumatic shopping experience since my head size often forces me into men's departments. This time I got lucky right off — a black lady's hat I liked, and it fit!

While I was waiting to pay, I saw Bob engaged in conversation with a sporty-looking older Japanese gentleman. He was wearing a windbreaker, in itself unusual, and standing beside his rickety bicycle. When I joined them I was impressed by the twinkle in his eyes and the lack of either superiority or subservience in his tone, only interest and fellowship.

"I've been retired for eleven years," he said. "For me, every day is now a holiday."

Leaping in with the penetrating questions, as always, I asked, "How did you learn to speak English so well?"

"I listen to Voice of America. At first I thought it was propaganda but ... " He threw up one hand and laughed. Then, to prove his point, he recounted the morning's news, that Clinton and Saddam were rattling sabres but not yet drawing lines in the sand.

"And you?" he asked Bob. "What do you do?"

"I'm a journalist."

"Oh, journalist. That is a very big thing in Japan. You know Japanese, 'very hierarchy.' Businessmen in suits walk very Confucius-like." He rested his bike against a tree and did a wonderful imitation of an important man walking with hands behind his back.

"You know, I am what you call a maverick, a nonconformist. Look how I dress. I used to dress worse. Big troublemaker. Not very good at consensus."

He was not deranged, only anxious to say as much as possible before we separated. He asked us to guess his age. I guessed too low and Bob too high. He was sixty-seven.

"And what was my job before?" This was tricky as well. To place him too high or too low would be embarrassing. He said we should try. He wouldn't be insulted — as he made clear, he was not a "typical Japanese."

I started. "Engineer?"

"No. Very wrong. I hate math."

"Something to do with driving?" We decided on the twenty-questions approach.

"Not at all. I drive a bicycle."

"A gardener?"

"No. No green thumb."

We should have guessed sooner than we did when he asked us, "Do you know what Shinkansen means? I will tell you. '*Shin*' means 'new'— like New York, New Hampshire, New Zealand, New Caledonia. And '*kan*'? This is '*kan*,' and he ran over and threw his arms around a tree. A 'trunk.' '*Kan*' is 'trunk.' And '*sen*' is 'line.' *Shin-kan-sen* — new trunk line!"

We told him we couldn't guess. "I was a teacher of English, but I never got very far. They told me that my English was too common!" He said he taught his students how to speak English but didn't give them sufficient drilling in grammar to pass the big entrance exams for university. They sent him to Hokkaido, I gather the Japanese version of Siberia, to teach adults only; then to Kurashiki where he either quit or was fired at age fifty-six.

Now he holds an employee's pass to the recently opened Tivoli Park, behind the railway station, a theme park modelled on Copenhagen's Tivoli Gardens. There he acts as something of an informal guide, without a uniform. "The Danish prince was there to open it. I was there, but I couldn't get close, of course. All these officials around in a big circle." He said that by reading Shakespeare, he'd learned about another Danish prince, Hamlet. The idea amused him.

"I was told that I am in an English guidebook — someone who welcomes people to Kurashiki, but I haven't seen it."

By then he'd escorted us to our hotel. "*Kokusai*," he said. "Do you know what it means? It means 'international,' but it's not really international." We said goodbye at the hotel steps, walked back to the ryokan, and returned with our bags to check in before setting out to do more touring on a quiet Monday.

As we walked around town, quite far from the canal and our new hotel, our new English-speaking friend popped out in front of us. "I have a present for you," he announced. "Open it."

Inside was a set of postcards of Kurashiki. We thanked him profusely, slightly embarrassed by his generosity. "These cards are more than ten years old, but look at this one." He took one from the series and handed it to us. "Look at this picture. Why this picture especially?" It showed a bridge over one of the canals and in the water, the usual sea of carp. Bob's turn to guess. "Because of something that's missing?"

"No," he replied, somewhat disappointed. "Because of something that is there. Look harder."

We did. Standing on the footbridge, looking into the water, was our own new friend.

"That's me. Same jacket. Ten years ago!"

He discovered his image on the postcard while writing to an American pen pal. Now he gives them to everyone he meets, adding his name, Mr. Yasuzo Sato, in English and Japanese, and his Kurashiki address. Bob gave him a business card while I took a photograph of the two of them.

Later that night, Bob and I wandered over to the bright lights of Tivoli Park — "internationalism," Japanese style. Make a replica of something foreign and famous, adapt it to Japanese needs, hire a few nationals from the imitated country for authenticity, and provide Japanese with the highlights of a foreign trip right in Japan. In Hokkaido there's an

Anne of Green Gables Land, staffed by a red-headed girl who lives there with her family and is now well on in age. There's a mock Dutch village near Nagasaki even though the authentic Dutch-influenced structures are being torn down. There's a British village not far from Tokyo where you're handed pounds sterling to buy lager and lime, Cornish pies, and Shetland sweaters. For the "host" countries, these theme parks are like a permanent trade fair.

At Tivoli Park there were Disney-like rides with a Danish overlay, "The Little Mermaid" and lots more Hans Christian Andersen. Instead of riding around in Alice in Wonderland's giant teacups, they offer the same pleasure in blue-and-white cups of Royal Copenhagen. As with Disneyland, once you buy your admission, all attractions are free, including several theatres. (The Disney model seems perfectly suited to the Japanese — no surprises, a chance to recapture childhood, and an opportunity to appear foolish in a predetermined way. Most Japanese, responding to a recent survey, said that "visiting Tokyo's Disneyland" was their peak cultural experience.)

Since it was getting colder, Bob and I slipped into a theatre. On this Monday night in November, it was about one-third full: parents and children, and parents without children, like us. The show was slick — pre-recorded music, endless pyrotechnics, expensive costumes, and a multiracial cast of fourteen young, high-energy performers, wasted on a banal story about a carousel coming to life and laid on top of a very loud through-score (as in opera or a modern Andrew Lloyd Webber epic musical). There are shticks designed to please the grown-ups: a trio like the Supremes and a Japanese Elvis Presley. Nothing Danish here, but who cared? The kids loved it.

After the performance, we bought skinny hot dogs and large Cokes and sat shivering beside a "lagoon." I can't explain why I love theme parks, but I do. I would like to "travel the globe" on the Japanese islands. We had a pleasant walk back to our "international" hotel with twin beds, locked doors, and a staff that plays by the rules.

TUESDAY, NOVEMBER 11

Himeji Castle makes a wonderful stage set, so it's not surprising that Akira Kurosawa used it for exteriors in *Ran*, his 1985 epic version of *King Lear*, with nods to *Macbeth*. Unfortunately, the interiors have been stripped of their former glory. Shirasagi, or the White Egret, the huge structure that's only part of the original, has been standing since the fifteenth century. Terumasa Ikeda acquired it in 1609 for services rendered in the Battle of Sekigahara. He was the son-in-law of Tokugawa Ieyasu, founder of the Tokugawa shogunate.

Unlike French or British castles of the same period, no attempt has been made at Himeji to recreate the castle's mood — the commonplace or the menacing. Just the opposite. Loudspeakers constantly reminded us of the present and our presence: they warned us against eating, drinking, or smoking on the site. One outstanding feature that remains is the separate wing for *seppuku*, or as it is crudely called *harakiri*, literally, "belly slitting."

Despite the Japanese renown for horticulture, they're hopeless with lawns. They don't mow them, they shave them, so the roots burn in the sun. There's been little rain in the six weeks we've been here, and I have not seen a single sprinkler and rarely a garden hose. As a result, everything is yellow and nasty. We've decided to skip one of the three great gardens on our list — the one in Okayama — since it's said to be remarkable for its lawns.

The towns of Himeji and Okayama, both with populations of about half a million, have grand boulevards running from the station, one to the castle, the other to Korakuen Gardens. This is town planning in the Baron Haussmann style, with the predictable effect in Okayama's case of a huge empty promenade at night with all the energy on the side streets and laneways, crammed with small shops and bright lights.

In Himeji, which looked like a port city on our map, I had an urge for the Inland Sea and a naive desire to practise my few words of Japanese. On leaving the castle grounds, I found my unwitting victim, a sweet taxi driver. I asked him to take us to an excursion boat. He said, "pier?" and I assumed that he and I had the same place in mind.

We drove past the railway station (I knew from my map that this was the right general direction), on and on past junkyards and dirty canals, until we reached a pier. But yipes! This was a big port! "My God," I said, looking at the rusting seagoing ship in the harbour, "the next stop is Vancouver!"

Poor taxi driver. Poor us. He realized that this wasn't what we'd had in mind. He couldn't leave us there, to catch an ocean liner. What to do? First, he turned off his meter, now about $30. Then he parked and ran into the customs office and came back with two chaps, one of whom stuck his head in the cab window and asked, "To Kobe?"

I tried to explain that all we really wanted was to get to Okayama, by water if possible. He suggested the JR. I told him that, yes, we knew about the JR. We'd come in that morning on the JR ... when Bob wisely interrupted with, "*Domo arigato*." In hopped our cabby, who didn't restart the meter but made a sign that looked like, and was, half. We agreed to designate the trip "one way," since we'd both been victims, and perpetrators, of miscommunication.

Our hotel was a model of bland modernism — low ceilings, dim lighting, acres of unused space, Scandinavian furniture everywhere. The simple, uncluttered style of the 1950s. A working time capsule.

In the morning paper, the *Daily Yomiuri*, I'd read a wonderful review of bunraku in Osaka and thought it would be fun to stop there on Thursday, on our way back to Tokyo. Bob agreed. Nothing like a little spontaneity in our well-planned trip. But first, tomorrow to Takamatsu on the island of Shikoku. It will be our first trip to another of the main islands. There are thousands of small islands in this archipelago nation, but only four major ones — Honshu (where we have been with a jaunt to the tiny island of Miyajima), Kyushu in the south, Hokkaido in the far north, and Shikoku in the Inland Sea. My reading assures me there will be plenty of excursion boats there.

WEDNESDAY, NOVEMBER 12

After a wonderful day on the road, coming back to our hotel room in Okayama for a second night was comforting. It's been almost a week since we've spent two nights in the same place.

We left at about 9:30 a.m. for Takamatsu, crossing over what I had heard from Cy Taylor was a most amazing bridge, except it was impossible to see while travelling across. When it was completed in 1993, it was the longest bridge in the world, 2.7 kilometres, and it incorporated every known feat of bridge engineering as it conquered different soil conditions from island to island. On the way back, as we rounded a corner I could see something of the engine, the bridge ahead, and a sunset blazing in the west.

Because buses are not tourist-friendly, we hadn't been on a regular city bus until Takamatsu, where we boarded our first local bus of the trip. It travelled from the train station to Ritsurin-koen (Ritsurin Park), a ten-minute ride. Although this is not one of the Big Three National Parks, the *Lonely Planet Travel Survival Kit* says, "it could easily be a contender."

The garden was completed after a hundred years of planning, planting, pruning, cultivating, and irrigating. There's a north garden that's more sprawling, and a south garden with six ponds and thirteen scenic mounds arranged so that as you walk the intersecting paths. According to Fodor's, there's always "a new view or angle to hold the focus of your attention. You cannot hurry through this garden: each rock, each tree shape, each pond rippling with multicoloured carp has a fluidity of motion enhanced by the reflections of the water and the shadows of the trees."

Rarely does a basic guidebook rave about any site, but I couldn't imagine anyone disagreeing with its assessment. Unlike Himeji, the authorities wanted us to enjoy our time with them; for ¥810 we could wander at will and enjoy tea and a sweet in the tranquillity and grace of the Chrysanthemum Moon Pavilion, a feudal-era teahouse built for the pleasure of the Matsudaira clan. There were benches and places to eat throughout the park, a rare phenomenon in Japan (one is usually expected to keep moving).

Especially remarkable was the park's siting against the backdrop of Mount Shuin, ablaze this time of year with fall colour. And the carp. We spent the better part of an hour sitting in a corner of the park, in front of a stand selling carp-feeding food, the Styrofoam baguettes. There were benches and a small waterfall where we could appreciate the glinting carp colours — gold, yellow, blue, green, red, black, and white, each carp bearing unique markings. They took turns darting forward, or lay motionless at the bottom of the pond. No wonder their shape is favoured by kitemakers: they move in water as if dancing in wind.

"I could stay here all day," Bob remarked, voicing my own feelings. "It's so restful."

"When I'm reborn, I want to come back as a carp," I announced, "and in a garden such as this." That went without saying.

As we were leaving the gardens, we saw groups of elderly Buddhists who were doing the famous pilgrimage to the eighty-eight temples on the island of Shikoku. Today, many make the tour in air-conditioned buses that drive them to within sight of each temple, transforming the exercise from a purely religious quest into a seniors' outing. Their costumes are stunning nonetheless — white apron, white wide-brimmed hat, white walking staff.

Bus back to the ferry dock and a lunch of peanuts, pretzels, and coffee for Bob and beer for me. At 1:10 p.m. we boarded the ferry for Shodo-shima, a large island about an hour away. Because there are now high-speed boats whisking people across the Inland Sea, there were only about four other people aboard who had not driven their car, bus, or truck into the bowels of our boat. I tried to imagine what the Inland Sea might have looked like before it became so highly developed, or the way it was when Donald Richie wrote his travel memoir *The Inland Sea* in 1971. Today, hydroelectric poles and ocean-going ships fill the horizon.

On board the ferry there was nowhere to buy proper food — noodles or bento — and that was unusual. I think that the Japanese have traded in their nourishing snack food for the fried and fatty American-style products. There are potato chips aplenty. One could still buy a package of dried seaweed, but there was nothing to compare with the variety of fresh and packaged foods I remember from ten years ago. And it shows in the fat and acne-spotted teenagers.

What might have been expected, although I'd never seen them before, were the places set aside for sleeping. Public napping has become institutionalized on ferries. On the largest deck, there was an enclosed, carpeted area where men, women, and children, truck drivers, housewives, and students take off their shoes, lie down on newspapers, and faster than you can say Shodo Island, fall into a deep sleep.

On the water my thoughts turned sentimental — the sort of time-passing thoughts one often associates with water travel. I have been with Bob for half my life: I was twenty-eight when we started to live together; we've been married for twenty-seven years. Japan has become a place of renewal. We find ourselves alone in a strange land with only one another for emotional support and intellectual stimulation, without work pressures or family diversions. For us, Japan has become an alternate reality, where all our senses and all our thinking are spent working out the world that's presented to us. I could not imagine Japan without Bob.

Although Shodo Island is not renowned for its tourism, I thought that I could spend an interesting day or so there. Its main industry is rock quarrying. At one site, far from where we docked, lies a mountain of cut stone, each piece with the name of the Edo lord who ordered it for his castle. He ran into unexpected difficulties and his order sits, hundreds of years later, waiting to be picked up.

I was miffed when something I was reading on the ferry mentioned that there were "frequent trips to the island from Himeji." Aha! I was right. Small consolation.

On the return trip from Shodo we were joined on the top deck by a high-school class, boys and girls in their mid-teens. There were the usual sleepers, the girl gigglers, and the boy clowns. One brave young man was sent over to ask us where we were from. "Canada? Yes, hockey!" and he proceeded to do a convincing pantomime of a stick-handling player who gets a bodycheck that sends him crashing into the guard rail. We all laughed. They were typical in that they gained courage from their group. I was certain that not one of them would have had the nerve to approach us alone.

Back in Okayama, without going to our hotel (I thought that, once in my yukata, I would never get out again), we set off for dinner and a restaurant that had a giant crab crawling up its exterior wall, like King Kong on the Empire State Building. Inside, we found a bilingual menu with pictures and ordered the house special, crab *nabe*. A heaping platter of cabbage, tofu, mushrooms, and crab arrived, more crab than I'd ever seen at one time, certainly more than I thought we could ever eat. But then, travel is full of surprises. The pace of eating was regulated by the cooking time — each piece needed about two minutes in the boiling broth, flavoured with sake and soy. It was a memorable meal, one of the best. *Nabe* in Yokohama, Miyajima, and now Okayama. I began to imagine a *nabe* tour, sampling local ingredients in every corner of Japan, a task for which I would gladly volunteer.

Over dinner we decided to skip a day-trip to Osaka, change our JR tickets at the station and leave for Tokyo directly from Okayama tomorrow. The thought of even this small negotiation would have made us a little crazy a week ago. Now I have learned to write down all requests and hand them over, since written comprehension is greater than oral. I'm also confident that the national rail system is probably the best in the world, that trains run so often on major routes that booking in advance, except on holidays, is unnecessary, and that having a JR pass allows *gaijin* like us to hop on and off.

THURSDAY, NOVEMBER 13

When we arrived back in Tokyo this afternoon, the always crowded streets between the station and our apartment were brought to a standstill in several places by police vans and roadblocks. Premier Li Peng of China was in town, the man who sent the army into Tiananmen Square. As our taxi crawled past the Diet we saw scores of police, many in riot gear, but only one small protest by old and infirm people who seemed to have nothing to do with the visit and were allowed to proceed. Li Peng's arrival coincided with news that the Chinese government had re-arrested a student dissident who'd recently been released from prison. The pairing of Japanese and Chinese flags lining the route to symbolize a détente between two former enemies seemed offensive in light of today's news.

The area close to our apartment was particularly slow, perhaps because the official state dinner was to be held later at the New Otani hotel, suited for the occasion since it has all the warmth of an official communist banquet hall. As I looked out from our balcony, the security seemed comical. Almost certainly the only killers for miles around were Li Peng and his henchmen.

The anxiety of the Japanese to prevent an international incident and their love of uniforms were even more apparent when I went out to do errands. There were men with fibreglass helmets covering their faces, walkie-talkies strapped to their sides, chic pale-blue uniforms like something from *Star Wars*, even special thick-soled, calf-high rubber boots in case they had to use fire hoses against crowds that were nowhere in evidence. Traffic barely moved. If there was to be an incident, I thought it might be started by drivers clubbing cops for parking their vehicles in the middle of arterial roads at rush hour. Of course, not a single horn could be heard, only a police helicopter circling overhead. I find this deference to authority frightening. Order makes life in this mega-metropolis possible and my life as a tourist enjoyable. But how to calibrate this kowtowing? Recently, I've noticed a small streak of anarchy in the Japanese psyche: they don't always follow the arrows designed to regulate the Up and Down foot traffic on subway stairs. They still have some distance to go before achieving an equitable balance between personal expression and collective imperatives.

Christmas decorations are everywhere. Christmas books, often in English, and presents wrapped in Christmas paper, contribute to a mock festivity that seems even more outlandishly commercial than in Canada. Fortunately for the merchants in this largely Shinto-Buddhist culture, the custom of giving elaborate gifts at year end closely coincides with December 25. Still, they have enthusiastically adopted the aesthetic of Christmas — tinsel, snowflakes, and jingle bells.

A welcome phone message from Illya, who wanted to change lunch from Monday to Tuesday, which is fine with me. She reported that the day after our visit to her house, I was "an entry" in her son's diary. His teacher said she envied his contact with so many foreigners.

FRIDAY, NOVEMBER 14

First thing this morning Mr. Akasaki, the building manager, arrived with a typed three-page set of house rules in English, updated November 1997, hot off the press — "hot" being the appropriate word since it was last night's alarm that no doubt brought it into being. I was heating sake on the cooktop and had forgotten to turn on the kitchen exhaust. All hell broke loose — phone calls from security and a visit from the heavily garbed gas inspector, who left satisfied that I'd learned my lesson.

After reading all the rules, I realized that we've been guilty of three other misdemeanours: we moved the living-room furniture around without consulting the management; we hung posters and postcards (using removable masking tape on doors and cupboards only, not walls); and we put laundry out to dry on the balcony. All are verboten. The furniture will stay as it is and so will the wall decorations. However, the clothes rack on the balcony has been removed to the spare bedroom. I consider this concession a reasonable compromise.

While Bob and Jun dealt with e-mail, I finished *Jishin*, a book about the 1923 Kanto earthquake by Lee Riordan, an American whose parents, a Russian-born mother and American-professor father, were young lovers trapped in the wreckage that left 140,000 dead in Tokyo. The book is an odd mix of fact and fiction, composed from stories his parents told him, with first-person accounts by a variety of Japanese survivors tacked on. I suspect that some of these were taken from published journals, but the author doesn't provide a bibliography. The story itself was so engrossing I forgave him.

I began another book, also by an American, on a tantalizing subject usually closed to those who don't speak the language. *The Encyclopedia of Japanese Pop Culture* is written by Mark Shilling, a journalist who has lived in Tokyo for years, is raising his family here, and writes movie reviews. Just when he'd whetted my appetite for Japanese television, our super-duper set stopped working. Did I have the nerve to bother Mr. Akasaki again? If I invited him into the apartment, would he notice our furniture re-arrangement? Would he rip the posters off the cupboards and doors? Careful thought must go into this decision.

Also on the technical front, Bob called John Harris's friend, Parmesh Bhatt, a travel agent and sumo enthusiast who has arranged an official tournament in Vancouver for 1998. He's an Indian-born Canadian who speaks many languages, including Japanese, and he's passionate about increasing Japanese tourism to our country. As he sees it, the Japanese don't know enough about Canada to be interested. In preparation for the tournament, Japanese television crews will fan out to make videos about how wonderful we are. One can't help but admire Bhatt's optimism.

While discussing other things, Bob mentioned our ongoing e-mail frustration. "It's your telephone," Bhatt said. Since his office is nearby, and he sounded so confident, Bob was inclined to believe him. He said that all Bob had to do was push a certain phone button, and he, Parmesh, would call the telephone company who would do the rest from their office. By Monday everything should be humming. Perhaps the age of miracles hasn't passed.

SATURDAY, NOVEMBER 15

Eventually, I suppose, the enormous Edo-Tokyo Museum will swallow both the smaller Fukagawa Edo Museum and the Shitamachi Museum, but that will be a shame. The Fukagawa area has a long history as part of the Low City in the late Edo period, before 1868, when shops and citizens moved across the Sumida River into posher neighbourhoods closer to the Imperial Palace. Old Shitamachi, beside the Shinobazu Pond at the bottom of Ueno Park (one of the five parks created early in the life of Tokyo), was a thriving neighbourhood at the turn of the century. Both museums are charming and manageable, history in bite-size pieces; both have restored shops, homes, and public places that re-create the world of ordinary merchants and artisans.

We decided to visit them chronologically. The Fukagawa Museum was in an area I'd never visited before, an unglamorous district of auto-body shops. We were slightly lost and corralled a young couple, who were clutching a newspaper ad for a shop where he was hoping to buy a motorbike. She had studied English at Christchurch in Coventry and was working for a company that makes elevators. As so often happens, they wound up taking us right to the door of the museum. They apologized for not speaking better English, and they meant it. I sometimes have a hard time remembering that we are in their country and not the other way around.

The Fukagawa Museum displayed scale models of an Edo-period tenement house, a vegetable store, a dockside tavern, and a fire tower, among others. "All the details of the reproduced buildings and displays, including nails," it was claimed, "are faithful to traditional construction skills and standards."

The Shitamachi museum was housed in a ramshackle building, lovingly guarded by old residents of the area. In their exhibits and literature they lamented the passing of the old ways: "In the modern living houses everything new was welcomed by people, and a large number of familiar daily utensils, even useful, were thoughtlessly discarded only because of old fashion." I was pleased to see the preservation of the stuff of everyday life that had managed to survive 1923 and 1945 and hundreds of smaller fires. I loved the table covered with board games and toys; we were even encouraged to play with them. These two museums brought each of us enormous pleasure. Bob continued his interest in Edo; I still favour Meiji and Taisho. Not irreconcilable differences.

We also went to a spot on the far side of the Sumida said to be the home of the seventeenth-century poet Matsuo Basho, the "inventor" of the haiku. Once again we had difficulty locating it from our map, which proved to be more schematic than exact. After wandering along the riverbank without much luck, we ran into a young man leaving his house, his up-to-the-minute sneakers still untied. "Basho Museum?" Bob asked, knowing that no matter how he said it, his pronunciation would be wrong.

"Basho Museum? Poet? Haiku? Basho?"

"Ah. Basho!" (It sounded almost like our version.) Then this sweet young man walked us five blocks out of his way to the gates of the museum. (I vow to repay our Japanese guides by showing equal kindness to Toronto's tourists. Saying, as I often have done, "Go left up there," or, "You just missed it. Go back three blocks," will no longer do.)

In Basho's time Fukagawa was a quiet, swampy area, and the *basho* (banana) tree planted by one of his disciples grew so luxuriantly that his cottage became known as Basho-an, meaning Basho's hermitage. The poet made Basho his pen name. (I suspect that the hot young Japanese novelist, Banana Yoshimoto, author of the hugely popular and extremely dumb *Kitchen* and *Lizard*, selected her name as a sly reference to Basho.)

Besides elevating haiku from pastime to literary genre, Basho wrote travel journals, including *The Narrow Road to the Deep North*, in Fukagawa. The pamphlet we picked up said, "We know that after Basho's death, the Fukagawa 'Basho-an' cottage was preserved as a

precious historical spot within the site of a samurai residence, but it disappeared at some time in the late nineteenth century. ...In 1921 the Tokyo government declared Tokiwa 1-3 as the historic site of the Basho-an." Construction of the museum wasn't completed until 1981. The museum also holds regular haiku meetings, and through a window on the lovely garden, we could see women gathered around a low table, reading or writing poetry. With its cases of travelling clothes and the sketch pads in which Basho painted illustrations for his travel pieces, this museum was charming even for someone as ignorant as I am about his work.

Basho the traveller would have laughed at us this morning, as Bob and I sat down to plan Trip No. 2. I know that we can do it but don't want to be too cocky. Travelling next week will be different as the weather changed the day we returned to Tokyo — warmer than Toronto but colder than we're used to. Japan is still hosting the Kyoto conference on the environment, and newspapers are filled with dire predictions of man-made disaster. So why are furnaces regulated by the calendar and not the temperature? This is, after all, a country with no oil, a fact that governs much of its foreign policy. All public spaces, including subways, were boiling today. This doesn't stop the fashion-conscious young people from wearing their newly purchased white or beige duffel coats however.

SUNDAY, NOVEMBER 16

Today, Amy Chavez, a columnist for *The Japan Times*, wrote about commuting, which she does by ferry from an offshore island five stops away from the mainland. She wrote that she finds the Japanese habit of falling asleep, often literally falling onto the shoulders of fellow commuters, annoying in the extreme. She suspects that the loud announcements of upcoming stops serve only one purpose, to awaken the dozers. The causes? The Japanese, in her view, get started too late in the day and waste their time sleeping on conveyances rather than reading or listening to improvement tapes on the way to work. Then they stay awake too late at night partying with co-workers. (Until reading this, I've never known a *gaijin* to criticize the Japanese for not working hard enough.)

From my small experience, it appears that the only places that open early are parks and shrines, where "opening" can mean a single person unlocking a gate. Public transport and the JR begin operations at 6 a.m. but stop at 1 a.m. Shops, libraries, museums, and department stores don't open until 10 a.m. I'm not sure why this is so, though I dare say there are historic reasons; opening hours, once they have been considered, discussed, and a consensus reached, could change in a flash.

To Ms. Chavez's comments I could add my own about holidays —

there are a remarkable number of them. Tomorrow, for example, there's another newspaper holiday, the second in less than two months. It can't be a union-provoked decision because there are no unions. The reason given — to allow delivery staff a break.

Still, I love this town and marvel at how well most things work and how much is accessible to an English speaker. I can't imagine being able to live with such ease in France or Italy, cultures much closer to my own. Perhaps I'm feeling particularly beneficent because Bob and I were able to find the View Plaza at Shinjuku and activate our second set of rail passes with little trouble. We booked reserved seats from Tokyo to Nagoya to Kyoto to Kanazawa and back. Will do the hotels tomorrow.

Then, after convincing Bob of the virtues of travelling with a suitcase on wheels, we hunted unsuccessfully around the station where I was certain I'd seen exactly the right thing a few days ago. Several lessons to be learned here: if you see something you think you might someday want while wandering in the maze that is Tokyo, buy it — you may never pass that way again. And, no matter how futile an expedition seems, there is always something interesting just around the next corner. Hence the discovery, while suitcase shopping, of a new bookstore in the Kinokuniya chain near Shinjuku.

There were seven floors with international books on the sixth. Generally, "international" or "foreign" means English. Not here. We saw books in French, Italian, Russian, and, most prominently, German. There were crowds on each floor, not just for video games, magazines, or pulp fiction, and not just browsing. Hundreds of book buyers. It warmed my heart.

I realized today that I've drawn two somewhat contradictory conclusions involving the relationship between public and private in Japan. Couples, except when they are on holiday, rarely speak to one another in public. In fact, the most animated public conversation I witnessed took place on the subway between a young man and woman — in sign language. On the other hand, Japanese alone imagine themselves within an airtight privacy-enclosure where, in fact, they can be seen indulging in fierce public nose picking. This is a puzzlement.

Tomorrow Bob has a meeting with Prince Takamado, who studied at Queen's, met his wife at a party at the Canadian embassy, and now works at the Japan Foundation. I will set out in a different direction to search for the perfect little suitcase on wheels. Never a dull moment.

MONDAY, NOVEMBER 17

It seems that all of Japan is converging on Kyoto next weekend. The first five hotels I called were full, but I finally booked one with the embarrassing name Hotel Rich. Doth it protest too much? They were willing to take us for two nights only, Thursday and Friday; now I have to find somewhere for Saturday. I called between fifteen and twenty more places — I lost track and suspect that I may have called some hotels twice. In each case, there was a huge intake of air at the other end. "Ah. So Sorry. We are ... not available."

"Could you recommend another hotel?"

"I think all hotels have no reservations." Quite right too.

In desperation, I asked one clerk, "Is there something special going on in Kyoto this weekend?"

"Nothing special. Just holiday weekend and a good time for touring."

Holiday weekend! I'd forgotten. People have been taking holidays to Kyoto for more than a thousand years, so why should they stop just because Geraldine's come to town and wants a room for three nights?

So we're on the waiting list at Hotel Rich and booked into hotels of our choice in Nagoya and Kanazawa. Everyone there is clearly going to Kyoto for the weekend.

Bob slipped out in the middle of all this to keep his appointment with the Prince who, besides his Canadian connection, is the youngest son of the youngest brother of the late Emperor Hirohito, which makes him the first cousin of the current emperor, Akihito. There should be a column there.

Parmesh Bhatt managed to get through on the phone during one of the short breaks between hotel rejections. "You should be able to get e-mail now in your apartment," he said. "Ask Bob to try when he gets home." He hasn't yet but I'm certain — hopeful? — that this will work.

At about noon I headed out in the rain for Iidabashi, where I just knew I'd find a sturdy, inexpensive (these things are relative in Tokyo) suitcase on wheels for Bob. Somehow I wound up in Ginza, entirely in the other direction and my second shopping choice. In the first store, Mitsukoshi, small suitcases cost between ¥100,000 and ¥500,000 ($120 to $600), which I thought outrageous. This was for a carry-on bag, not a set of Louis Vuitton! At the second store, Matsuya Tokyo, prices were more ridiculous — starting at ¥210,000. Humbled, I returned to Mitsukoshi and grabbed the little plaid number I'd briefly considered and initially rejected for a mere ¥105,000.

When Bob saw my purchase he was predictably horrified and I was predictably annoyed. "But it's *plaid*!" he moaned, as if I hadn't noticed.

"Yes. That's right. It's plaid." A subdued plaid, browns and greens like a Burberry coat. "Fine, then. No problem. We can trade. You take my black one. This bag has character! Look at the outside zipper compartment? Perfect for books and magazines. Believe me, you'll be sorry!" Actually, he seemed relieved.

While I was traipsing around the Mitsukoshi basement looking for a place to eat, I stumbled into the children's clothing department. There, the entire staff, all grown women, were dressed alike in larger versions of a dress on the racks — a black Holly Hobby outfit with frills at the neck and a white frilly apron, accessorized with frilly ankle socks and black patent-leather Mary Janes.

Back in the non-commercial, grown-up world for the evening, we heard a lecture by a woman with the memorable name of Dallas Finn. She was speaking at the Goethe Institut about her recently published book on Meiji architecture, and she was as unique as her name. Looking as if she'd come straight from her hospital bed, Dallas Finn was a plucky, fragile, eighty-something Radcliffe girl with a Harvard Ph.D., a member of the American Occupation generation.

She had two carousels of slides to illustrate the speed with which Japanese builders learned Western techniques and arrived at their unique blend of the traditional and the borrowed. She argued that the speed at which Japanese culture remade itself, materially, was unprecedented and has never been duplicated. Until that time, the only large-scale buildings were temples and palaces. But, to stage the social and economic revolution that was necessary to compete with the West, they needed factories, schools, courts, jails, a parliament, train stations, and happily, very early on, museums.

While many of the original buildings have disappeared, a broad sampling of Meiji-era architecture has survived, some within theme parks such as Meiji-mura. There are some Meiji buildings in their original locations, such as the Museum of Transportation at Tokyo station, and a few that still operate as designed. Many corporations have turned the private estates of powerful merchant families such as Mitsui and Mitsubishi into private clubs for company honchos. These Western-style guest houses were built in chateau-like grandeur for Western guests while their Japanese hosts stayed in the comfort of their traditional homes. Akasaka Palace, built for the unfortunate

Emperor Taisho, Hirohito's short-lived father, has survived and is used as a guest house for visiting state officials.

Mary Taylor had suggested that we might want to attend one of the Goethe lectures because they were generally excellent. She also recommended the dining room and so we stayed for a German dinner that didn't disappoint — rolled beef, beets, spätzle, with a large, German-size glass of splendid Riesling. (The Japanese drink wine from glasses so small they might be sake cups.)

Dallas Finn and the man who'd introduced her, an aged priest from Sophia University, sat beside us in the dining room. He has known Dallas and her husband since they both arrived with the Occupation, and when he thanked her at the end of her talk he mentioned that her husband could not attend because he was, at that very moment, working with the Japanese government, redrafting their constitution. While they were eating, two men approached their table to thank her for her speech. She looked up at one of them and said, in her clipped Eastern-seaboard tone, "I think you're a friend of my great friend, Ed Seidensticker?" I did not hear his reply.

What a generation that was! Besides the two Donalds, there are the two Eds: Edwin O. Reischauer, born and raised in Japan, a Harvard man who served as the American ambassador in the 1960s and author of the landmark book, *The Japanese*; and Edward Seidensticker, a Columbia graduate, translator of the *Tale of Genji* and author of *Low City, High City: Tokyo From Edo to the Earthquake, 1867-1923* and *Tokyo Rising: The City Since the Great Earthquake*. I envy them their opportunities, and am grateful they had the wit to seize them.

TUESDAY, NOVEMBER 18

This not very profound thought occurred to me today as I strolled through my neighbourhood: the one North American trend that has not crossed the Pacific is rollerblading. This shattering thought struck as I watched a tall foreigner on large rollerblades create a stir in this pretty cool midtown area. If bicycles can wheel their way through crowded streets, it should be a snap for a kid on rollerblades. A fortune awaits some savvy entrepreneur.

At a slightly higher level of technology, Bob was unsuccessful in his attempt to hook up our e-mail. He tried again late at night with

Professor Bowers instructing by phone; no luck. Abandon all hope, I say. We leave Japan in two weeks and starting tomorrow we'll be away from Tokyo for a week. As Donnie Brasco would say, "Fa-ged-aboud-id!"

Lunch with Illya was terrific. I realized how much I missed intimate girl-talk. I did not expect to have it in Japan with a Japanese woman, but what value is travel if it doesn't shatter false assumptions? She told me more about her family. Her mother was a nurse who was forced to stop working by a demanding, traditional husband.

"He never even made tea! He'd say, 'Tea,' and my mother would rush to make it. When his toenails got too long she'd be on her knees, 'Clip. Clip.'" Illya was an only child, and her mother was extremely bored. "She told me, 'I was a nurse, but you could be a doctor!'" Hence the emphasis on Illya's education in good Catholic girls' schools.

As in universities in the West, Japanese women graduates outnumber men. And as in North America, women in Japan are marrying later. Not only is closeness before marriage not considered necessary, it's widely believed that knowing someone too well only accentuates his flaws. Japanese women look for men with the "three highs," as they're called: high education, high income, and "high physically" (tall).

I mentioned to Illya that I'd read the situation was changing: recent figures show that six out of ten married Japanese women work outside the home. Illya pointed out that many have rejoined the workforce after raising their children (often only one child, rarely more than two). These women usually find only low-level, part-time jobs in the service industry. Among highly educated women with young children, Illya's an exception.

"When we have alumnae meetings," Illya said, "I'm the odd one. I would say 95 percent don't work. They're just housewives." Many of Illya's friends look with disdain on American supermoms. These educated Japanese women know they lead relatively easy, privileged lives, and they'd like to keep it that way. We talked about our own choices around working and having children — how much time we stayed home after each baby (three months for me, four for her).

She told me that because her regular secretary was on maternity leave, the embassy needed a replacement, a Japanese fluent in English and French. One woman who applied had worked for a tire company where she'd met her husband. As soon as they married, she was let go — a practice common in Canada forty years ago. When Illya called the company for references, she was told: "Oh, she's very aggressive. Stand out. Pushy." Perhaps because of this recommendation, or despite it, the embassy hired her.

"And you know what?" Illya said, bemused. "She's wonderful. Very good at her job. And she's very Japanese — not pushy at all!"

A recent study reported that Japanese women have long been willing to accept male domination in major areas of society and to use their feminine wiles to keep their men ambitious, hard working, and devoted to their jobs. For their part, men have played along, even if they recognized the female ploys used against them. This game, played by mutual consent, is now regarded as one of the driving forces behind Japan's rapid economic growth in the 1960s. In the current economic slump, the old pattern no longer works: many women are being forced to provide a second income.

Illya wanted to know if I had been "a pioneer" in broadcasting in Canada? She was surprised to learn that, on the contrary, when I started at CBC Radio in 1966 there had been a score of women producers and a few administrators far ahead of me. We decided that, at least where women in the workforce are concerned, Japan is forty years behind. If either of us is a pioneer, it's Illya — and her husband.

"When I stayed home for four months each time I had a baby," Illya recalled, "my husband said he could feel waves of frustration greet him at the door, so he never suggested that I stop working." The real problem was child care.

"There was a very good nursery school about five minutes from our house when Shota was born. The problem was, there were eight openings and over a hundred who applied. Many of the spots went to women with part-time jobs or who worked in family businesses, like a restaurant." To get a spot, Illya and her husband had to devise a winning strategy: *he* would go for the interview and when they saw that a man had to take a day off work to worry about child care, well ... that was serious. Shota got in.

At the end of lunch we exchanged presents — a book on Japan for me, a bottle of wine for her — although her real gift to me was her candour. We hope to meet again on the twenty-eighth, when Bob is scheduled to speak to the Canada-Japan Friendship Society. I hope, for Bob's sake, it's more rewarding than his recent address to Meiji journalism students.

Before leaving for lunch I'd decided to inform Mr. Akasaki, the superintendent, about our neurotic television. After all, I thought, they might decide after we leave that we damaged this massive Panasonic and charge us for it. This time, to bridge the language barrier, I brought down the channel changer, and through an interpreter in his office, tried to explain, and illustrate, that the television was broken.

Mr. Akasaki disappeared and returned a minute later with another channel changer. I shook my head and persuaded him to follow me to our apartment, where we each toyed with the set. Finally he looked up and said, "New one. Afternoon. Okay?" When I returned from lunch, there it was. A brand new set.

WEDNESDAY, NOVEMBER 19

On the road again and it feels great. Bob pulling my little black bag; me, his lovely plaid. Where to? Shinkansen. *Hai.* Where shall we buy our bento — platform or train? Beverage. Cold coffee or Coke? Standing in the correct spot to board our car. Then straight to our assigned seats. Not a hitch. It's 10:30 a.m. Time to eat. Did you find the Western toilet? This car or the next?

Nagoya, largely destroyed in the war, is Japan's fourth-largest city. Six-lane roads as far as the eye can see. We walked the short distance

from the station to our hotel, the Plaza Castle. Outside the main entrance was a mock wedding chapel complete with white wrought-iron chairs and three mannequins — bride, groom, and clergyman in dog collar, all Caucasian. There are four floors devoted exclusively to the wedding business on which this hotel, like many others, survives.

After checking in we took a local bus to the Tokugawa Museum, repository for more than twenty thousand objects once belonging to the Owari branch of the family. Unfortunately, they allowed us to see only a couple of dozen. Very frustrating. Although they own most of the surviving fragments of the twelfth-century hand-painted scroll of the *Tale of Genji* — the greatest work of classical Japanese fiction — it was deemed "too fragile to be on continuous display." Instead, there was a reproduction, along with a fake tea room and a mock daimyo's residence.

Since time was running out, we grabbed a cab. We had to get to Atsuta-jingu, "the second most important tourist attraction in Nagoya" by sunset or we'd miss "one of the three most sacred Shinto shrines in Japan." Unfortunately it was located at what must be the other end of the city (Nagoya: population 2.5 million). Since we're not going to Ise, site of the most important Shinto shrine, we thought this visit was worth the expense.

I love the Shinto aesthetic but loathe the purpose to which it was put in the recent past — state Shintoism that created a divine emperor, putatively the direct descendant of Amaterasu, the sun goddess. In fact, this historical link had all but disappeared until it was revived about 120 years ago. Government leaders wanted to end the shogun's powers and install an emperor as head of Japan. When the "restored" emperor, Meiji, visited the sacred Ise shrines in 1869, he was the first monarch to do so since Empress Jito at the end of the seventh century.

Part of the reinvigorated Shinto includes *miya-mairi*, something like a Christian baptism. Month-old infants are taken to the local shrine and presented to the deity, whose protection is invoked by a priest. The next rite of passage occurs at this time of year, when little girls and boys in traditional dress are brought, once again, by their parents to the tutelary shrine to pray for protection. We saw them all around us, like little dolls. The ritual is called Shichi-Go-San (literally, "seven-five-three"); girls participate when they are three and seven, boys when they're five. Cameras flashed everywhere, and a professional photographer had set up nearby.

This shrine is rumoured to house one of three pieces of Imperial regalia — the Sword that, according to legend, was plucked from a dragon's tail. It's part of the imperial mystery that we not know exactly where it is, even though we are (perhaps) in its proximate presence. The two other elusive pieces of regalia, the Jewel and the Mirror, are said to remain at Ise.

Back to the hotel. Sad images on television of the four newly married Japanese couples who were killed yesterday by Islamic terrorists while honeymooning in Egypt, made sadder by the intense wedding paraphernalia that surrounds us. Turned off the television and turned to the reading matter available in the bedside table — *The Teaching of Buddha*, donated by the Bukkyo Dendo Kyokai, the "Buddhist Promoting Foundation," the local version of the Gideon Bible Society.

"Do you think it would be all right to steal it?" I asked Bob. I have come to trust him on ethical issues. He thought not.

THURSDAY, NOVEMBER 20

I'd like to write to the editors of the guidebooks we've carted around Japan and tell them that when it came to Meiji-mura (Meiji Village), they were way off the mark. For example, Fodor's said: "The 19th-century buildings and Western architecture make this park more appealing to the Japanese than to Westerners. An exception may be the lobby taken from the old Imperial Hotel, which was designed by Frank Lloyd Wright." Nonsense. Anyone interested in architecture, or cultural anthropology, or how to design an architectural theme park, will love Meiji-mura.

We left the hotel later than anticipated, and I'm pleased I had the wit to change our return tickets so we had two extra hours to browse. Still, I could have spent more time and seen more buildings than I did. Despite a few drops of rain, it was perfect strolling weather.

Meiji-mura proved the Dallas Finn thesis that no other society absorbed another as quickly as Japan took in the West. It's apparent in buildings completed less than a dozen years after 1868, the year Japan was opened to the West. Some Japanese craftsmen trained with Western architects but insinuated an Edo flavour into foreign structures, adapting techniques applied in wood and reed to stone and brick.

The site itself is magnificent — a million square metres of hills beside a lake. Sixty-seven Meiji-era buildings have been rescued and rebuilt here. Many more were lost in the 1923 earthquake, the Second World War, and the construction boom of recent years. The outdoor museum was opened in 1965. Remarkably, the credit for this park has been given to two individuals, Yoshiro Taniguchi and Moto-o Tsuchikawa, very unusual in a country that prizes teamwork. But typically for Japan, they were old friends from high school. One, the vice-president of a railway company, no doubt helped in the installation of the two rail lines in the park. Steam-powered trains move along the lines, a reminder of their crucial role in transforming Japan.

Especially wonderful for me were the reception house of Marquis Saigo Tsugumichi, where he received foreign guests; Lafcadio Hearn's "summering house," now turned into a candy store; the Kanazawa prison; and the Kureha-za Theatre from Osaka.

Inside the theatre, I could imagine seeing Edo-period kabuki. I might have sat on the tatami floor, divided into squares by horizontal wooden beams, each square accommodating four or five people. Or I might have been seated with the elite in the wraparound gallery, with a better view of the two *hanamichi* and the small stage with a centre area that revolved for scene changes. (The Japanese invented the revolving stage.) There was such a sense of intimacy that guests must have felt like extras rather than audience members. Bob and I arrived in time to join a young woman leading a small group of slightly older women on a tour. I think I must have felt giddy since I recall striking a *mie*, or pose, one hand above my head, as she led us onto the stage. Bob stayed upstairs while I descended the steep steps under the stage to see how the turntable was moved by the stage crew working like donkeys at a millstone.

Other wonders included a church and a cathedral dedicated to St. Francis Xavier, several bridges, a brewery, a lighthouse, a barbershop, a railway factory — and, most memorable (here the guidebooks are correct), part of Wright's Imperial Hotel, more eccentric and splendid than it appears in photographs. There's something at once Aztec and art nouveau Charles Rennie Mackintosh about it, both in the design of the building itself and the furnishings. Overhanging the lobby was the original mezzanine, now a tea room. There we sat on Wright chairs, listened to piped-in chamber music, and lamented the destruction in 1976 of this masterpiece. Still, I was grateful for what had been preserved.

In Lee Riordan's account of the Great Kanto earthquake of September 1, 1923, *Jishin*, he describes the role played by the Imperial Hotel. Because the quake occurred on the day the hotel was to be officially opened, many foreigners were gathered there. Because Wright had floated the foundation on thousands of short concrete pillars, the building withstood the tremors. Because he used no gas, the quake caused only a small fire in the kitchen. And because there was water in the reflecting pool outside the hotel entrance, a bucket brigade kept the roof moist and fireproof. That same reflecting pool was itself rescued for Meiji-mura; it was a thrill to see it still guarding the hotel entrance.

When we arrived in Kyoto, we found that the Hotel Rich was indeed badly named. Hotel Small, or Hotel Seedy, would have been more suitable. Our room (about $150 for two) was so tiny I thought we would have to sleep curled around our suitcases. Even so, they have nothing available for Saturday unless there's a cancellation.

Ted arrived and went out with us for a lovely dinner — yakitori, the same sort of place we went to ten years ago and the same reaction from the staff when Ted not only ordered in Japanese but made jokes. Everyone in the small restaurant thought he was a hoot. And, as in the past, we ate tons.

"First, tofu and beans for the Yin," Ted explained, almost seriously. This was followed by plenty of Yang — skewers of mushrooms, onions, okra, chicken, meatballs, and best of all, wild duck. "Kyoto is famous for its wild duck," Ted assured us. It was served with a pile of chopped green onion and a mound of crushed garlic.

Ted was full of good humour and kindness, as he had been on our previous trip. We'd seen one another several times during the intervening ten years but somehow meeting in Japan is special. Ted has been here since the spring and will stay out the year. The last time we met was in April at a Japan Foundation party in Toronto to launch *The Oxford Book of Japanese Short Stories*, for which he was the general editor. In our copy he'd written, "For Geraldine and Bob, Let's keep meeting in Japan (at Tsukiji?) or wherever." Here we were, in a little yakitori restaurant down the street from Hotel Rich, Kyoto. And it was lovely.

Ted told us about John McGee, the Canadian-born Japanese tea master we hope to meet in Kyoto. (Katherine Ashenburg met him during her trip here, then again in Toronto in 1996, when he was the guest of honour at a dinner she hosted.) Originally a farm boy from Georgetown, Ontario, John first came to Japan in 1970 for the Osaka Expo. Unlike William Thorsell, he fell in love with the country, especially the tea ceremony. He wanted to study with Soshitsu Sen XV, the grand master of the Urasenke School, the largest tea ceremony school in Japan and the only one to have established branches overseas. John sought an audience, but the master would not see him. He returned, day after day, and waited with fierce determination. This, I gather, is a prerequisite for a disciple. (I remember seeing a similar situation in one episode of the *Kung Fu* series on television.) John's patience paid off; he's now second-in-command of the entire school, with branches all over Japan and abroad. He and Ted have become close friends.

"The summer was unbearably hot," Ted told us. "John let me stay at his place outside Kyoto so I was able to get some work done." The place is a seventeenth-century house John bought and restored, filling it with exquisite antiques. The house has been featured in *Architectural Digest*.

Ted told us that he was leaving the next day to appear on NHK on a TV show called something like "Intellectual of the Week." (Last week's guest was Donald Keene.) He's to speak from a prepared text for about three minutes, then answer questions. His subject? The future of Japanese literature. He'll tell them it may lie with immigrants or long-time non-Japanese residents, and he will use Canada as a point of comparison — Michael Ondaatje, Rohinton Mistry, and Neil Bissoondath, for example. We were happy to offer Ted our apartment for two days of his stay. Much of what I've learned about Japan I've learned from him, and I know I'm not the only one he's taught and inspired.

FRIDAY, NOVEMBER 21

Ridiculous as this may sound, I was not looking forward to visiting Kyoto again. I'd had such a marvellous time ten years ago I wanted my Kyoto memories intact even though I knew I'd merely skimmed the city's surface. There are 1,600 temples in Kyoto, several hundred shrines, a dozen museums and galleries, great shopping and eating, more than ten centuries of history, including about a thousand years as the nation's capital. Although some marvels have been lost because of fire, earthquake, and warfare, many treasures remain. Moving the capital to Edo, renamed Tokyo, in 1868 saved Kyoto from Allied bombs. I knew I wouldn't be bored, but could I squeeze more from the experience than I had a decade ago when I was there a week compared with only two days this trip?

I have sympathy and disdain for people who have only two days in a lifetime to visit Kyoto, the same disdain — and I hope sympathy — long-term visitors and residents have for me: lifetime total, nine days. Then there was the hotel issue. I spent about an hour trying to find a place for tomorrow (Saturday night). "Sorry. No reservation." "Rooms full." "Not possible." In short, no luck. Bob retreated to the lobby while I worked the phones; there's no room in our space capsule for two people to sit comfortably. Pitiful to think that I would kill to keep this room for an extra night. While I was upstairs dealing with rejection, Bob was downstairs planning our day. I refused to shoulder another ounce of responsibility. It turned out that he had far greater luck than I did, but not before another glitch.

When Katherine Ashenburg had the dinner for John McGee in Toronto, I was unable to attend but Bob was there and enjoyed John's company enormously. "He has a writer's mind," Bob had reported,

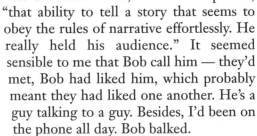

"that ability to tell a story that seems to obey the rules of narrative effortlessly. He really held his audience." It seemed sensible to me that Bob call him — they'd met, Bob had liked him, which probably meant they had liked one another. He's a guy talking to a guy. Besides, I'd been on the phone all day. Bob balked.

"What am I supposed to say? 'Hello. We're in town.' Then what?" I think he found it hard to believe that people he enjoyed talking to might also have enjoyed him. Lots of people come to Toronto, people Bob has never met, people who don't even speak English, for God's sake, and he takes them to lunch and sometimes it's painful but just as often it's interesting, even thrilling.

"Why don't you ask him out for dinner? That way he can say he's busy if he doesn't want to see us."

Bob called and John accepted. Apparently he had known we were in town and expected to hear from us. He would call our hotel at about seven o'clock to complete arrangements. I was of course full of misgivings that the evening would be a disaster, and whose fault would that be?

About the day — Bob had taken his assignment to heart and charted a route that sounded perfect. We would cover part of eastern Kyoto, starting at Ginkaku-ji, the Temple of the Silver Pavilion, wander down the Philosopher's Walk that runs between a canal on one side and boutiques on the other, and wind up at the Nomura Art Museum.

We went first by subway to Kyoto Station, a supersonic, bustling, and chaotic place, polar opposite to the contemplative temples that are the city's main attraction and entirely rebuilt since our last visit. At the information booth we bought two-day passes for public transport and asked about accommodations for Saturday night. The woman behind the desk said to come back tomorrow morning to see if there were last-minute cancellations. I'm not good at dealing with uncertainty.

Then, joining millions of other tourists — well, a long line of them — we boarded the #5 bus and headed for Ginkaku-ji, about a thirty-minute ride. I'd forgotten how wonderful both the buildings and the gardens were, reason enough to return to Kyoto. Our reading says that the shogun Yoshimasa Ashikaga (1435–1490) built this villa for his retirement. He began in the 1460s, but it was not until 1474, after he became disillusioned with politics, that he gave his full attention to its construction and to the arts, particularly, "romance, moon-gazing, and the tea ceremony," which he helped develop. He died before covering the pavilion with silver foil, and his personal sanctuary became a Buddhist temple. After the decline of the Ashikaga family, many buildings were destroyed, but not the pavilion with its moon-viewing platform or the tea ceremony room. All the buildings were designed with their backs to the city and their facades to the mountain so that Yoshimasa could forget that Kyoto was burning and thousands were dying in the Onin War.

He epitomized both the aesthete and the moral monster, a dichotomy found too often in both East and West — think of Picasso. He was said to have hired Soami, a famous gardener and artist, who divided his monumental work into sections: one with a pond, bridges, egrets, and carp; the other, a Zen stone garden with raked ribbons of fine white stones, smooth then rough — often called Sea of Silver Sand because of moonlight sparkling on its surface.

The second original building, the *hondo* or main temple, contains an intimidating bust of Yoshimasa carved in cypress. A Japanese guide

was leading a tour but, because we were *gaijin*, allowed us to wander at will through the five rooms and across the stone bridge. There we entered the Togu-do, a National Treasure, one of the original buildings from 1484. It contains the Dojinsai, a four-and-a-half-mat tatami room with a window framing a view of the mountain that is considered the model for all tea ceremony rooms. Although the pavilion was crowded, there was a respectful, even reverential, silence.

Feeling suitably pensive, we headed down Philosopher's Walk, the 1.7 kilometres we'd walked with Ted ten years ago. Our first stop along the way was at the Honen-in temple, a peaceful and unpretentious place suited to the Buddhist sect that began here, the Pure Land Sect. I don't think I appreciated the many Buddhist options until this trip: novels are filled with interdenominational squabbles of the sort that beset Protestantism in the past. This temple was built in 1680 in honour of the priest Honen (1133–1212), who could be compared to John Wesley in that he brought Buddhism to the people by preaching human equality and focusing prayer on the all-merciful Amida Buddha's name, the *nembutsu*, "Namu Amida Butsu," which he is said to have repeated sixty thousand times a day. Afraid of his influence, the established Tendai sect spread the usual rumours of sexual corruption, in this case involving noblewomen, and the reigning emperor banished Honen and executed several of his disciples. He was later pardoned and returned to Kyoto. He is said to have starved himself to death at age seventy-nine.

We stopped for tea and a tapioca sort of goop eaten with a spoon, and later to buy a pair of knitted gloves, each digit a different colour, for Margaret. At the end of the path, at 3:30 in the afternoon, when we were almost ready to pack it in, we came to Zenrin-ji, or as it's popularly called, Eikan-do, in memory of a popular eleventh-century priest, Eikan. It's a magical place I'm so glad we didn't miss.

If I can make another religious comparison, Eikan was like the Jewish Baal Shem Tov, the Polish seventeenth-century founder of

Hasidism, who believed in understanding God through joyful worship. Of Eikan it's said that once, while he was dancing in front of the Amida Buddha, the statue came to life and joined the dance. Eikan was so shocked, he slowed his steps and the Amida Buddha turned its head back, as if reprimanding him. That's why, as legend has it, the statue of Amida Buddha in the Amida Hall depicts him with his face turned to one side.

The buildings that climb up the side of the maple-covered mountain are all sixteenth-century reconstructions of the originals, which were destroyed in the Onin War. Room after room was filled with eye-catching treasures; especially beautiful to me were the Muromachi period (1333–1567) painted screens with their spare, monochromatic scenes. White space was as important as the sparse brush strokes that created the sense of a cloud or a tiger. Then the temple bells sounded, prayers were to begin, and our feet gave out.

Back at Hotel Rich — that we now know is pronounced "Rish-ay" — we received John McGee's call. He said he'd fax us directions to his house, where we would have drinks and then go out to a restaurant in his neighbourhood. It sounded perfect. Although this was not the fabled country house, I knew it would be lovely — located along the Philosopher's Walk — and it was.

We ascended stone steps into a garden, all bamboo and rocks, fallen leaves and dramatic lighting. There was no bell at the front entrance, at least none we could find, so we trailed around to a side window where we could see two men and they could see us. One was unmistakably John; the other, his partner, Alexandre Avdoulov, from Russia.

John motioned us to return to the front, where he let us in. His appearance is as improbable as the rest of his story. He's large, taller than Bob, rather beefy, and dressed in a business suit and socks. As he greeted us and we struggled with shoe removal (like boots in Canadian winters), a young cat darted out the door.

"Geraldine's allergic to cats," Bob said. Without having discussed it, Bob and I had come to some tacit agreement that my complaint sounded less off-putting coming from him.

"Oh, Misha hardly comes into this room," John said. "Let's go in here. I'll put him in the kitchen."

We entered a Western-style reception area that ran across the front of the house, overlooking the entrance and attached to the tea room. We admired the wonderful wooden chests, the clay bowls, and watercolours until John returned with our drinks: Coke for Bob, something brown in a tall glass for John, and for me a tumbler of room-temperature sake, the way I like it. I asked John about the tea paraphernalia and he told us that the next day he was beginning a three-day seminar for mostly non-Japanese teachers of tea who are learning to teach the Way of Tea to other foreigners. This will be the thirty-fourth in a series started a dozen years ago by the Urasenke grand master, part of the internationalization of the tea ceremony. There have been over a thousand graduates who now form the Urasenke International group, which John supervises. He himself teaches tea each summer at York University in Toronto. I asked if cooking for all those people wasn't a huge job.

"We're going to have it catered, thank God. To do the whole *kaiseki* thing, sweets, the whole meal, takes ages. Alex and I will still have plenty to do." He told us that the heavy Western furniture in this room would have to be moved elsewhere in the house. I found it all fascinating and was a little taken aback when John interrupted himself and said, "Oh, let's talk about anything but tea!"

It might have been the sake, the lack of food, the excitement of the day, the nervous anticipation of this meeting, combined with John's expansive personality, but I got rather silly and so did John. I think we must have appeared particularly outlandish to Bob, who doesn't drink. When you're sober and others aren't, the rapier wit of your companions might seem slightly dull. John was attentive to our needs and after a short time commented that I seemed to be scratching my eyes rather a lot.

"Let's move into another room," he suggested. "That might be better."

It seemed that we had passed some test because we were let into the inner sanctum, and John invited Alex to join us in their gorgeous living room, large enough for a Yamaha grand piano. "I think," said John, "that it's one of the first ever made — 1909." Alex, who spoke perfect English, as well as Russian and Japanese, was as feline and playful as Misha the cat. He'd been in Japan for seven years, had a background in theatre, and now lived and worked with the tea guru John.

As time passed, I think we all felt more comfortable, at least I did. They told the charming story of their first meeting, when Mikhail and Raisa Gorbachev came to town and had tea with the grand master, John's boss, Soshitsu Sen XV. Alex translated from Russian to English, and John, from English to Japanese. They also mentioned that Alex's parents had just completed a six-week visit.

"It must have been a bit of culture shock for them," I remarked.

"You mean, John and me?" Of course I hadn't, but my denial made no difference. "Well," Alex continued, "that's 'culture' too, you know, and boy, was that a shock!" As a parent I wanted to suggest that perhaps it hadn't been a shock at all, but I kept still.

More light-hearted chat all around; more persistent eye-scratching from me. Stupidly, I'd left my antihistamine at the hotel. Bob gave me Coricidin he keeps handy for frequent sneezing fits, and I took a couple of good snorts of my asthma inhaler. "I think we should leave and have some dinner," John suggested.

I felt it appropriate for us to invite Alex as well. He said he'd love to join us, and I rubbed my eyes some more.

I could tell by the look on Bob's face that he was concerned, perhaps wanting to end the evening right there and get me back to the hotel. I said, "I'm fine. Really." John was already contrite. "Misha's new. We'll have to start asking people how they are with cats before they visit."

"In Russia," Alex added, "I never heard of such a thing — 'Allergic to cats!'" John sprang to my defence and said that it was quite common in North America and Alex would have to get used to it. John had recently bought an old sea captain's house in Lunenburg, Nova Scotia and was set to remodel it. (The new version will no doubt result in a second appearance in *Architectural Digest*.)

On the walk to the restaurant we all seemed to find one another hysterically funny as we talked about ice hockey, about my ancestral home of Mogilov (Alex said it was now a big city), and about Alex applying to become a landed immigrant in Canada. We had heard something of this from Ted: Soshitsu Sen XV is now seventy-five; his son and heir is standing in the wings, waiting for his father's death or retirement. Whatever happens, the new master will bring in his own acolytes and John will be retired. There have been discussions about building a teahouse at York University, where John could teach. He has such energy, charm, and skill, I'm sure there are a number of things I could do, as could Alex.

The restaurant, Omen, a block west of Philosopher's Walk, was, as the guidebook said, "inexpensive, popular, and known for its homemade white noodles." However, by the time we arrived, one of my eyes was red and puffy, almost closed. I looked like a Cyclops. My nose was running non-stop. But I wasn't wheezing so I saw no reason to end the fun. We sat at the counter, drank sake out of square cedar cups with salt around the edges, while John ordered a variety of fish and meat and rice, all delicious.

"They've just opened a branch of Omen in New York, in SoHo," John told us. "It's supposed to be a huge success."

Too soon the management interrupted to announce that it was ten o'clock, closing time, and we were forced to leave. We walked together to a main intersection and hailed a cab. I invited John and Alex to visit us on their next trip to Toronto in August 1998.

I hadn't looked at a mirror before we returned to the hotel, and I was a fright. I should have had the good sense to take a shower before bed but I was too tired and too happy to bother about a little thing like a swollen eye. So, two Benadryl and to bed.

SATURDAY, NOVEMBER 22

Woke up with eye still puffy but feeling fine. Tried again unsuccessfully to get a room in a Kyoto hotel but no luck. The idea of trekking down to the station with packed bags, hoping the tourist office had a room so we can try to duplicate yesterday's wonderful "shrining" experience was unappealing. Too uncertain. On top of that, it was raining. The Evil Geraldine was thinking: "Let them come to Kyoto, those usurpers of my room. Let them try to enjoy themselves in the rain!" Kanazawa for an extra day also didn't seem a good idea because it was an outdoor sort of place, and what if it was raining there, too? We'd been so blessed with great weather it seemed ungracious to moan about one wet day. Think of those thirsty lawns.

The answer? Go to Osaka and catch bunraku in their home theatre, which is exactly what we did. Perhaps because I'd heard so many negative things about Osaka ("The best thing about Osaka is the road to Kyoto") or because I am at heart a lover of big cities, I was charmed by Osaka. I even appreciated the Holiday Inn Osaka — in a great district, one subway stop from the theatre — and was proud when we navigated underground from the train station to Namba, the stop near our hotel. After a frustrating morning of relentless rain, travel plans collapsing, regrouping, changing tickets so we could go direct from Osaka to Kanazawa tomorrow, we were standing with our luggage in an Osaka subway car. Bob turned to me and said, "I think I love you because you're the only other person I know who would think this is fun!" Perhaps there are one or two other reasons, but I won't quibble.

Bunraku started at 4:15. It was two o'clock and we hadn't had lunch, so after unpacking we walked through the bustling business district on our way to the theatre and climbed to a small, second-storey Sri Lankan restaurant. Our waiter, a middle-aged man of dignity, pride, and curiosity, was also the owner.

"Where are you from, please?" he asked after we'd finished our meal.

"Canada," I answered, "Toronto."

"There are many people from Sri Lanka there, I think."

"Yes. One of our best-known writers was born there, Michael Ondaatje." I'm not sure he knew who I was talking about but something encouraged him to tell his story. He'd come to Tokyo seventeen years ago to study. He was an electrical engineer in the field of superconductivity and worked for IBM in Japan, then in the United States. When he returned to Japan, he left engineering (why was not too clear) and opened the first of three restaurants. "I actually live in Kyoto," he explained. "And I had to shut one of my places after I started doing work for the Sri Lankan government."

When we were paying our bill, Bob noticed a picture over the cash register of our "host" — an impish, balding, bearded chap, up to his eyeballs in some sort of green plant.

"That," he said, pointing over his shoulder, "was in recognition of the twinning of Uji in Japan with Ceylon City in Sri Lanka, two tea Meccas." There he was, in a field of green tea.

I liked this man so much I wanted to find out everything about him. Was he married? Where did he meet his wife? What language does he speak at home? I managed to ask how he liked living in Japan.

"Well," he said, thoughtfully, "it's very hard for foreigners. Not for me now, but in the beginning."

Perhaps that's one thing I liked about him — his foreign-ness, and his nerve. Immigrants who survive and even flourish in Canada seem heroic to me. But here, it's a bloody miracle. Each year Japan admits only one or two refugees and allows only a few hundred immigrants to become citizens. It doesn't consider a foreign baby Japanese even if the child is adopted by a Japanese couple. Seeing this man reminded me of all the things I admire about life in Canada.

The National Bunraku Theatre in Osaka had all the charmlessness of the National Theatre in Tokyo. (Does the word "National" ensure banality?) Accustomed to theatre in Tokyo, we assumed there would be an explanatory audioguide in English. Wrong! Here was a real test: would I still admire bunraku with only a miserable little plot summary to read beforehand? The answer was emphatically yes. Once again I was transfixed by the personality of the puppets. Because there was nothing speaking into my ear to distract me, I could pay more attention to the puppeteers, although one is not supposed to. On stage was Bunjaku Yoshida, the master puppeteer we'd visited backstage ten years earlier. He looked much the same, more highly buffed, perhaps, like a piece of ivory. His puppet was the tragic wet-nurse who kills herself when she thinks her young charge has lost his voice.

One of the narrators was dazzlingly wonderful, playing five separate characters, each with a distinctive pitch and style. An assistant always leaves a glass of water beside the lectern on which the script rests, but there was never a pause, nor did there seem to be any need for him to refresh himself. Many young people in the audience appeared to be theatre or literature students who followed the text of the first play, *Hana no Ueno Homare no Ishibumi* (*The Glorious Stone Monument at Ueno*). We left before the second act, feeling pleased, and walked out into a rain-free Osaka Saturday night just as the whole city seemed ready to party.

Although our room was on the fourteenth floor, it sounded as if a helicopter was idling a few feet outside our window, dropping scrap metal onto the barge in the canal below. Perhaps to distinguish themselves from Tokyoites, Osaka drivers ride their horns and party most of the night. Could all this self-generated enthusiasm be a reaction to the Second City blues? I mean, who thinks of fun when they think of Osaka? I was awakened at about two o'clock and waited for the festivities to end, which they did, eventually, at about 3:30.

SUNDAY, NOVEMBER 23

I suppose I will board the plane for Toronto a week from today, on schedule, but I'll try not to think about it for now. Up early, subway back to the station, boarded the Limited Express that skirted the Japanese Alps with Takayama off to the east. Arrived at Kanazawa, the furthest north we've been in Japan, and met the first seriously cold wind of the season. Stopped at the tourist office in the station for information and a map that listed about a dozen hotels, none of them The Prince, a name I'd selected from the *Lonely Planet* guidebook and where I'd reserved for two nights. Our worst suspicions were confirmed when our cab pulled up in front of a dump. We entered the lobby not to check in but to phone around for better accommodation.

A new hotel, the Kanazawa Citymonde, took us. From the front desk, we faxed Toronto our change of itinerary — always the lingering worry of the emergency call that must get through — and headed into the chilly autumn air, across the Asano River to a gentrified geisha district that leads into a pleasant loop of slightly rundown temples and small ryokans. Because Kanazawa had no strategic military installations, it was spared heavy Allied bombing and is now a thriving tourist town full of delights. Much attention and money are spent on preservation, and there's an appreciation of the traditional arts, which continue in Kanazawa much as they have for centuries. We wandered past a tiny shop that produced tatami, and the smell of fresh rushes was intoxicating.

Obviously, every temple can't be maintained and some we saw resembled rundown churches in the American South — rotting wooden buildings, plastic bottles, and wrecked motorbikes on the lawn, gates creaking on their hinges. From tiny ryokans without English signs, we saw men scurrying with bowls and towels to a nearby communal bath.

So far, I think Kanazawa has something of a French air about it, at least in the food department. Had a sandwich lunch in Les Anges, decorated in art nouveau posters, in a renovated house in the geisha district, and a bouillabaisse dinner, local fish and seafood cooked in the French manner, in a dining room in our hotel.

The city (population 450,000) is crowded with Japanese tour buses — as many, I think, as we saw in Kyoto — so it's early to bed, early to rise for Kenrokuen, which is sure to be jammed. One of the Three Great Gardens. And it's maple-viewing time as well.

MONDAY, NOVEMBER 24

It was only after a day of almost non-stop touring that I realized we'd managed to visit only half the places of real interest. We started at eight o'clock at Kenrokuen, under cloudy skies that cleared at about 10 a.m. while we were still walking blissfully in the park — the term "garden" doesn't really do it justice. The area I loved best was Gourd

Lake, shaped, obviously, like a gourd with a waterfall that broke over strategically placed rocks. The garden was created over two hundred years ago under the protection of the samurai Maeda clan, the most powerful in the Tokugawa shogunate.

Since wealth was measured in rice and since the land in Ishikawa Prefecture around Kanazawa was, and is, rich in rice production, the Maedas had the wealth and leisure not only to build an exquisite garden but to foster the arts, including painting on silk, pottery, wicker, and lacquerware. The extent of their power, and the uses to which they put it, suggested the Medicis of Florence.

Because of its northern location, Kanazawa used to receive a thick, wet cover of snow each winter. To protect trees, shrubs, and hedges they devised an intricate arrangement of bamboo and rope called *yuki-tsuri*. Today, even though weather conditions are not as extreme, this tradition continues. A single bamboo pole, or a tepee of poles, is erected to a height greater than each tree or bush. Then the spaces are filled in horizontally, creating perfectly symmetrical cones of bamboo and rope, each knot identical.

Although Kanazawa was of no strategic importance in the Second World War, it was a crucially important naval and army base in the Japan-Russia War (1904–1905). We visited a history museum housed in three grandly renovated Meiji-era brick army barracks. The staff provided translations of key wall texts that were both helpful and disconcerting. The Second World War began in 1930 and ended in 1945 (this seems to be the orthodox ruling here). They see the "China Incident" resulting from China's reluctance to join the rest of Asia in "a social and economic co-operation entity" controlled by Japan. The Pacific War was America's response to Asian domination of Asia. So much of the official view of Japanese history seems at odds with the views held by the rest of the world.

Perhaps because my taste runs to the expression of a personal rather than corporate aesthetic, I was more charmed by the intimate garden of the Nomura family than the epic Kenrokuen of the Maeda clan. The Nomura house stands out in an area of original and reconstructed samurai houses, the Nagamachi. The house was rebuilt at the turn of the century by an industrialist with exquisite taste. The drawing room is made of cypress wood, elaborately embellished with rosewood and ebony. On each of the sliding doors is a great landscape painting by Senkai Sasaki of the Kano school. And facing the living room is the garden, my dream garden — a waterfall, curved bridge, stone walk, reflecting pool, and of course, carp.

It's no surprise that Japanese tourists love Kanazawa. When we told friends we were coming here, their eyes lit up. "Ah, Kanazawa! My favourite place," was the reaction of many. It is in some ways unique: the Maeda clan had power and taste; the climate favoured preservation; and it was not bombed. Civic pride is exhibited in the Ishikawa Prefectural Art Museum, which displays the work of local artisans, past and present, all beautifully displayed with some items for sale. As we were preparing to leave, a young curator asked if we would mind "testing" an audio tour tape. We agreed. She gave us two headsets and we went back through some of the exhibits. We were glad to report — and she was pleased to hear — that the text and the delivery were perfect.

After a visit to another merchant's house, a silk-dyeing establishment, the home of a writer whose name we were not able to figure out, and another stroll through our local spruced-up geisha quarter, we returned to dinner in our hotel. They do French so well, why not Japanese? It was a lucky choice. The *kaiseki* was perfection, with one dish unique to Kanazawa, *jibu*. Ruth Stevens, in *Kanazawa: The Other Side of Japan*, says *jibu* is the finest example of Kaga cooking, the local cuisine. It's a stew made with chicken or white fish (ours was fish), spinach, shitake mushrooms, and *sudarefu* (don't know what it is, but it's local), all combined with dashi stock (made with dried bonito), soy sauce, sugar, and rice flour, which makes a rich gravy. Everything was delicious. The tempura was the lightest and crispiest of the trip.

TUESDAY, NOVEMBER 25

Intrepid travellers that we are, we awoke early, checked our bags at the station, then hit the nearby Omichi Market, which was said to feature "local products from land and sea." It did, except that it didn't open until nine o'clock and we were too rushed to enjoy it.

On the way back to the station we passed a row of chi-chi boutiques, including several hair stylists with names like Next and Louis Ferrand. Inside one place, a young woman dressed in black (the manager?) was addressing the stylists — six men and two woman, lined up in a row, all in uniforms, some sporting orange spiked hair, all with their hands clasped behind their backs. They appeared to be giving their full attention to the young woman facing them. Hairdressers everywhere are an iconoclastic bunch; I can't imagine them lining up for their morning pep talk, or whatever it was, in any country but Japan. I wanted to stay and watch, but we had a train to catch.

Changed trains in a bit of a rush at Kyoto, and neglected to buy bento. Forced into a pretty poor dining car, our last on this trip. Seem to be ticking things off — events, places, days. Five until we leave for home.

Read the lovely thank-you note Ted left for us in the apartment and then left for my last household shopping. Made a simple supper, did the laundry, and read Lafcadio Hearn about the Japanese being like their bonsai trees — pruned and twisted into impossible shapes, holding the form long after the gardener, that is, social restrictions, demand it. Such a graceful writer, so astute.

WEDNESDAY, NOVEMBER 26

What did Tokyoites do on this miserable, soggy day? First, they went by subway to Kiba station on the Tozai line (last visited by Bob and Ger when looking at a hellish apartment). There they pushed their way through a phalanx of umbrellas stretching around the block to get on a bus packed with dripping, steaming passengers and made a half-hour trip to see La Collection at the Tokyo Museum of Contemporary Art. While the Centre Georges Pompidou in Paris is being renovated, Tokyo was the eager recipient of 127 works by eighty artists. The pieces were carefully selected and intelligently displayed in yet another mega-museum, this one built in 1995. (Oddly enough, when Bob called to find out how to get there, he was left with the impression they would be thrilled to see us and we might have the place to ourselves.)

There were thick clusters of people around certain paintings, singled out for special attention by the show's audioguide. There was also the same tropical temperature we have to contend with in all public spaces. The Japanese seem oblivious to heat and humidity. Some gallery-goers walked around in their duffel coats, wool hats, and mittens the entire time. The blank-faced "guards," all young women with bangs, sat on chairs in each room wrapped in woollen blankets, double folded.

Except for the temperature, the show was a treat. I even discovered two Chagalls I could admire. There was Picasso's three-storey-high set for Diaghilev's ballet *Parade*, a Jean Tinguely gizmo that played bells, horns, gongs, and whistles for twenty minutes each hour, and a Jean Dubuffet cave so large it could accommodate a dozen people walking around inside. Only the Japanese (at the time this show was planned), or the oil-rich Gulf states (if they sanctioned contemporary art), could afford to insure, transport, and install such an exhibit. It will run three months, is a huge success, and must have cost the sponsors millions of yen they might now regret spending.

We toured the permanent display as well, about 150 pieces from their collection of 3,500. There were some fine Hockney prints and excellent Pop Art stuff. Most of the Japanese work was mediocre, but two pieces caught my eye: Tomio Miki's *To Charlie, Love From*, a 1977 painting, and Jiro Takamatsu's *Shadows on the Door*, an installation on the subject of the atomic bomb that's more evocative than anything I saw in Hiroshima. A happy confirmation of the power of art and imagination over brute realism.

Back in our district, Bob suggested lunch at one of the thirty-odd restaurants inside the New Otani hotel and we discovered, to our surprise and delight, that there was a perfectly good reason a person would pay ¥26,000 for an inferior clubhouse sandwich in the cavernous room: the Garden Court Restaurant actually looks out over the four-hundred-year-old garden, complete with teahouse, waterfalls, bonsai and all, once the private preserve of the samurai family who owned this piece of Edo. There are, as well, two restaurants in the middle of the garden and one can imagine the parties of brides and grooms dotting the landscape on dry days. Since we'd been living across the street for about six weeks and had often walked through the hotel, this discovery proved, once again, that Tokyo is one surprise after another.

The combination of a postal strike in Canada and the fact that there is no way we can tap into e-mail means we'll have to get home for news of family and friends. I do not miss general current affairs, the sort that occupies me every morning over newspapers and coffee. There's more than enough news of that sort right here. Yesterday, for instance, was the twenty-seventh anniversary of Mishima's suicide on the grounds of the Self Defense Forces headquarters, just up the road at Ichigaya. *The Japan Times* reprinted its original story. "The life and death of Yukio Mishima, one of Japan's literary giants, demonstrated a Japanese proverb: 'The only difference between a genius and a madman is a margin as thin as a piece of paper.'"

As thoughts turn to home, I find my resolve not to go into a gift-buying frenzy dissolving. Yesterday, on the train back from Kyoto, our fellow travellers were loaded with gift-wrapped boxes of *presentos*, some in bags marked KIOSK (one of the many franchised platform sweet-sellers), but a gift nonetheless, and most likely something "typical of the region" they'd visited. In this the Japanese are like the French; despite the fact that a person can buy almost anything the country makes in either Paris or Tokyo, it's always more prized if it's actually bought close to where it was grown, distilled, or manufactured. Several people in our car had boxes of beautifully displayed crabs from seaside holidays, and any number of variations on the red beanpaste sweet.

Last night, lying in bed, I was certain that I felt a slight tremor. I know from reading about the 1923 earthquake that slight tremors are good. They keep the big rumble in abeyance. Quiet is bad.

THURSDAY, NOVEMBER 27

It was hot today, really hot. Went shopping in a shirt and a silk skirt that I've worn a lot on this trip because it's comfortable, fairly indestructible, and the sort of green/brown colour that hides dirt. It once belonged to Barbara Frum and was given to me by Murray and his second wife, Nancy Lockhart. It wasn't until I took it off today that I noticed it came from Japan, an Issey Miyake design. The cleaning instructions are in Japanese. We returned to Japan together.

I did much of the shopping I was determined not to do at Isetan, billed as Tokyo's Bloomingdale's. Not quite, but they do employ a wonderful staff in exactly the ratio I appreciate — two clerks to one shopper. In short order I figured out that going to the souvenir section, filled with silly and expensive things, was pointless. Items in the stationery and houseware sections were all nicer and cheaper. I'm especially attracted to the wooden spatulas (*shamoji*) used to scoop rice. Besides their simplicity and usefulness they are traditionally considered the symbol of the female head of the house. When a mother-in-law finally relinquishes domestic control to her eldest son's wife, she literally hands over the *shamoji*. This formal changing of the kitchen guard is not done in haste; often twenty years of apprenticeship passes before a reign change.

I had to step lively to avoid having all the gifts, even spatulas, wrapped in Santa paper. Everywhere, the improbable shopping bags featured an all-white 1940s Norman Rockwell family hugging at the front door. Over and over on the public address system the announcement kept repeating, in Japanese and English: "For your shopping convenience during this holiday season, Isetan will stay open every evening until December 31." Excuse me. The holiday being discussed is not Christmas but Japanese New Year. Such a cultural mishmash. If Norman Rockwell only knew!

I treated myself to a long-awaited broiled eel lunch, as wonderful as I remembered it — oily and sweet. Then home, Shopper Triumphant.

While I was out spending money, Bob was absorbing culture — although I consider the sort of shopping I was doing a cultural experience of great depth and magnitude. He'd gone to the local fire department museum, one we'd passed half a dozen times when shopping for groceries. In the Edo section, Bob said he'd learned that fire fighting in Japan was done by groups called *hikeshi*. In some cases they were samurai and other retainers organized by low-ranking daimyo. In Edo itself the job fell to groups of boisterous commoners, organized in teams and dressed in striking costumes. Several groups would answer the alarm and race to the blaze. The first there would plant his "team's colours" — staking a claim, as it were — and others would stand clear or be clubbed away. Since water was either scarce or non-existent, as were pumps, they contained the fire with their axes — tearing down all the adjacent buildings. Given the materials of construction at that time, wood and paper, this seems an intelligent solution to tame "the flowers of Edo."

I took down and rolled up the family scroll in the living room, afraid if I didn't I might forget to take it with us. I'll re-establish it in my own tokonoma on Lynwood Avenue. Other things winding down: unable to close bank account without going to branch in ARK Mori, so we will leave Japan with ¥700 on account. Bob called Ms. Iino at the Japan Foundation to find out if we could hitch a limo to the airport. "Sorry. It is not possible." We'll probably leave via one of the thousands of buses that stop at the New Otani. We think that Mr. Akasaki said to leave our apartment keys in his office. I feel as poorly prepared to leave as I did to arrive. What else is new?

FRIDAY, NOVEMBER 28

Our twenty-seventh anniversary and Bob's speech to the Canada-Japan Friendship Society. Spent the morning sorting through accumulated papers. Because we're both clipping and collecting like mad, this was a big job. Pleased to chuck pages of documentation on our apartment hunt; happily, I'd already forgotten most of it. Despite the fact that we have filled a large green garbage bag with cast-off clothing, and have an extra suitcase, it will be a tight squeeze.

Perhaps because we were already thinking returning-to-Toronto thoughts, we forgot to bring the invitation with us to the Ana Hotel and the information desk had never heard of our Friendship group. Raced across the driveway to the Japan Foundation office, where we

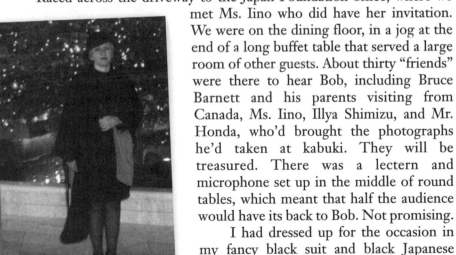

met Ms. Iino who did have her invitation. We were on the dining floor, in a jog at the end of a long buffet table that served a large room of other guests. About thirty "friends" were there to hear Bob, including Bruce Barnett and his parents visiting from Canada, Ms. Iino, Illya Shimizu, and Mr. Honda, who'd brought the photographs he'd taken at kabuki. They will be treasured. There was a lectern and microphone set up in the middle of round tables, which meant that half the audience would have its back to Bob. Not promising.

I had dressed up for the occasion in my fancy black suit and black Japanese Ladies' Travelling Hat, as I call it, from our time in Kurashiki. I had it rakishly pulled over one eye (it had lost its shape and this seemed the only option). We were joined at our small table by a woman who was introduced as a member of the lower house of the Diet. (Note: 100 percent of the parliamentarians we met on this trip to Japan were women.) She asked about the places we'd visited on our trip. "Ah yes," she remarked. "They say that a person from Osaka gets poor because he loves to eat well. A person from Kyoto gets poor because he loves to dress well. I would say that you are like a person from Kyoto." I demurred, confessing that in my heart, and my stomach, I had a greater affinity with people from Osaka.

The president of the association, the former Japanese ambassador to Canada whom we had met near the start of our trip on the way to the races, introduced Bob in a rather casual way that seemed to set the tone for the speech. Bob seemed uncomfortable in this room, with these people, and his script failed to lift off the page, nothing like the animated talk he'd given to a roomful of nodding Meiji students.

To celebrate our anniversary we returned to the Korean barbecue in our district, and it was as good as I remembered. Then, because it was a lovely night, we walked along Shinjuku-dori and its little side streets, where John Harris had taken Bob for lunch yesterday. Before the war, John had told him, one side of the street was a Burakumin ghetto.

The name Burakumin means simply "people of special hamlets." They are racially and historically Japanese whose ancestors had the misfortune to be assigned to occupations considered ritually impure — butchering animals, working in leather, handling the dead. Even though the Meiji government outlawed discrimination against Burakumin in 1868 and said they should be called *shin-heimin* ("new common people"), they continue to live for the most part in six thousand segregated communities around Japan and to be limited in the education they receive and the jobs they can take. Even those who are willing to abandon their families and try to "pass" find it nearly impossible to hide their origins, thanks to the Japanese household registry system. (From the Meiji era, the household registry system provides the government with information on all its citizens; the system was retained in the Civil Code in 1947, so that each couple must register their marriage and the birth of their children, as well as divorces, deaths, and out-of-wedlock babies. This information, required for job applications, can result in discrimination.) I've never discussed this issue with a Japanese. There's no way of knowing how the subject would be greeted. Poor excuse, I'm afraid.

The other side of the street, opposite the Burakumin, was once a geisha district. Little trace of this past life exists, except perhaps on one or two wiggly lanes dotted with jazz clubs and groovy restaurants including a place considered to be the best French bistro in the city, run by a Japanese man.

We stopped off for a nightcap at Dunkin' Donuts. This branch serves not only doughnuts but also dim sum steamed buns, congee (Chinese cooked rice cereal), and Japanese seasonal confections. Every table but one was taken by students doing homework. They looked old enough to be in university but they were working from books that looked like elementary school texts — all multiple-choice questions. It's been ten years since I first heard about pending Japanese educational reform, and I'm sure discussions started long before that. The only change I could see as I looked around the room was the presence on each table of a pocket calculator, a cell phone for each student, and a full ashtray, but that's not new.

The Japanese are only beginning to become concerned about smoking. It isn't allowed in subways and there are a few non-smoking tables in restaurants, set right against smoking tables. There are smoking sections in theatre and movie lobbies and just about everywhere else. It's expected that *gaijin* don't smoke.

Home and bed. The telephone rang at 11 p.m., Tokyo time, and I nearly choked on my heart. It was our friend from Siena, Laura Ferri-Forconi, calling to confirm that the Toronto-Siena Centre at the University of Siena wanted Bob in January. They'd been trying to contact him by e-mail without luck, and Laura needed Bob's confirmation. "You can come by train to Siena," she said. "Who knows? You might meet someone interesting!" (It was on a train from Genoa to Pisa in 1991 that we met Laura and have stayed in touch since then.) I'll be going on this trip too. It's my firm belief, though I've seldom been lucky enough to manage it, that everyone should end one trip with the prospect of another on the horizon.

SATURDAY, NOVEMBER 29

Spent the morning packing because the torrential rain made the idea of venturing forth unappealing. Bob picked up a cart from Mr. Akasaki to help take our luggage tomorrow to the New Otani, and set out across the street to buy newspapers and our airport bus tickets. Departure time, 12:50 p.m.

We were determined not to let the weather, or the fact that our plastic umbrellas were riddled with holes, deter us from a trip to the Tokyo Metropolitan Government building designed by Kenzo Tange. Subway to Shinjuku, then most of the rest of the way underground, miles underground, to the monster complex that was completed in 1991, "when the bubble burst." It's referred to as "Notre Dame" because the twin spires remind some of the Gothic cathedral. They are two forty-eight-storey towers, each with an observation deck. Thirteen thousand people work there. I don't think that the bleak, Alphaville-appearance of the compound, including the massive square, was entirely attributable to foul weather.

In *Tokyo: A Guide to Recent Architecture*, Noriyuki Tajima wrote that although Tange's design was said to have won the 1986 competition because of its "symbolic appearance and highly formalized structure" it seems there were political forces in play. "The outcome of the competition might have been prejudiced by the fact that during the election for the leader of the metropolitan government, Tange, a highly respected establishment figure, had openly supported the re-election of Suzuki as governor of Tokyo."

Every time I visit one of these high-rise buildings on the west side of Shinjuku Station, I worry; they were built to conform to a structural engineering theory that has never been tested in a large quake. Bravely, we lined up to take the elevator to the top of one of the towers. Six thousand visitors do the same each day, to look at "the new downtown," but there were few of us today. Not surprising, since we could see nothing but Four Views of Grey Soup. Had coffee amid the rain clouds and headed down for some last-minute shopping.

At the back of Keio department store's sixth floor there was an extensive area set aside for holiday presents — all food, with prices ranging up to $3,000. Display boxes generally featured a single product — tea, for instance, or fish. There were whole fishes, as well as a seafood smorgasbord, including delicacies such as eyes and heads. There were hams, mushrooms, and fruit, all samples, many in plastic. About fifty saleswomen in uniforms were taking orders for delivery. Looking around, I felt it would be hard for me to distinguish between a gift and a bribe, between pleasure and obligation.

Picked up bento and came home. Lunch had more or less cleaned out our food supply. Despite the purchase of really fine clear plastic umbrellas, our clothes were so wet I threw everything into the dryer. Waiting to leave is a drag.

SUNDAY, NOVEMBER 30

On the plane home with turbulence ahead; I've taken a Gravol as a precaution. Went in the morning for one last run through the bookstores of Kanda. Even though it took us longer than anticipated to get there, many of the stores I wanted to browse through were still closed. Had some luck in the English section of Sanseido, but didn't find exactly what I wanted: books about the Japanese obsession with food, about wedding customs, about Miss Kitty (the cunning little feline we see everywhere on kitschy items who had just celebrated her twentieth birthday). I did find *The Anatomy of Self* by a psychiatrist, Takeo Doi, a sequel to *The Anatomy of Dependence*, which I'd found helpful in trying to come to terms with the notions of "inner" and "outer" and the prominent position of silence in Japanese culture.

Then, something of a rush. One last sweep through the apartment, final packing, dropped off the keys, made two trips to the New Otani parking lot, returned the trolley. Bob, in a sweat, regretting, I could tell, that he'd gone along with my hare-brained scheme for last-minute book shopping. We were both frazzled but not a harsh word was spoken. One of the unexpected pleasures of travels — dependence breeds forbearance.

On the way to the airport we passed mammoth developments on the man-made islands in Tokyo Harbour. If the bubble has burst, no one seems to have told these people. Caught a glimpse of the new

Fuji television location, a giant spaceship of green glass. And further on, the only slightly more fantastical towers of Disneyland.

It's been a glorious journey, one I'll never forget. Even if I never see Japan again, I won't stop thinking about it, my alternate reality. Nothing can stop me from trying to fit the pieces together, even though I know a final, fixed image will always elude me.

ACKNOWLEDGMENTS

My two trips to Japan were gifts from the Asia Pacific Foundation and the Japan Foundation, to whom I'm enormously grateful. Without them, my long-standing dream would not have been realized. Special thanks to Ron Richardson of the Asia Pacific Foundation and Masamichi Sugihara of the Japan Foundation.

To prepare me for my travels, I had two mentors — Ken Richard, of the East Asian Studies department at the University of Toronto, and Ted Goossen, of East Asian Studies at York University. In 1981, when I was executive producer for *Ideas* on CBC Radio, we worked together on a five-part series, *Canada and Japan: Images and Realities*. Ken took me to my first tea ceremony in Don Mills, Ontario. And in Japan, and while writing this book, Ted generously shared his time and knowledge.

Among Canadians in Japan I'm indebted to Tim and Betty Armstrong, Cy and Mary Taylor, David and Jill Bond, Russell Mark, Wendy Wortsman and Tom Stolberg, Bruce Barnett, Stephane Jobin and Annick Goulet, John McGee and Alexandre Avdoulov. Among the many Japanese who offered insight and hospitality were Mr. and Mrs. Hideo Tomiyasu, Atsumi Karashima, Hiroyuki Matsumoto and his family, Hajime and Takiyo Tsujimoto, Bunji Yokomichi, Dr. Kimitada Miwa, Fumitomo Horiuchi, Marie Suzuki, Naomi Iino, Osamu Honda, Toshiaki Aoyagi, Rui Umezawa, and Tomoko Illya Shimizu and her wonderful family.

Gratitude also to my family: Philip Sherman, my late father, the first person I knew who owned enamelled Japanese chopsticks and used them; Sadie Katzman and Frances Fulford, my late grandmother and mother-in-law, encouraging onlookers at the start of the journey; Helen Sherman, my mother, facilitator, and enduring fan; Margaret Fulford, my stepdaughter, computer teacher, and supplier of exquisite Japanese books and postcards; Rachel Fulford and Sarah Fulford, my daughters and other two passions.

Canadian friends and fellow enthusiasts shared information and offered excellent advice, especially Katherine Ashenburg, James Quandt, Judy and Danny Stoffman, Larry Richards, Andrew Watson, Janet Inksetter, and the late Peter Day and Barbara Frum. Others might consider me daft, notably Karen Levine and Michael Enright, Julian and Anna Porter, Murray Frum and Nancy Lockhart, William Thorsell, Marjorie Harris and Jack Batten. They, too, have been helpful: a true believer should occasionally have to explain herself to atheists.

Linda McKnight, of Westwood Creative Artists, was the first person outside our house to read these diaries. Without her I would not have found Kim McArthur, my enthusiastic publisher, who had the good sense to hire as editor Meg Taylor, whose knowledge of Japan greatly improved the text, and as designer, Linda Pellowe of Mad Dog Design and Karen Johnson, who made it beautiful, and Pam Erlichman, who trolled for errors, followed by the vigilant volunteer, Florence Rosberg. Thanks also to Tereza Penollar, an indispensable aide.

For Robert Fulford, my travel companion, in-house editor, and husband of almost thirty years, words, for once, are not enough.

INDEX